Escape from the Nazis

Escape from the Nazis

Benjamin Mandelkern
With the Assistance of Mark Czarnecki

James Lorimer & Company, Publishers
Toronto, 1988

Canadian Cataloguing in Publication Data
Mandelkern, Benjamin, 1916-
Escape from the Nazis
1. Mandelkern, Benjamin, 1916- . 2. Mandelkern, Helena. 3.
Holocaust, Jewish (1939-1945) — Poland — Biography. I. Czarnecki,
Mark. II. Title.

D810.J4M35 1988 940.53'15'09240438 C88-094499-4

James Lorimer & Company, Publishers
Egerton Ryerson Memorial Building
35 Britain Street
Toronto, Ontario M5A 1R7

Printed and bound in Canada

5 4 3 2 1 88 89 90 91 92 93

To the memory of my dear parents, my brothers and their families and the six million Jews who were murdered by the Nazis; the righteous Gentiles who put their own lives on the line to help my wife and me survive the hell of 1939-1945; my dear wife Helen, whose love of her family, character and disposition were the source of our strength to rebuild our lives.

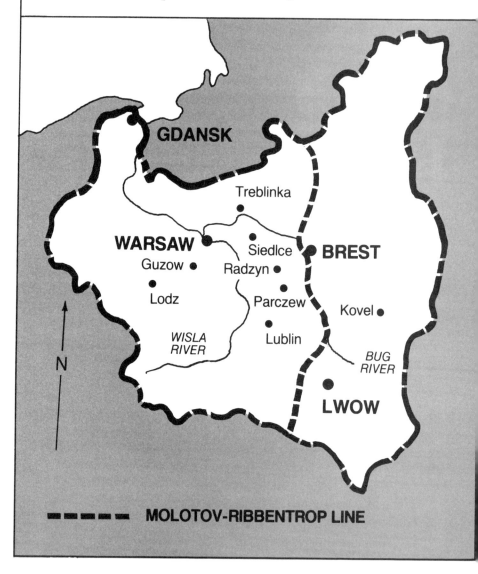

POLAND
September 1, 1939

GDANSK

Treblinka

WARSAW

Siedlce

BREST

Guzow

Radzyn

Lodz

Parczew

Kovel

WISLA
RIVER

Lublin

BUG
RIVER

N

LWOW

- - - - - MOLOTOV-RIBBENTROP LINE

Acknowledgements

My first thanks I owe to my children, who, after reading my first stories, encouraged me to go on writing. At first I thought that their motivation was the idea of being nice to father, and pleasing him. But then, to my amazement, my oldest daughter and her husband presented me with that modern writer's tool, a word processor. They read everything that came out of the machine, and that convinced me their support of my writing was genuine.

Acknowledgement number two goes to my cousin Pamela Levitt from Chicago. One midnight, she called to tell me that she had just finished reading my manuscript, and was very taken by its contents. Pamela, a professional editor, offered her help in the form of some adjustments to my language in the manuscript. I accepted her offer and liked her work.

The history of my manuscript took an unexpected turn when I met Ms. Heather Robertson. On a routine visit to the North York Library I read about the "Writer in Residence" programme organized and supported by the Government of Ontario. Encouraged by the leaflet concerning that programme, I showed Ms. Robertson a sample of my writing and...everything started snowballing. Needless to say, I was very pleased with the fact that Ms. Robertson, an accomplished and known writer, gave me credit for my way of writing, but more than anything else, I was impressed with how much emotional involvement in the subject Ms. Robertson showed.

Last but not least, a great acknowledgement is due to Mark Czarnecki, my collaborator. I have to admit that when I first met him I was a bit apprehensive. I thought him to be too young and therefore likely to be more interested in current events than in the history of almost a half century ago. But I was pleasantly surprised by the degree of compassion he showed in the work. I especially appreciated the fact that

Mark, in the reorganization of the material, showed a great deal of concern for my feelings.

My list of acknowledgements would not be complete if I did not mention that living in this country made it possible for me to tell in writing about my experiences in that dark time of history. With all my heart and mind, and with all my might, I say "Thank you, Canada," for giving me the opportunity to regain the most precious commodity a person can possess: *Dignity.*

Prologue

This book is about war, suffering, love and the human determination to survive against all odds. It tells the story of my struggle, and my wife's, to escape the Nazis in Poland during the Second World War. Every word of it is true.

I was born in Parczew, a town in central Poland, on April 7, 1916. After graduating from high school in Lublin in 1935 I spent a year in Parczew helping my father in his fish distributing business. I wanted to study for a medical career but had to give up the idea because of the severe restriction on the admission of Jews to Polish medical schools; eventually, I decided to study political economy at the Szkola Glowna Handlowa in Warsaw. I was still a student there when war broke out in 1939.

My wife came from Parczew, too. We were childhood sweethearts, but our real romancing started when I finished high school. When I moved to Warsaw she came with me and started work as a bookkeeper. We were married in early 1940 and carried on our romance, filled with devotion to each other, until her death in 1984. Our love was one of the main reasons we were able to survive the hardships of the war.

In this book I refer to my wife by different names. Her real name was Hinda, but I called her Hindele. In Warsaw before the war we changed the name to Helenka or Helena, and during the Nazi years she assumed the Aryan-sounding name of Krystina Lydia Bartkowska.

After liberation, my wife and I left Poland for Sweden, where we lived for three years. During that time I became convinced that a war between the West and the Soviet Union was a real possibility, and knowing only too well what such a war could mean for civilians, I wanted to get my family out of Europe as soon as possible. Accordingly, we immigrated to Canada in the Spring of 1950, settling in Montreal.

The first years in Canada were not exactly easy, but my wife and I did not complain. After our experiences during the war, we accepted material hardships, reassuring ourselves that better times were ahead and that our most prized possession was our freedom from fear.

I did not like my first two jobs — in a lingerie factory and a grocery store. But things improved when in 1968 we moved to Toronto and I joined a diamond tool manufacturing company. My past schooling came in handy as I learned about metallurgy and the process of producing diamond components for tools to be used in road-building and the stone-cutting industry. For the first time in many years, I felt creative.

When I retired in 1981, I turned my attention to hobbies, especially woodworking. And one day I began to write. Why?

One of my grandsons, then four years old, wanted me to tell him a story. At first I told him a made-up story about two fishermen who were so successful on one of their expeditions that they were able to save their village from starvation.

My listener did not find the story interesting.

I then made up another story — about two boys who wandered away from home and couldn't find their way back.

No, that story didn't take either.

A third try still did not elicit much interest, and my grandson looked at me with disappointment in his eyes. I then put imagination aside and told him how evil people once captured a young man and put him on a train to a faraway place, where they planned to kill him. Why they wanted to kill him, he didn't know. Not wanting to die, he started thinking of ways to escape from the locked car of the speeding train. Using a little knife he had hidden in one of his pockets, he cut an opening around the door-lock, opened the door, and jumped off the train.

My imagination was not working while I told the story; my memory was.

When I saw how my little grandson concentrated on each and every word of the story I was telling him, an idea occurred to me: I should write down my story for the sake of my family. Learning about what had happened to me and my wife would help them to draw the right conclusions about how to conduct their own lives.

Why didn't I think of writing about all that sooner? The numbness that comes from pain — the pain of remembering tragic experiences — was a major reason. Another was the fact that, by not telling our children about our wartime experiences, my wife and I had hoped to protect them from the horror of the past. Yet, as I began writing this book, I changed my mind. I now realized that what I was doing was not only worthwhile but absolutely necessary. In telling my story I was bringing back to life the people who were dearest to me: my family and all those other Jews who died so tragically. I was giving them back their dignity.

Some of my friends, on reading the manuscript, asked me how I could remember so many details after forty-five years. My answer was that, while I was writing about one event, others came to my mind and I could hear voices calling to me, "Don't leave us out, tell everybody that we lived, that we had families we loved dearly — since we died before our time in so unnatural a way, revive us at least in words." To avoid forgetting anything important, I jotted down in a notebook one- or two-word headings referring to long-gone events — the details followed later. Needless to say, the dialogue in the book is not a verbatim transcript of past conversations, but an imaginative reconstruction. Still, I am sure that the spirit of this dialogue is very close to the spirit of what was originally said.

Readers may wonder about the fate of some of the characters in this book. Mieczyslav Tarwid, the major in the Warsaw Blue Police who played a critical role in shielding my wife and me from the Nazis, disappeared in the war. Despite my efforts after the war, I could find no trace of him. He still, however, looms large in my memory, following me around wherever I go. Ludwik Golecki and Mrs. Felicia Trochimczuk, two other Gentiles who befriended us, survived. Golecki still lives in Poland and in late 1986 he received a special medal from the Yad Vashem Institute in Jerusalem for the help he offered to Jews during the war. Mrs. Trochimczuk, the first Polish woman to give shelter to my wife in Warsaw, still lives in that city.

It is my hope that readers of this book will come away from it with a better appreciation of the horror and evil of Nazi Germany, and that, reflecting on what they have read, they will never, never forget what happened in those dark days. I also hope that what I have to say pays fitting tribute both to those people who died so needlessly and so brutally, as well as to the righteous Gentiles who risked their own lives to shelter Jews.

But enough. It is now time for my story.

Note that in Polish, the letter "w" is pronounced like the English "v." The words "Pan," "Pani," and similar forms of "Pan" are terms of address like "Mr." and "Mrs."

Chapter One

Parczew was a dull place no longer. That Sunday morning, and again the following day, two German bombers flew very low and dropped incendiary bombs. They didn't encounter any answering anti-aircraft fire. There was no garrison in Parczew, no military installations of any kind. It was obvious that the Germans' target was the beautiful local church: luckily, they missed it. There were no casualties, but it took a few hours each time to bring the fires under control. The German strategy was to spread panic, fear, and intimidation among the civilians.

The Polish faithful believed that their church had been protected by the saints. At mass that Sunday the church and the huge courtyard were packed with worshippers giving thanks for the miracle that had taken place only hours before. The priest made it clear during his sermon, I was told, that the Great Protector would punish these "pagans" from the west.

The look of our town was changing from hour to hour. Strangers, with their meagre belongings on their backs, crowded the streets. They were mostly Jews from neighbouring small communities — men, women, and children of all ages. They were leaving their homes because their neighbours of German descent, the *Volksdeutsche*, had begun harassing them. In this they were aided and encouraged by anti-Semitic Poles.

Other Jewish families came from much farther away. They told horror stories of how the invading Germans treated the Jews. Most of these homeless people continued on to the east; they hoped to reach the area beyond the River Bug where, according to the non-aggression pact between Germany and Russia, the Russians would hold the eastern part of Poland.

Local Jewish charitable and social organizations did their utmost to help, giving shelter and economic assistance to those refugees who decided to remain in our town. But every day new waves of homeless people arrived. *Ad hoc* benevolent societies did their best; the young people made sacrifices. But despite their efforts, everyone felt a growing fear that their help would not be enough. It was heartbreaking to look at people whose clothes, words, and behaviour all testified to the fact that no more than a few days ago they had been living normal family lives in their own homes. What would become of them now? Complete helplessness seemed inevitable. Foreboding settled deeper and deeper in every Jew's mind.

Parczew was far from the main strategic roads. The few German or Russian military units that passed through rarely stayed even as long as a day. Hoping for a miracle, we wondered whether our area might be taken over by the Russians: that way we'd be spared the German boot. But all the Russian officers could tell us was "Maybe we'll stop at the Bug, or maybe we'll march right to the Atlantic. Our leader, Stalin, is smart and our army is invincible."

About ten days later our fate was decided. There were no more Russian troops. The German Wehrmacht had arrived and begun to round up Jews for forced labour. There was some mistreatment, but it was not yet severe. The German soldiers made it clear to us, though, that things would change when Gestapo units arrived. More and more rumours about atrocities, especially against Jewish males, were reaching Parczew from places where the Gestapo units had already established themselves.

We held a family conference in our house, to decide whether to go east, where there might be a chance to wait out the war in safety. It was settled that the male members of the family would go over to the other side of the River Bug, organize a place to stay, and then get the rest of the family over. I was heartbroken to have to leave Parczew without seeing my sweetheart, Hindele, whose Polish name was Helena. She and her younger sister, Dula, who had been in Warsaw when the war broke out, remained there to help their older sister Gienia and her family. They were in great danger, for the Germans were bombing Warsaw every day now.

Fourteen males of our family set off in two rented horse-drawn wagons, taking only essential food and supplies. No one planning to go east ever mentioned his decision to neighbours or acquaintances for two reasons: to avoid speading panic, and to give no opportunity to people who might want to blackmail him.

The scene of parting from mothers, wives, sisters, and cousins was heartbreaking. Would we be able to return for the women and young children? No one knew. There were open tears, concealed tears, and sad faces. A few of the men put on brave faces, assuring those left behind that everything would work out. We climbed aboard the wagons. Another kiss from a young wife, a mother. A father's kiss for a small child. Goodbye again, and we were off.

My father was the most optimistic of our group. "It's going to be tough with the Russians too, but at least they won't bother Jews just because they are Jews. With the work of our hands, we'll be able to live modestly but peacefully."

Our first stop was in a village about eighteen kilometres from Parczew. At slightly past midnight, we knocked at the door of our Uncle Shea's house in Sosnowice; he was my grandfather Eli Lerner's brother. He had worked for my father for many years and had visited our house quite often; Uncle Shea was good natured, and everybody loved him.

He did not approve of our plan. "Where are you going — to Russia? To that 'paradise'? Do any of you know what it means to be homeless, a refugee, in a strange country? I do, I was one during the last big war — I can talk about it for hours. Tell me, Leibel," Uncle Shea turned to my father now, "how can you, of all people, agree to that kind of plan?"

"Shea," my father answered, "you haven't heard the news of what the Germans are doing to the Jews, especially the young ones. We want to protect our sons."

"Leibel, once these Germans have won their military victories, they'll leave us Jews alone again. I know the Germans from the last war: they were strict with us, that's all. The same thing will happen now. Maybe we'll suffer more than in the last war, but to be homeless is worse."

Despite his warnings, we decided to continue our journey. Uncle Shea embraced every one of us, saying goodbye. The lenses of his glasses reflected the moisture of his eyes. "I hope to see you all again," he told us, and then could not hold back his tears, for he didn't believe he ever would.

We travelled on. No one had the heart for conversation. When we crossed the River Bug we noticed crowds of people in the small towns and small villages we passed, crowds that seemed to wander aimlessly. Were these the homeless people Uncle Shea had spoken of? We were beginning to understand. We decided to go on to Lutzk, one of the bigger cities in the area. In Lutzk, the streets were literally jammed with people. In that sunny, hot September of 1939, it was easy for the refugees from west of the Bug to sleep outdoors. But where would they go in winter?

Everywhere on the streets, groups of people stood talking. Others walked around — up and down the streets. We met some people from Parczew who had arrived two days before us; happy to see familiar faces, we listened eagerly to their experiences. "Lutzk, as you can see, is overcrowded. We were told that it was a lot easier to find accommodation in Kovel."

It was decided that we would all go on together to Kovel. It was not as crowded as Lutzk. We managed to rent one large room on the outskirts of the city. We bought some straw-sacks, filled them with straw, and put them on the floor; the rented wagons and their owners returned home. We slept well that night.

Our second day in Kovel, we met more people we knew from back home. There were hundreds of different plans and opinions about the situation. Some who had left their families behind thought of going back to get them, then heading east again. Others said that newcomers would be sent deep into Russia.

Life became harder by the hour. Basic food was harder to find and buy. No storekeeper or farmer wanted to take the Polish zlotys; they all asked for Russian rubles or for valuables like gold rings, watches, or diamonds. To get rubles the refugees found that they could sell their watches to the Russian soldiers, who were fascinated by western timepieces; the bigger the circumference of the watch, the higher the price they paid. The face of the Russian soldier would be full of pride as he rolled back his sleeve and showed you three or four or even more watches on his arm. It didn't matter much to him that some of these "tchasis" didn't work. The Russians were buying everything. They loved coloured scarves and ladies' coloured nightgowns. Trade with the Russian army was the only way to get rubles to buy food.

Rumour had it that some people had opened two freight cars at the train station and found them loaded with salt. Anyone could go and take as many bags as he could carry — this was wartime, and we had to survive as best we could. Four of us ran to the station, grabbed a 50-kilogram bag of salt each and carried them back to our room. It was a precious commodity: you could sell it for rubles or barter it for food with a storekeeper or farmer. We found more men and all ran back for more "gold." Too late. All the salt was gone. There were more closed-up freight cars on other side-tracks, but they were now guarded by armed Russian soldiers. "Everything belongs to the state," they said.

One day I saw Russian trucks moving slowly along the main street of Kovel, with the soldiers who rode in them shouting to get off the road. Then a column of Polish officers appeared, in full military dress, each carrying a small back pack. Their insignia were of different army ranks: from lieutenant right through to general. They marched in orderly ranks, six abreast, and at every fifteenth row an armed Russian guard marched along beside them. They were prisoners of war. Hundreds upon hundreds of officers passed by, their faces set and grim, but their pride still evident in their upright bearing. I felt tears coming to my eyes. When I looked around I saw many people wiping away tears.

Still the ranks of officers passed. I couldn't help thinking of their wives, their children, the young women they were planning to marry, and of their parents. For two hours, column upon column marched through town. There must have been thousands of them. And where were they going? How would they be treated?

I wondered how many of them, after the official political surrender, might have changed to civilian clothing and escaped being taken as prisoners of war. Probably their pride did not allow anything of that sort. The Polish military had always cultivated a tradition of honour: a soldier did not defect, even after defeat. They carried that patriotism even into a prisoner of war camp. Yes, that's how it was.

These officers knew that the Geneva Convention would protect them. The cultured European nations agreed that once you surrendered on the field of battle, you could no longer be considered an adversary, and your civil rights as a prisoner of war would be protected. Why, then, throw away the military uniform, the symbol of one's belonging to a country one loved? Once the war was over, each prisoner of war would return home a hero, with his honour unblemished; and his children would tell their children that grandpa was a true patriot, a warrior of high moral standards.

Later in the afternoon, people were saying that these Polish officers had surrendered to the Germans, who had handed them over to their new friend, Stalin. It was said that that was part of the deal between the two moustached leaders. Only after the war was it disclosed that Stalin killed 12,000 Polish officers in Katyn.

We had been in Kovel for five days. The heat wave of that September never let up. We were tired, exhausted from the heat, and even more from the news buzzing around us. We talked to people; people talked to us; everybody repeated what he heard from someone else about the latest news on the radio. From what we could gather, the German army was destroying the last positions of the scattered Polish resistance. The German occupation of Poland was complete, except for Warsaw where brave Mayor Starzynski continued his heroic fight. According to recently arrived refugees from the vicinity of Warsaw, the Germans were mercilessly bombarding the Polish capital, from the air and on the ground. There were stories of hunger and thirst, of thousands of victims in that surrounded city.

"Will I ever see my Hindele again? Why did I leave Warsaw without her?" These were the questions that tormented me.

The new German-Russian border was not yet defined. German bombers were flying low over the territory that — according to the political agreement — was expected to go to the Russians.

One day, trying to escape from the city heat, our group went out to the meadows beyond the city limits. We were sitting in the shade of a tree when a German bomber dived over the area — as if the pilot were looking for people. Someone, a short distance away from us, inspired by either desperation or stupidity, decided to fire at the bomber with a hand-gun from a hiding-place in the bushes. The pilot, or his companion, must have noticed the flash from the pistol-shot because they turned the plane around and flew right in our direction. We ducked, instinctively covering our heads with our hands. We heard three salvoes from a machine-gun. We could hear then the fading sound of the disappearing airplane and the screaming of people not far from us. One person had been killed and four wounded by the machine-gun fire.

The next day was Sabbath, and my father came back from the synagogue with surprising news: two Russian officers had been there, praying with the others. It turned out that these Communist "atheists" had been raised as Jews. The two officers told him that this was the first time they had been outside Russia. "When we saw Jews carrying prayer shawls in their hands, going to the synagogue, nostalgia took hold of us and we came to pray too," they had said.

My father told the officer about our group and our growing frustration. The man replied, "I think you should go back, get your wives and your children and return as fast as you can. Every day counts now. Once the border is closed the Germans won't let anyone out and the Russians won't let anyone in. Yes, comrade, hurry. Don't entrust your family's fate to the Germans."

We talked over the Russian officer's suggestion, and decided to go back to Parczew and get the rest of the family. I was especially happy with that decision — I wanted my Hindele back. Once again, we hired two horse-drawn wagons, and two days later we were back in Parczew.

My mother and the other women in our family were greatly relieved to see their husbands, sons, and fathers back, but their joy was muted. Who knew what tomorrow might bring for the Jews? So far Parczew had not been subjected to any brutality from the Germans, but the news from other parts of the country was worse every day. The only ones showing open joy and happiness at our return were the little ones. My older brother Bunim's two-year-old, Kubush, was all over his father, jumping and giggling. The baby, with his long, bright blond hair, couldn't contain his laughter when his father threw him up in the air; he kept asking for more and more of the same. When father got exhausted, little Kubush ran consecutively to grandpa, to my eldest brother, and to me. The child's overflowing happiness made us forget for a moment the danger all around us. What power a little child can have to influence the grownups!

The family consulted together about what to do next. For the women one thing, and one thing only, was the most important: "Whatever you men decide — to stay here or to leave and cross the River Bug, we will do it together. No more splitting of the family. Whatever will happen will happen to all of us together."

As soon as we were back in Parczew, I went over to Hindele's parents' house. I ran the whole way. "Have you any news from Hindele in Warsaw?" They had not heard from her. Mrs. Falkovitch embraced me and cried bitterly. "The news is bad," she said. "Everybody is talking about the terrible bombardment of Warsaw. They say there are thousands of people dead, there is hunger, and epidemics. Will I ever see my children again? Why don't the defenders of Warsaw surrender?" We were glued to the radio, in hiding, of course, listening to the still operating Polish Radio Warsaw and then to the German broadcasts calling on the defenders of Warsaw to surrender or face the complete annihilation of the city. The victorious Germans, in their calculated drive to demoralize the people of Poland, spared no terrible details in their reports of what they were doing to Warsaw: "Not a single stone in the city will be left in place unless you surrender immediately."

"Hindele," I said to myself over and over, "why didn't you leave Warsaw with me? Why did I agree to let you stay there? Did fate part us forever on that day?" There were no answers to my questions.

Every day now was filled with tense expectation of an unknown future. Every day young Jewish people were rounded up by the German soldiers as they passed Parczew. Usually the Jews were ordered to do cleaning jobs in and around the military quarters. They were given food while they were working and let go at the end of the day. The rounding-up routine was repeated every day. It didn't seem so very serious. The Jews wanted to believe that with the war progressing so well, and with victory, the Germans would temper their anti-Jewish plans.

September 1939 was coming to an end. Warsaw, the capital of Poland, surrendered. With no more military supplies, no military help from the allies in the west, no food, no medicine, the city in ruins, the brave but physically exhausted leadership gave up in order to save what was still left.

The radio blasted out new German orders to the people of Warsaw. The moustached idol of the supreme race entered Warsaw in an open car. The Germans were quick to publish photographs in the newspapers, showing their "superman" standing in the slowly moving car, his hat visor positioned at a forty-five-degree angle, looking out in triumph. That devil's look of his seemed to say, "You haven't seen a thing yet. Wait a while. You'll soon see what our master race can do."

Hungry people were leaving Warsaw. Had Hindele made it? Would she be back soon? My parents felt my anguish, but explained that there was no regular transportation to and from Warsaw yet. It would probably take up to a week, if not longer, for Hindele to find her way back. Mama and Papa Falkovitch told me that during the day they were glued to their windows waiting for their children to arrive from Warsaw. At night they listened, waiting for the knock on the door. "Benjamin," said Shoel Falkovitch, the man with an impeccable soul, "*Mimamaakim karati yo* (from the depth of my heart I keep asking the Almighty) to see my children alive and well." Mama Falkovitch's eyes had the stare of kept-back tears, but she made no loud complaints. Mother dolorosa.

Our prayers were answered. Hindele and her younger sister, Dula, reappeared from Warsaw. My sweetheart was back! The instant I received the good news, I ran to her parents' house, and as I ran I thanked God. "Hindele, my blond, blue-eyed love is alive, and in a little while I'll see her graceful face. Oh God, how grateful I am to you!"

She was waiting for me. We embraced and kissed each other. But her kiss was cold and remote.

"Hindele, how are you?"

"Fine."

This short answer was disappointing. "Is anything wrong? Has something hurt you?"

"I'm all right."

I was afraid that something had come between us, that our love, which had begun four years before, was in danger. Was this what war could do to young people in love? How could I win her back again?

Hindele's features, and those of her sister, Dula, had changed. Their faces were sharper, more chiselled, and their eyes appeared deeper-set than before, their expression more serious. They had grown thinner. But they were alive, and they brought news that their older sister, Gienia, her husband, Seweryn, and Wiktor, their little boy, were safe for the time being.

It wasn't until the third day after their return that I was able to talk with Hindele. "Ben, forgive me for my strangeness," she said. "I can hardly control myself. I keep seeing corpses of grownups, children and babies strewn all over the streets. It was horrible. All I still see is blood and death. Do you think I will ever regain my balance?"

I was relieved that my fears about our love were unfounded. "Hindele, dear," I said, "we will work at it together."

Chapter Two

It was clear now who our new rulers would be. One Saturday morning, three senior German officers and a dozen or more soldiers from the regular army, the Wehrmacht, arrived at city hall. They called on the mayor and ordered him to summon the ten most prominent Jews of the town. The mayor chose to call the former Jewish aldermen. When a messenger came for my father, telling him he must appear in city hall within half an hour, I offered to go instead.

"Father, I'll go. It's likely that all the Germans really want is a set number of people to appear before them to comply with whatever demands they may want to make. Whatever happens it'll certainly be easier for me than for you. Besides, I speak good German. I'll have no trouble communicating with them."

When I arrived at city hall, all the other former aldermen were there. The three German officers appeared. One was in his forties, the two others looked older, maybe in their early fifties. The younger one stepped forward and said, "It's eight-thirty in the morning. I'm giving you four and a half hours, until one o'clock that is, to collect a 15,000-zloty contribution to the German army. If you fail to come up with the money at the set time, all ten of you will be shot in public, in the market square. Go to your people and collect the money. One of our soldiers will accompany each of you to help you. That is all for now."

The three officers went back into the city offices. The German soldiers knew their orders. They approached us: "Come, don't waste time." I explained to the soldiers that we, the hostages, would have to have a short conference, to divide the districts where each of us would be "working." "Do it fast, your life is at stake."

I didn't take the threat to our lives seriously. I couldn't believe that they would take us and just kill us for no reason. I knew that 15,000 zlotys was a lot of money — it would be hard to get all of it, but when the Germans saw our honest effort, surely they would understand and let us get away with a lesser amount. Why kill us? Why? We were civilians, they were regular army; everybody knew that army men didn't just kill civilians for killing's sake. No, it was impossible. All these thoughts flashed through my mind. The ten of us quickly decided who would collect on which street, and we dispersed, each one accompanied by a Wehrmacht man carrying a rifle.

Saturday morning in Parczew. It was still the beautiful, sunny September of 1939. The streets were quiet. The Jews were probably getting ready for their prayers inside their houses; it was dangerous to gather in groups. Only the very religious Jews would go to the synagogue and pray with a *minyan*, a Jewish customary quorum of ten men. In the middle of all that, I had to ask for money. Money on a Saturday morning? What was going on?

I talked, and explained, saying the same thing in each and every house. I asked my companion, the German soldier, to wait outside while I went into the houses to ask for the money. I didn't want my fellow Jews to feel terrorized. He agreed, but warned me, "Don't run away. You know what will happen to the others if you do." No, I didn't mean to run away. I would fulfil the mission imposed on me: I had no wish to be the cause of tragedy.

Patiently, I talked to people. I asked for the largest possible contribution. When the amount offered seemed small in comparison with the look of the surroundings, I gently asked for more. People responded positively to my request. Some scenes were touching. In one house, the insides of which clearly indicated that the family was poor, I spoke with a man who looked to be in his early sixties; I told him what I came for, adding that I'd understand if he felt unable to contribute to the fundraising.

"My dear fellow Jew," he replied. "I can't give a lot, but I would be ashamed if I didn't give at least a small sum." He went over to an enclosed bookcase, opened it, took out one book of the Talmud, and pulled a bank note from between the pages.

"It's only ten zlotys. It's from my meagre savings for food. Please take it. When lives are in danger, I have to contribute too. I'll be grateful if you will take my ten zlotys."

News of our "work" spread quickly among the Jews that Saturday morning. As the day progressed we had to do less and less explaining.

By twelve-thirty in the afternoon, we ten gathered in the front of city hall and counted the money. There was only 12,000 zlotys. At that moment I realized that our lives were really in danger. The soldiers, the plain Joes of the army, knew their officers' methods better than we did. When they saw that we had not collected the sum asked for, they began to speak as if our execution was imminent. They seemed very concerned, their faces grim.

One of the soldiers took the money and went into the city hall office, to the officers. I was nervous. So were the other nine Jews. We were silent, waiting. Waiting for what? For our end? No, it was impossible. I couldn't believe it.

The youngest officer came out and said to us: "You are short about 3,000 zlotys of the required 15,000. The German army does not make jokes. You have one more hour to come up with the extra money. I repeat, your lives are at stake. It'll be all your own fault if we have to shoot you." He disappeared.

After a few minutes of consultation, we decided to approach five or six people, the richest people we knew. We got them together in the Jewish community building and told them about the danger to our lives. We didn't have to bargain long; we got the missing money. When we returned to city hall, one of the soldiers said in German: "They are lucky guys."

For several years, Hindele and I had planned to marry. But with the outbreak of war we put off our wedding plans indefinitely, and I was extremely surprised when one day early in 1940, my father said: "I talked it over with your mother and we've decided to ask you whether you and Hindele want to get married."

"Of course we want to, Dad, but why are you asking me this now? In the middle of a war?"

"Whenever Hindele comes to our house I can see how devoted she is to you. She loves you and you love her. You should be together. Both of you are young and willing to fight it out together. I hope you will. Yes, you should get married. Mom and I want to see you married."

When I told Hindele about my father's suggestion, she said: "I want so much to be together with you, but it's wartime. I can't make up my mind. Who knows what might happen? But your father is helping me make up my mind. What do you think? Should we get married now?"

"Yes, we should. It will give us a new strength to fight out our future together. Your parents and my parents want to see us married. I'm sure that their wishes are as dear to you as they are to me."

"I always wanted our wedding to take place in a joyous atmosphere, not at a time like this."

We looked at each other, both thinking the same thought.

Hindele went on. "All right, we have to consider our parents. Let's have an official ceremony now and we'll throw a great party right after the war."

We talked to both Hindele's and my parents, and they got together and set the wedding date.

In the winter of 1939-40, life for the Jews of Parczew under the Germans was still bearable. The on-and-off military rule was replaced by a permanent gendarmerie, or police administration. The chief of the new police force in Parczew instructed some former members of the Jewish community council to select a *Judenrat*, or council of Jews, that would be responsible for carrying out his orders. The police chief immediately presented them with all kinds of requirements: money to run the station, furniture for their officers, people to clean the requisitioned homes, and so on. To help them meet these demands, the new *Judenrat* approached my father and asked him to speak to the new rulers on its behalf. Although my father had never before been officially involved in the council, he considered it his duty to help in any way he could.

The *Judenrat* was at that time composed of the most honest people, and did its best to temper the German orders. It seemed then that what the Germans were mainly after was bribes, bribes and more bribes. The *Judenrat* paid and the local German authorities limited their demands by asking only for workers to do jobs in or around Parczew. These workers were paid by the *Judenrat*.

Many Jewish women gathered courage and started to copy the Poles who smuggled food to Warsaw to sell, bringing back to Parczew all kinds of manufactured goods, especially linen, shoes, cloth and so on. That trading (smuggling, because officially it was forbidden by the Germans) was the only way left of making a living for these Jewish women who were now their families' sole breadwinners.

Hindele's parents received letters from relatives living in Lodz, the second biggest city in Poland, asking for food parcels. The bigger the city one lived in, the harder it was to obtain enough food to feed one's family. The Falkovitch family in Lodz offered to pay for food with textiles, of which the city of Lodz was the biggest producer in Poland.

Hindele listened to her mother reading letters from Lodz, and came up with an idea: she would travel to Lodz, taking with her as much food as she could carry. That would help the family there, and in return, they could help her with new linen, towels and other household articles at a reasonable price — and they were all things she would need when we married.

I thought the trip would be too dangerous, but Hindele dismissed my objections. "Benush, after what I went through during the siege of Warsaw, I learned not to be afraid. Besides, I can rely on my 'Aryan' looks: blond hair, blue eyes and my smile. No, there's no reason at all to be afraid. Another thing is that the Germans don't seem as ferocious as we were told they would be. And I'll buy the nicest linen, nightgowns for me and pyjamas for you. Won't it be nice to have all that and use it as soon as we get married? It isn't a long time away now, just about three months. What do you say? Ah, say whatever you want to say, but please don't say no to my plan."

"It's true that it's easier for a woman to be a smuggler. The Germans are more lenient towards them. But I will worry about you until you are safe at home."

"I promise to be careful."

I helped my official bride pack all kinds of food — butter, beans, rice and other nourishing products — and she set out in good spirits. It wasn't easy waiting for her to return. Each day seemed to last forever. I decided that once she was back I'd never let her go again.

Hindele returned after a week, and she promised me she wouldn't go to Lodz again. "It was terrible to see how the Germans took all the luggage from the Jewish women travelling on the train. No amount of begging was any use. They'd do the same to me if they recognized me as Jewish." Then she opened her bags. "Benush, I'll show you what I bought for us — very nice things. I pray that we'll use them with pleasure."

Jewish life in Parczew in the few weeks after Hindele's trip was still such that we thought somehow we would outlast the Germans. It was unpleasant, yes, but then, our history had always been full of terrible events. In the end, we always survived our oppressors.

But one day something happened — a terrible thing that disrupted our community to its innermost core. It was Friday in the deep, deep cold of the first winter under the German occupation, and the members of the *Judenrat* had gathered in their building on Zabia Street. It was a routine meeting to take care of the daily Jewish problems. There were always some people in the community who needed help, whether it was food, clothing, wood for heating or medicine for children. Then a message came from the local gendarmerie saying that a large number of Jewish prisoners of war would be passing Parczew shortly, and the *Judenrat* was ordered to prepare places for them to stay and to supply them with food. They would stay in Parczew for only a very short while. Their destination was Biala Podlaski, about fifty kilometres away.

The *Judenrat* lost no time. A call went out to all the young adult women to come to the *Judenrat* building to help. Food and warm clothing were the main items needed. The women divided the work among them: some cooked meals, others collected clothing. Shirts and bedsheets were made into bandages. The young and energetic Boruch Reich co-ordinated everything. He was a smiling, good-looking, streetwise man with a heart of gold and inexhaustible initiative: day or night, he never tired of helping out people in need.

But the POWs never came. First it seemed that there was a delay; everybody began to be anxious, fearing the worst. The *Judenrat* decided to send a few men to Lubartow, where the POWs had supposedly stayed the night before, to find out what had happened to them. The group was supplied with horses and wagons, in case there were people who had trouble walking in that 30-below-zero weather. Three hours later the wagons were back. They were empty. The men reported that only a few hundred were on their way to Parczew. "Hundreds, or maybe thousands, were machine-gunned. The Germans didn't let the wagons come near," they told us.

Helpless despair swept over the community. Thousands had been murdered, prisoners of war machine-gunned. Would they spare the remaining hostages? We waited, tense and despairing. All we could do was wait: no one knew what would happen next.

The POWs arrived late that evening. The *Judenrat* immediately approached the escorting Gestapo men, who agreed to allow the former soldiers to be housed in the old synagogue for the night. The Gestapo also consented to let us take food to the captives.

What a sight! Exhausted Jewish soldiers, most of them young, dressed in Polish military khaki, entered the old synagogue on a Friday night, but no, they were not entering the *shul* to greet the arrival of the Sabbath. These men entered the *shul* now as degraded Jews. They couldn't pray, they didn't even know that it was Friday night. Their days had no names now. You could hear the religious people of Parczew asking: "God, where are You? What are You doing to Your chosen people? It's a sin to talk to You this way, but all our lives we have been taught that killing innocent people is the greatest sin. How can You, the Almighty, let us be so shamelessly murdered — we who were the first ones to make a covenant with You?"

The Gestapo went to the local restaurant, Mrs. Witkun's. Three members of the *Judenrat* went too, to "negotiate" with them. German guards were posted around the *shul* so that nobody could escape.

The young women immediately swung into action. Dressed in white coats like nurses, they brought in pails of food and medical supplies. Courageously, the women bribed the guards with chocolate so that they wouldn't watch their activities too closely. Then, when they were outside for more food or water, the "nurses" put on men's clothing, rolled up the trouser legs and hid the extra garments under double white smocks. Once inside, they quickly passed the civilian clothing to the more daring prisoners. White coat over street clothes, white cap, some dishes in their hands, and the disguised soldiers got out of the *shul*. About ten escaped that way. It was dangerous, because the Germans had counted the number of POWs they allowed into the *shul* and if they had checked their numbers before leaving town the Gestapo might have gone wild with reprisals.

The women also found out how it all was with the POWs. The four thousand of them had left Lublin and were supposed to go on foot to Biala Podlaski *via* Lubartow and Parczew. On the way to Lubartow, anyone who could not walk fast enough in that bitter cold was shot. Now and then the group was stopped in an open field, and a few hundred at a time were lined up and machine-gunned. The Jews who survived estimated that between Lublin and Lubartow more than two thousand POWs were shot to death. Between Lubartow and Parczew, large groups were taken out of the barns they had been put in for the night, and shot. Thus only a few hundred reached Parczew.

At Mrs. Witkun's restaurant the begging and pleading and bribing of the representatives of the master race was continuing. My father, Boruch Reich and another member of the *Judenrat*, helped by Mrs. Witkun, tried to get all the hostages freed in Parczew. "No, impossible," said the guards (who had killed almost four thousand of them), "we are responsible for delivering them to Biala Podlaski."

The *Judenrat* begged now for permission to transport the POWs on horse-drawn wagons to Biala Podlaski. They were allowed to, if they could collect two kilograms of gold by the following day. So, again on a Saturday morning the *Judenrat* members went from house to house asking for gold: "We have to save the lives of the remaining POWs and also pay the last honour to the bodies of the victims strewn between Lubartow and Parczew." Whoever of the Jews had golden wedding rings or golden earrings gave them away for the sake of the two holy causes.

The next day the gold was delivered and the POWs left for Biala Podlaski in wagons. We supplied them with whatever covering we could to protect them from the bitter cold during the journey. We hoped and prayed that they reach Biala safely. But what would happen to them in Biala? Would they be freed? We paid for their safety generously and we did it from our hearts; how could they not be saved?

Back to the holy work in Parczew. All Jewish wagons and horses, as well as some rented non-Jewish wagons, were sent off in the direction of Lubartow on the grim errand of collecting the bodies of the killed soldiers and bringing them back to Parczew for burial. Young Jewish boys volunteered for that work. The wagons with their tragic load returned to town late that Sunday. All the bodies were brought to the cemetery.

What we saw next morning was more terrible than the human mind can imagine. The bodies were frozen; some were frozen together — probably they fell on each other when they were shot. The blood on the uniforms was frozen and was forming lines in all directions over the bodies depending on the way the victim had fallen. One victim was frozen in a begging position on his knees with his arms up. Probably he was begging for his life.

We counted 161 dead. Our men couldn't find more bodies, the ground was covered deep in snow. At the time we thought we would find more bodies in the spring and bury them then. Then we started the sad work of identifying the bodies. There would certainly be relatives looking for every missing person, we thought, and only a sure identification could establish the reality, whatever it might be. The bodies had been robbed of whatever possessions the men had been carrying. Their pockets had been turned out, personal papers and photographs strewn all over. Some of the victims had even had their shoes stolen. None had been left with a watch or wedding ring.

We registered each name, from the name tags hanging around the neck of the victims: they were men from twenty-one to fifty. We found pictures of fathers, mothers, wives, girlfriends and small children, all pictures taken in happy times, the faces laughing and happy. Now there lay the dead, frozen bodies of husband or friend, father or son, brother or cousin. We found letters to the dear ones about life in camp; love poems to girlfriends, poems expressing hope of being united again; letters to children telling them that Daddy would be back soon to play the game of riding on his back, or hide-and-seek, or throw and catch the ball. "Don't cry, Shloimele, don't cry Sarale, Dad will come back to you soon. Honestly." Every shred of paper was carefully catalogued for the families that would some day come searching for them.

We started to dig two mass graves, each one for eighty of the fallen. But the frozen ground resisted being dug. One of the diggers remarked: "Mother Earth is trying to shame God." The gendarmes sent over two officers with a message to the diggers: "Complete the burial today, or else...."

We brought in long ice picks and, using the fallen branches of nearby trees, started a number of small fires to soften the ground. And we dug. It seemed that all the male population of Parczew was digging the two graves for the innocent victims. All of us were the burial society now. All of us paid the last respects to the dead. The frozen ground responded with sparks to the blows of the steel picks. A foot and a half down through the top soil, the digging was easier.

We laid the dead side by side in the two graves. We buried them in their uniforms, with no white shrouds, because they did not die natural deaths. They were murdered because of their religious beliefs, and those are to be buried, according to Jewish tradition, in the clothes they wore at the time of their death. Maybe these *Kadoshim* (pious) would appear before the Almighty in their uniforms and urge him to revenge their death.

We covered the dead with earth and smoothed the top of the graves. One hundred and sixty-one lives. For what? Complete silence around the grave. A swaying figure covered with a prayer shawl started out: "*Yitgadal V'yitkadosh...*" the prayer affirming the eternity of the Almighty.

Chapter Three

L ife in Parczew after the POW tragedy continued.... There was no other way. Life, if you can use the term to describe those troublesome times, was full of new hardships every day. The mood of the people changed by the day. When a day or two had passed with no new restrictions on the community, the eternal human optimism made people begin to hope and believe that the hard times would not last forever and the Germans would stop being so cruel.

The political arm of the German occupation was the Gestapo. They established their headquarters thirty kilometres from Parczew, in a town called Radzyn. And they ruled over the whole district from there. Their representatives came to Parczew and commanded that the established *Judenrat* should now consist of twelve prominent Jews. From now on, these twelve Jews were showered with orders and demands for all kinds of things: money, workers, jewellery, clothing. New demands, and new restrictions: for identification, every Jew had to wear a white armband with the star of David on it. Anyone caught without an armband was mercilessly punished. Once again the *Judenrat* asked my father to act as a go-between.

The Germans' orders became increasingly brutal and my father was always the negotiator to temper these orders. He went to the Gestapo accompanied by his secretary, Max Weinreich, who told of an incident that made his listeners weep. He and my father had been ordered into the presence of a Gestapo commanding officer, who ordered my father to undress. The officer then told his accomplices to whip that Jew ten times.

"Ten times, no more," he said.

When the whipping was over, he told my father to get dressed. He then ordered him to return the following morning at 7:00 sharp with fifty workers and 3,000 zlotys. In a composed voice, Leib Mandelkern answered: "Obersturmführer, I'm sure you have had your satisfaction in having me whipped. Let us be reasonable. I'll find workers, but I don't know how many — the same thing about the money."

"Have you brought anything for me now?"

"Max, bring in the two parcels from the wagon."

Max returned with the parcels, and the Gestapo officer said, "I couldn't have acted differently; after all, you are only a Jew. See what you can do about the workers for tomorrow morning."

The Germans' demands and our degradation went on and on. Gloom overtook the most optimistic of us. My father never ceased to try to make the Germans' orders at least a little bit more bearable, even when trying meant risking his life.

Our wedding day was approaching. I talked to Hindele. We decided to ask our parents to postpone the wedding until better times arrived. But Hindele's parents, as well as my own, said that according to Jewish tradition, the set wedding date must not be changed. "It will be a small official wedding, with only the closest relatives attending. God willing, we'll have a big party for both of you when peace comes," my parents said.

The wedding took place in Hindele's parents' house. Only about sixty guests, close relatives of both families, attended. Many of the invited guests didn't come, for fear that if the Germans heard of a big gathering they would surely attack us. In normal circumstances, when an invited guest failed to come to a wedding it was considered an unforgivable insult to the parents of the bride and groom — but not this time. Who knew what might happen? Our parents understood the situation and honoured the guests who did come to the wedding for their courage.

The ceremony was short. Hindele looked beautiful in her white gown, but she behaved strangely during the *hupa*, under the wedding canopy. While I was placing the wedding ring on the index finger of her right hand, she was giggling. Just giggling. Surprised, I looked at her, trying to make her realize that this was not the time for giggles. But she continued, though in a suppressed way, laughing for the duration of the *hupa* ceremony.

Everyone wished us *mazel-tov* (good luck). As a precaution, we had decided against the customary big meal. Drinks and cakes only were offered to the guests. "Good luck to the bride and groom, good luck to their parents," people said to us. "May your wedding mark the beginning of better times for all Jews," said one of Hindele's religious uncles.

The vodka inspired a better mood and everyone tried to say something cheerful. "On behalf of the bride and groom the Creator will give us all good luck."

"Amen."

"I don't want to sound as if I were — *has veholile* (heaven forbid) — a non-believer, but He should take more care of us," said Uncle Yosef.

One of my father's brothers, Uncle Hershel, who was a born optimist, stepped forward. "All those gathered here, listen, everything will be better, good times must come again. God is our Father. Now let's form a small ring and have a *rekidele* (little dance). I want us to dance to a quiet song."

People responded to Hershel's call. They formed a ring, joined hands, chanting quietly "Let the redemption come soon." The people turned one way, then the other way. For safety reasons, the dancing didn't last long. Everybody wished us *mazel-tov* again and then quietly left the house.

The whole wedding lasted a little over an hour. After the guests left, I asked my wife why she had been giggling under the canopy. "I don't know," she replied. "I realized that it was not the right thing to do. I tried to stop, to compose myself, but I couldn't."

"Were you nervous?"

"Maybe. I don't know...I always expected my wedding to be the most joyful affair of my life, but the circumstances made it impossible. Yes, I suppose I was nervous about that."

"We'll make it up when Hitler is gone. We'll have a big celebration then." We were young; we had the right to hope for the best.

After our marriage, we lived in the house of Hindele's parents.

One morning, there was a sharp knock at the back door. It was very early and still dark outside.

"*Aufmachen!*"

Open up! That order was like an electric shock to us. My in-laws were on their feet in an instant. So were my wife and I. Our first thought was that they were coming to get me, the young man. My mother-in-law whispered to me to stay in my room.

Now we heard a kick at the door and, "Open up quickly!" I heard my in-laws and Hindele opening the door, and two men walking into the house.

"Good morning, don't be afraid. All we want from you is two towels. Where is the closet with your towels?"

Now I could hear my mother-in-law's footsteps, and the Germans following her. I was sure now that the two early visitors had not come for me, and I came out of my room. The two men were not from the local German police or the Gestapo; they were soldiers from the regular army (the Wehrmacht). They had come to do a little plundering in a Jewish home. Why not? There was no chance that anybody from the authorities would stop them indulging in such a natural activity.

Both soldiers were taking out towel after towel from the closet, putting them in two piles. Then they reached for the sheets lying in the same closet. "Karl, did you notice everything is brand new, unused? *Die Juden*, they have got everything."

"You're right, everything is brand new. I'll send some stuff to my *Bubchen* at home. Do you think she'll like it?"

"I'm quite sure she'll like it. I'll send new bed-sheets to my Gretchen. I'd like to see her face when she gets this parcel."

One of the soldiers turned to my mother-in-law: "Everything is brand new. You must be dealing in these things. Where else do you have more linen? Show us the hiding place."

My wife stepped forward and said: "We are not dealers and we have no hiding places. Everything is new because my husband" — here she pointed at me — "and I were married only two weeks ago. These are our new sheets and towels. Take some and leave us the rest."

The two soldiers looked at my wife and then at each other. "I'll just take two towels and two sheets, Karl. You do the same, don't take any more than that."

"No, Hans, I don't want anything. If I survive the war and come home, I'll always feel ashamed of this morning."

"I'll just take two towels."

"Hans, no, don't take anything. It might be bad luck to take away anything from a newly-married couple."

Karl turned to my wife: "You are not a Jewess."

"Yes, I am a Jewess."

"But you're so blond and you have such blue eyes. Is this man your father?"

"Yes. His eyes are blue, too."

"To me you look more like a woman of our race."

"Hans, let's go. You people, don't tell anybody that two German soldiers were here asking for towels. Goodbye."

"It hurts to see our business disappearing right before my eyes," said Rivkele Goldreich, Hindele's best friend. "Imagine, the business was started by my grandfather Hersh Mordechai. Then my father worked as hard as he could to develop it into a family enterprise — and now what?"

Rivkele was visiting us and we were sitting talking about the Goldreich wholesale business, which figured prominently in the community. Her father, David Goldreich, had developed his business on a grand scale. Before the war, trainloads of sugar, rice, barrels of herring (which was a very popular item in those days) and groceries in big crates arrived in Parczew to be distributed by the Goldreich family. Rivkele, the youngest in the family, had begun to work in the business late in the 1930s.

Retailers from a radius of 100 kilometres around Parczew used to come to them to buy their supplies; the Goldreichs were known for the quality of their service as well as respected for their honesty. But when the war broke out, their little empire, which had taken many years to build and develop, started to shrink. Not only were the goods now longer available, but non-Jewish customers began to be afraid to buy from a Jewish firm. The mass propaganda had worked very quickly.

Rivkele, Hindele and I were talking about the changing circumstances. The Goldreich business faced complete ruin. "Maybe we should take a non-Jewish partner into the business, who would be a storefront person," I suggested.

"You think we'll be able to find a non-Jew who wants to involve himself with Jews now? And he has to be honest or he'll steal everything," Rivkele said. "My sister Hesse and my brother Yankel and I thought of your idea already. We approached two non-Jews but both of them said that they were afraid to get involved with Jews."

"Rivkele," Hindele said, "let me talk it over with my father-in-law. I'll do it today. He knows people; I'm sure his choice would work out well."

My father suggested Ludwik Golecki. "He is young, courageous and he seems to me to be a straight, honest person."

The Goldreichs were surprised. "Golecki? Ludwik Golecki? Your father must be making a mistake," said Hesse. "The whole Golecki family is very anti-Semitic. I remember Ludwik from school, and he was the biggest troublemaker. He was always out to give the Jewish kids the most trouble. Can he have changed that much?"

"Hesse, why don't Benjamin and I talk to Ludwik? Just the two of us. You won't be involved, so there won't be any obligation on your side."

We asked Ludwik over for a talk. When he heard the proposition, he replied, "Mr. Mandelkern, I want to be honest with you. I have worked for you a number of times, and I think of you as the most decent person I ever met. But tell me, honestly, don't you think that by associating myself with Jews in business now, I'm risking my future?"

We assured him that the risk was not great, and that he would be helping people in distress. "You don't have to put in any money but you'll share in the profits," said my father.

Ludwik talked it over with his wife, Lola, and agreed, on condition that I was involved as well. We all met and worked out a deal. I put some money into the business, Ludwik gave his name. There were now three equal partners in the new firm: the Goldreichs, Hindele and I, and Ludwik Golecki. The new business was a far cry from what it was when the Goldreichs alone were running it, but then everything had changed as a result of the war. It was hard to obtain supplies and customers had less money to spend. Neither I nor any of the Goldreichs, not even Hesse and Rivkele, were working in the front of the store. If they had it might have created the suspicion that the Golecki deal was just a fake, and "friendly" people, especially the non-Jewish storekeepers, would have denounced the Golecki deal to the Germans as just a convenient set-up for the Goldreichs.

The front of the store was run by Ludwik's wife, Lola, and by my wife, whom very few people knew, since she had grown up on the periphery of the town and had been away in Warsaw for the last few years. We decided that she should go by the name Helena, the Polish form of Hindele, which she had used in Warsaw. Former out-of-town customers of the Goldreichs were buying now from the new firm of "L. Golecki Wholesale Supplies," and they never suspected that blond, blue-eyed young woman of being Jewish. Mrs. Golecki told them that Helena was her girlfriend from Warsaw, whose house was bombed during the siege of the city in September, 1939, but just to be careful — and not be caught lying — Lola Golecki never talked about Helena as if she were Catholic.

Ludwik was the travelling buyer. He travelled to Warsaw by train and brought back all kinds of goods. The Goldreichs' connections from before the war were very helpful. Ludwik, who had been an anti-Semitic kid, the kid from an anti-Semitic family, now showed the gentler side of his character. Travelling around, he had seen the Germans in their true colours. He had observed what the occupying Germans were doing to Poland and the Polish people — and not only to the Jews, whom the Germans used as bait to gain support from the misled Poles. The new Ludwik decided to help out the Jews whenever he could. At my request, he sought out friends of mine in the Warsaw ghetto, and risked his life bribing German guards so that he could take food into the ghetto and save our friends from starvation.

Ludwik and I spent many hours talking about what was going on around us politically. "I'm getting scared," he said. "As you know, I was an officer in the Polish army. Wherever I travel and talk to people, I hear that the German Gestapo is systematically arresting and sending to Auschwitz all former Polish officers. I keep hearing about these arrests more and more often. I was at the Witkun's beer parlour, right here in Parczew, and I heard undercover police talking about former Polish officers. I'm afraid to sleep at home. I built a *kryjowka* (hiding place) near my house, and I sleep there now." Ludwik described to me, in precise detail, the location of his *kryjowka* and how to get there unnoticed. "Benjamin, I'm trusting you with that information, because one day you might need to use that place yourself, who knows?"

Oh, how right Ludwik was.

The business Ludwik's wife, Lola, and "Helena" were running was doing quite well: three families had a decent income, which was an enormous achievement at that time.

One of the out-of-town client-retailers behaved differently from the others. Mr. Mrozowski bought large amounts of goods and always paid cash; he never bought on credit. When he reached for his money to pay his bill, he always seemed to have a bigger than average bundle of banknotes. The two curious salesladies asked him where he got so much more money than the other retailers, who never had enough to pay their bills. Mr. Mrozowski replied, "I'm a good businessman. I run three stores in three villages. I also deal with the Germans, and they are good customers. I sometimes even supply them with entertainment...you're grown up, you know what I mean."

Mr. Mrozowski was always very polite. This very short man had a soft way of speaking, he was gentle, always ready to help with moving a heavy parcel, always trying to be nice. "I don't trust him," Helena told me. "I have no definite reason to say anything bad about him, but something in his eyes scares me."

Karl was a policeman with a big beer belly, a big face, red cheeks, small blue eyes. He was of German origin, *Volksdeutsch*, but he spoke good Polish. One day, he walked into the store, and found Helena there by herself. Lola had gone out for lunch.

"Tell me, where is the Jewess hiding? Is she there in the back room?" he asked.

Hesse Goldreich's husband and I were at the back of the store unpacking goods. When we heard the German's voice and his footsteps coming towards the back room, we quickly ran out the back door.

"You're making a mistake," said Helena. "There's no *Zydowka* (Jewish woman) here. The store owner will be back soon. You can wait for her if you wish."

"Sure, I'll wait. She must be the Jewess I'm after. I don't mind waiting for her if I can talk to such a good-looking woman. You're so blond and blue-eyed, your father must have been German."

"I don't think so. He never told me that he was German."

"Where do you live? I'd like to come to your house."

"My father wouldn't like it. I'm going out with a boy and my father wants me to marry him."

"Do you like that boy?"

"We're in love with each other."

"Still, I'll be coming here more often now, because I like to talk to you. You have such a smiling face."

Mrs. Golecki walked in. Before Karl managed to open his mouth, Helena told Lola aloud the reason for the German's visit. She kept laughing as she talked, ridiculing the idea that there might be a Jewess working in this store. Lola, a former stage actress, started to laugh, too. Karl now seemed convinced that he had been misinformed. Assuring them that he would be back to see Helena, he left.

A friend of ours, Nahum, who had helped us out in the business many times, was nearby and saw the policeman, Karl, come out of the store. Nahum watched as he walked over to a young Jew and slapped his face: "You liar, you made an ass out of me." Another slap. "There's no Jewish woman in that store."

"Karl, I looked in the store when you were inside. You talked to her all the time. She is blond, with long hair, you talked to her."

Karl ran back into the store. Helena was gone. Lola started to charm the German, and to calm him down, she opened a box of chocolates and treated him.

"I can't believe that a Jewess could be clever enough to fool me."

"She is very nice, too," said Lola.

"And pretty," added the calmed-down Karl. "Listen, when you see her, tell her to come back to the store. I won't bother her at all. Tell her, I'll be back to talk to her, I like her."

Karl kept his word. He was a frequent visitor to the store, and once told them what the young Jew had told him about Helena: "She pretends to be Polish, she doesn't wear the armband with the star of David. She's rich — you'll get a lot of money from her."

"Helena and Lola," Karl used to say. "I'm away from my home and family. I enjoy a lot coming here for a chat."

Chapter Four

The family Aronbrot lived in Lublin, about sixty kilometres from Parczew; they were related to my sister-in-law, Gienia, and that's how I happened to know them. They had a well-established business of buying rags for recycling. The small retailers of the entire district of Lublin sold their wares to the Aronbrot wholesalers.

When the Germans invaded Poland in 1939, they allowed the Aronbrots to continue their business. After all, these Jews had the expertise in their line of work, so why not let them go on, for a while anyway, with their work? The German war machine could always use recycled materials. To protect the Aronbrots from being harassed by the different German organizations, like SS, SA, SD and other groups with different initials, the German war department of supplies had given them special status. The Jewish firm was instructed to set up a network of rag collectors in different locations. Instead of the white band with the star of David, each man was given a green armband that identified him as a *Lumpensammler* (rag collector). With the armband came a certificate, stating the name of the collector and asking all the German uniformed units to give assistance to that Jew, who was performing "useful" work for the war apparatus.

When one of the Aronbrots came to Parczew to set up rag-collectors there, I spoke to him and he agreed to take me into the group. I was given all the necessary documents and instructed how to achieve good results. "You should bear in mind that these Germans mean business. They promise protection but they check on us often to make sure we are fulfilling their requirements."

With the green band on my arm and the *Ausweis* in my pocket, I moved around more freely. I told everyone, Jews and non-Jews, to bring any kind of rags they could find to my warehouse, and I'd pay for the useful waste by weight. I was employed, and protected from being harassed — or so I thought. I even travelled to Lublin by train. No star-of-David-banded Jew was allowed to use the train.

My trips to Lublin, taking loads of rags to the Aronbrots, served another purpose, too. My Aunt Dvoshele and her family lived in Lublin, and during my last year of high school I had lived in her house. Now I could bring her food — which was easier and cheaper to obtain in Parczew than in Lublin. Dvoshele's husband "enlightened" me about appropriate behaviour if I were stopped by a German on the street. For example, if the Germans noticed two or three Jews talking to each other, they would ask what they had been talking about. Each Jew would be questioned separately about the subject of the conversation, and if the answers were different, the Jews would be taken away to the Gestapo quarters for a severe beating. So, the first thing two or three Jewish friends did when they met was to decide what they would answer in case they happened to be asked what they had been talking about. A long list of standardized, innocent answers was created: "We were talking about cheaper and better bread being sold on Szewcka Street." Or: "The weather is getting colder. Good thing my old coat is still in one piece." Or: "The potatoes you can get now from the farmers on the market are half spoiled."

"Remember," my uncle told me, "never have long conversations on the street. You can be sure that you are being watched by the Germans." I followed the instructions.

I was sitting in the train on the way to Lublin when a uniformed German walked into the compartment. He put his suitcase on the luggage rack above the seat, loosened the belt on his uniform a bit and sat down. The two of us were alone in the compartment. He looked me over for a while. I was now, deliberately, puttering around with my little suitcase and taking discreet glances at my companion. He was wearing a plain army uniform with no insignia on it. He looked to be in his mid-thirties, blond, tall, a little on the heavy side. I didn't feel too comfortable. I didn't know what to expect next, but I didn't have to wait too long.

"*Jude?*"

"*Jawohl.*"

"What are you doing here? Oh, yes, you're wearing a green armband. You are the useful kind, eh?" I didn't say anything. "Is that armband yours or did you borrow it from a friend to get on the train? Can I see your special certificate?"

Reaching for my *Ausweis*, I said: "I didn't know the Wehrmacht was interested in those documents. Here is my I.D. card."

"*Jude*, don't make smart remarks." He checked the I.D. number on the band and on the card, then read the card and gave it back to me. "You won't be using that document, or the privilege that comes with it, for very long," he said, so matter-of-factly. I said nothing in response to his remark. He pursued, "Aren't you going to ask me what I meant by that?"

"Frankly, I don't know whether you want to hear me talk."

"You can talk, your German seems quite good. You must have learned it in school."

"Yes, I did."

"You see, that's one of the reasons we hate you. You are always trying to reach inside our culture, mingle with us and then exploit us. I may be a simple man but I read a lot, especially about the tricks of you Jews. Our Führer will put an end to all that now."

"I hope you won't feel offended if I mention that Jews have contributed a lot to German culture. Mendelssohn to music, Professor Ehrlich to medicine, Einstein to physics — just to mention a few."

"Our professors, in the hundreds, are proving now that your Einstein and his theories are a big bluff. The same thing goes for the other Jews as carriers of German culture. You manipulated our lives. We don't want you in our midst, and we'll get rid of you."

"Do you know how the German authorities are planning to get rid of the Jews?"

"I don't know. The last I heard was that the Jews would be resettled as far to the east as possible. There is also talk of shipping you out to Madagascar. I think that would be even better for Germany: the Jews out of Europe, with no right ever to come back. But it will be up to our Führer to decide the Jews' fate. If he finds it more beneficial to the Aryan race to take more drastic measures against the Jews, he'll do it. And we Germans will always be behind our Führer."

The soldier now reached for the German newspaper that was stuck behind the strap of his suitcase. There was no more talk during the remainder of the one-hour trip to Lublin. What was I thinking about? I couldn't figure out how anyone could talk about inflicting pain on millions of people with so much indifference in his voice. Am I not human, or is he not human? I'm not talking about destroying, he is. So, he is the one who is not human; his Führer is bent on destroying us and the Germans are trained to follow orders, no matter how bestial those orders may be.

The German soldier across from me calmly read his paper. I kept thinking about the future of the Jews. Could we still do anything to save ourselves, or was it too late?

During a routine trip to Lublin to deliver some bundles of old rags to the Aronbrots, I noticed that there were very few people on the streets — in a neighbourhood that had always been packed with people of all ages. Something was very wrong. I walked faster; I wanted to reach my friends' house as soon as possible.

I didn't make it. Someone grabbed me from behind and pushed me into the courtyard of one of the houses. It was a Jewish policeman who had grabbed me. When I saw that between thirty and forty people had been rounded up and herded into the courtyard, I knew I was in trouble. I showed the policeman who brought me there my armband, and told him that he had no right to stop me.

"You can stick your armband you know where," he said, "or better yet...." He tore it off my sleeve and took it away. "Put in a day or two's work on Lipowa and you won't get hurt."

There were six policemen armed with clubs guarding the group. A few more young men were brought into the courtyard. Among them, I recognized a neighbour of Aunt Dvoshele's. I pushed through the crowd to speak to him: "Where are they taking us? Shlomo, what's happening? Tell me!" I shook his arm.

"What's happening? Did you just come from the moon? They are taking us to Lipowa, that's what happening. Now do you get it?"

"No, I don't, I just came to Lublin from my home town this morning."

"Forget your home town. You won't see it again. Every day in the last two weeks the Jewish police have arrested people and delivered them to the Gestapo on Lipowa. Nobody has come back from there alive yet." Shlomo was looking frantically in all directions.

Was this the end of my life? It seemed impossible, unbelievable. The policemen lined us up in marching formation, in fours. I made sure

I was in the outer line, hoping that maybe a little brawl or mix-up on the two- or three-kilometre march to Lipowa might allow me a chance to escape. I looked around, searching all the faces. A tall young man stood on the sidewalk. He turned around. I knew him. It was Zvi Silverberg, who used to come to our house, campaigning for the Zionist-revisionist movement. I waved at him, and seeing me, he ran over to the policeman beside me, said something to him, then grabbed me by my arm and pulled me away from the group. Holding hands we ran into the nearest house. I was shaking.

"Hey, calm down. I remember you. You are from Parczew, aren't you? Your father lent me his horse and wagon before the election to the Zionist Congress."

"Yes. I remember you well."

"I told that policeman that you were once my right hand, my buddy, and that I need you now. I know all these bastards. I have some influence with them."

"You saved my life."

"I do whatever I can every day. But, for heaven's sake, what are you doing in Lublin? Are you crazy or what? Stick to your own holes in Parczew." I told Zvi about my green armband and my work collecting rags. "All that means nothing now. Don't be naive — you can't rely on the green band. Where are you staying in Lublin? I'll take you there."

Zvi escorted me to my Aunt Dvoshele's house. Before I went in, I thanked Zvi. He looked at me seriously and asked: "You think we'll make it?"

We shook hands. I never met or heard of Zvi again. He didn't survive. (Dear Zvi: If there's a place where your soul is staying and you can hear me from there, I want to tell you this: Thanks to you, I survived Hitler. I lived to see our enemy smashed to pieces. I lived to have that satisfaction; and I want you and all the others so dear to us to share that satisfaction with me. That is our vengeance.)

Everyone, especially the young men, was constantly afraid, constantly on the alert. News reached Parczew that the Gestapo were rounding up young Jews in neighbouring towns and taking them away to unknown destinations. People said "they," the Germans, showed up early in the morning and had left by sunrise, speeding out of town in trucks specially brought in to carry the young men they had rounded up.

Rumours were spreading that a raid on Parczew was imminent. Groups were formed to keep watch at night on the highways: looking out for approaching German trucks. These trucks were always preceded by two or three cars, carrying the commanding officers. The moment a line of headlights appeared on any of the highways leading to the *shtetl* (town), the young men would be warned immediately and they would take cover in the prepared hiding-holes. These anti-Jewish actions intensified when events on the Russian front in the late fall of 1941 began to turn against the German army.

I was part of a group that included the young males of the Goldreich family and a few neighbours of theirs. We used the Goldreichs' house as a lookout. From the front windows on the second floor we could clearly see the highways leading to the city. As we watched, we played poker and discussed the war — how long it might last, how hard the Germans would oppress the Jews and how the Western powers did nothing but talk: as one of us said, "If the war could be fought with well-phrased slogans, the West would easily win." We took shifts: while one of us watched, the rest of us slept. In our clothes, naturally. We had to be ready to run to the "hole" in seconds.

The hole was behind the building we were in, in one of the Goldreichs' warehouses. Preparing the hole had taken a lot of time. We had to remove many cubic metres of earth and dispose of it without anybody's noticing. The hiding-place was three by four by three metres high. We put up a ceiling of wooden boards and over the boards we put earth to the same level as the rest of the floor in the warehouse. We used that hiding-place several times when the local German police units, instead of requisitioning workers from the *Judenrat* in an orderly way, used "round-ups" just to create panic among the Jews.

Life became more depressing with each passing day. Besides the round-ups, the Gestapo dropped by regularly in their Mercedes-Benzes from their headquarters in Radzyn. Each time we saw the grey cars, sometimes only one or two of them, we knew that a new order, a new command against the Jews was imminent. Attached to the back of each car was a box on two wheels. The box was about one cubic metre in volume (approximately ten cubic feet). Unexpectedly, the *ketchel* — that's what we called the box — would stop in front of a house. The

Germans would walk into the house, take out one or two people, stuff them in the box and drive off with them to the headquarters in Radzyn.

The first victims were intellectuals, who might have organized resistance or sabotage. After an initial beating and interrogation in Radzyn, those arrested were sent to Auschwitz as political prisoners. If they were Jews, we never heard from them again. Other people to be taken away in the *ketchel* were Jews who were suspected of being rich or having jewellery or gold. All the victims' families were blackmailed, then the arrested ones were tortured to death. To this day, in the late 1980s, the sight of a Mercedes or BMW car brings those images to me: the images of the *ketchel*, with its "load" to be brutally murdered.

Chapter Five

Karl, the beer-bellied German to whom my wife had once lied about being Jewish, came into the Ludwik Golecki store one morning.

"Helena, it's good that you are here. I've got to talk to you. Let's go to the back of the store. I don't want anybody to see us talking to each other."

I was in the back of the store and Helena knew it. To give me time to get out through the back door, Helena said:

"Sure, let's go to the back. But just a moment — I want to take a sandwich with me, I'm hungry." I went out the back of the store. What did Karl want?

"Helena, I'm German, but I'm not all bad. I want to help you. You have to be honest with me and tell me the truth. Only then I'll try to help you. Do you promise to tell me the truth?"

"What truth? I told you already that I'm Jewish, what other truth can I tell you?"

"Do you promise or not?"

"Yes, I promise."

"Listen, Helena. I know who your husband is. They say he comes from a well-to-do family. Now. Did you marry him for his money or because you loved him? Tell the truth, Helena. If you are lying, you'll be in trouble. When you lied to me the first time, telling me you were not the Jewish woman I was after, I forgave you. I liked your courage then. But it'll be different if you don't tell the truth now."

"Karl, I married my husband because we have loved each other since childhood. This is all the truth that I'm telling you now. My word of honour, that is the truth. Why do you want to know?"

"Listen. There's a list been made up at the station, a list of those to be arrested tonight or tomorrow night. We've received instructions from the Gestapo in Radzyn to arrest some educated people. We asked around; your husband's name is on that list."

"Karl, can you help? Help me, Karl, I beg you."

"I have helped you — by warning you. Your husband will have to hide for at least a week. He must not stay or sleep in the house until this blows over. I'll talk to you then."

"Karl, I'm so thankful to you. Can you tell me who else is on the list?"

"I know the names, but I don't know who they are and I don't want to know. My advice to you is: take care of yourself and keep your mouth shut. If you talk, you'll be the loser."

I went into hiding in Ludwik Golecki's hideout. Two days later, a German from the police station came to my house looking for me, claiming that they wanted me to do some translating from German into Polish. My mother-in-law told the policeman that I was at work. Later, Karl told Helena that he had been listening and had heard no talk at the station about chasing me. After that incident, Karl kept coming to the store to talk to the two ladies. Although he was the joking type of person, they were always suspicious of him.

Every day I wondered how long my luck would last. I had been saved by a warning from a German who admired my wife Helena's quick wit. In Lublin my green armband and special *Ausweis* were supposed to give me security, but they hadn't protected me from the Jewish police — only Zvi Silverberg, and probably my luck, had saved my life. I decided to become invisible, or as close to invisible as it was possible to achieve.

Every day at dawn, a group of between forty and fifty Jews went to work at a sawmill in Pohulanki, a place six kilometres away from Parczew. It was dark when they came back to the city. I thought that by working all week long — from sunrise to sundown — in the sawmill, I might avoid the "evil eye." Perhaps nobody would think of me — out of sight, out of mind; I joined the group.

Before the war, the sawmill in Pohulanki was one of the enterprises of the government-run forestry industry. The forests around Parczew were rich in pine, birch and spruce trees. When the Germans arrived, they took over the lumber industry. They brought in private entrepreneurs from Germany who leased the sawmills from the German government and sold the wood products either to German builders "*in dem Reich*" or to the military, which always needed wood for bridges, barracks or other purposes.

When I joined the group, the manager of the mill was a man by the name of Heinz Erlbacher, an Austrian. Short and slim, always neatly dressed in a suit and a darkish hat with a Tyrolean feather, his face narrow with prominent cheekbones, he seldom spoke to us, but when he did, it was only to harass us. Once he ordered the foreman to have the workers take a sorted pile of cut boards and turn it around 180 degrees. When the boards were brought out of the milling shop to the yard we had to sort them out by length and width, stack them two metres high and arrange them with one end even. And here came that Austrian and told us to take a pile apart and arrange it straight at the other end. He was an unbelievably vicious man.

One day I remarked to my father, "Look what happened to all the efforts you and Mom made for my education. Now I have no choice but to work at sorting out lumber. My hands are so hardened that I almost never get a splinter in my skin."

"My dear son, if with God's help we survive all this, you'll still possess great capital. That capital — education — nobody can take away from you."

One evening my dear Helena told me she was pregnant. "Dear Ben, I know what this means, how hard a time we can expect, with me being pregnant, but I don't want to think about an abortion. I just pray it will be a girl. Just in case. You know what I mean."

My family and my in-laws supported Helena's wish for a baby. My own reaction was mixed. When it was quiet for a day or two, I thought, "Wonderful! my wife is pregnant. We'll have so much pleasure when the baby arrives." But when terrible things were done to our community, I felt just the opposite.

Every day, after I came home from work, Helena and I talked about the coming baby. "Ben, I want so much to have him. Who do you think the baby will look like, you or me? Maybe everything will change for the better when our baby arrives. What do you think? Say something, Ben!" In answer, I kissed her. "Let's pray for a lucky baby," Helena said.

As the months went by, Helena gave up working at the store except for the odd day when she felt comfortable. Still, I asked her how business was, and about the customers I used to know — the ones from out of town. Helena talked a lot about Mr. Mrozowski, who had three stores. "He is still as polite as ever: he keeps telling me that he is ready to help me at any time I might need any kind of help. I still don't trust him."

After my day's work at the sawmill in Pohulanki, we were talking about events in town. There was never a shortage of events to talk about in those days.

There was a knock at the door, and two soldiers walked into the house. They ordered me to go with them. Helena tried to explain that I had just come home after working a full day.

"We need a young man to do two hours' work." Helena and my mother-in-law's pleading did not help. I had to go with them. "We will even pay him, we are the Wehrmacht, you know."

I dressed again for the cold winter night outside and we went out. With a soldier on either side of me, I walked in the direction indicated by them. It was a clear, cold night, with lots of stars in the sky. I wasn't expecting to come to any harm: after all, these two were just soldiers. They'd probably make me work for a while, then let me go. An everyday occurrence.

About three hundred metres from my house, the soldiers stopped in front of a dilapidated building. It was unlighted: all the windows were dark. The entrance door was half open. One of the soldiers told me to get inside. In a split second, there came to my mind the thought that, once I was inside, the soldiers were going to shoot me, just for the fun of it. I made a sort of gesture hesitating to go inside.

"*Gehe mal in, habe kein Angst, schnell* (step inside, have no fear, quick)."

I had put one foot over the threshold when I saw the light beam from a flashlight, and heard a man groaning. Oh, my God, something bad is going on here, was the thought that flashed through my mind.

The light beam turned on me and before my eyes had a chance to adjust and see who was holding the flashlight, I was kicked with a terrible force, right in my groin. I bent forward in pain and instinctively moved two or three steps backwards. I couldn't run out of the house:

the two soldiers were behind me, silhouetted in the doorway. If I had tried to escape, they would have shot me and I couldn't run fast anyway, with the pain in the groin not yet subsided. Such pain makes one's thoughts run through one's mind with the speed of light.

After kicking me, the man with the flashlight turned slightly away from me and I recognized him as the tall German with the baby face whom everybody at the police station called "the dog." This animal never walked the street alone. There was always a German shepherd dog beside him which was trained to attack Jews at his command. Whenever any of us noticed "the dog," — Ili was his name — we immediately ran into hiding. Ili was feared even by his police comrades, because he was a Gestapo plant whose job was to watch and report on the activities of the other Germans.

Oh, God, "the dog," I thought. He was holding in his right hand his short stiletto. The German shepherd, his eternal companion, sat on his haunches, just watching.

The groaning was louder now. It was coming from someone lying on the floor. "The dog" turned to me and said, "Tell that *Jude* in his own language to show where he is hiding the leather, or I'll kill him."

I approached the figure sprawled on the floor. I recognized him. It was the tall, red-headed Enoch "Kepke." Kepke was not his real surname, just a nickname, of the kind people in small towns often give to each other. Enoch was a leather dealer and shoemaker. There was a pile of leather on the floor.

I told Enoch in Yiddish what "the dog" had told me to tell him. In a groaning voice, Enoch answered that he had no more leather. "Everything...I...had...I...gave...already." Enoch's voice was barely audible. I repeated his answer to the German.

"*Der Schweinhunde Jude, warte* (pig-dog Jew, wait)." "The dog" walked over to the bleeding Enoch and stabbed him slowly with his knife, saying in a low voice: "*Jude*, you have more leather. Where is it? Tell me, tell me or you'll die."

"The dog" stabbed Enoch slowly, repeatedly, talking all the time for what seemed to me then another fifteen minutes. Then he ordered the soldiers to move Enoch outside. Enoch's groans were getting weaker.

"The dog" was going around now, using a wooden stick to poke the floor, inch by inch, looking for a hollow spot, a possible hiding-place for leather under the floor. Then I was ordered to take the leather lying on the floor and bundle it together in two sheets pulled from the beds. The two soldiers carried one bundle; the second they lifted to my shoulders.

"Follow us," they told me. "The dog" and his companion dog went off in a different direction.

We were going towards the German police station. With the bundle of leather on my back, I passed the place where my in-laws had once lived. There was the glassed-in veranda, where I had spent so many pleasant evenings talking to Hindele. And now?

When we reached the police station, "the dog" was already there. He told me to go home. It was past midnight. I asked for a *Bescheinigung* (certificate) in case somebody stopped me for being out so late. "The dog" uttered a short laugh: "Nobody will stop you. And if somebody kills you, well...you are only a Jew." Another short chuckle. I turned around and started to walk, expecting to be shot in the back by that monster. When I reached home I found that no one had gone to bed. Everybody was waiting for me to return.

The following morning, before going to work to the sawmill, I heard that Enoch "Kepke" had been found dead, frozen in a pool of blood about thirty feet away from his house.

In the winter of 1941-42 the Jews of Parczew were kept hard at work on projects the Germans did not need; once they were given plenty of bribes, however, the Germans agreed to consider the projects useful for *das Reich*. The *Judenrat*, through bitter toil, did its best to provide the neediest with food and clothing.

Then a new figure arrived on the scene: Rudi Kresh, a German Jew in his mid-thirties, who dressed like a German, always in a long leather coat. When he was out walking on the street with his beautiful wife, there was always a dog on a leash at their side. Somehow, he became an intermediary between the Gestapo, or the local gendarmerie, and the *Judenrat*. His way of communicating with the *Judenrat* was official, German-like. Only one member of the *Judenrat* recognized that a new element had come into our lives. His name was Shulim Fuchs; and he joined forces with Kresh. Giving the Germans exactly what they wanted, Fuchs and Kresh grew powerful. A needy Jew could not communicate with them; they were unreachable. The old guard of the *Judenrat* tried to intercede, to temper the zealousness of the new team's "co-operation" with the Germans. They seldom succeeded in their efforts.

The Germans were becoming worse and worse in the demands they made on the Jews. The Jews, for their part, looked for a silver lining in all those clouds: and they found one. The news filtering through from the eastern German-Russian front told of hundreds of German soldiers being transported back west, terribly frostbitten. Even the German press wasn't hiding the fact that the German army had been halted at the front. The Jews, having developed through millennia the art of hoping for better times to come, compared the situation of Hitler's army in Stalin's winter land to Napoleon's situation in 1812, in the same part of Russia. This was the beginning of the end of Hitler — or so the Jews said, and hoped.

The leaders of the Gestapo who were close to the Führer at that time were probably plagued by a vision of their defeat. The Jews were praying for it. But the beasts decided that, even if nothing else could be achieved, they would succeed in at least one of their programmes. The Nazi programme for the liquidation of the European Jewry now became the ultimate goal. Goebbels, with his crippled mind, wrote constantly in his weekly *Das Reich* of the imminent destruction of the Jews. The minister of propaganda couldn't talk about the German army immobilized in Russia; instead he talked about Jews.

That winter, the Germans ordered the Jews to hand over, on pain of death, all their furs and pelts — apparently it was all right for furs from "dirty" Jews to keep the "clean" Aryans warm on the eastern front. It seemed, from the Germans' complaints, that many Jews had not complied. Helena told me one evening that she had cut up her seal coat into small pieces and buried them in a deep hole behind the barn of her parents' former landlord. "I loved my coat," she said. "I bought it with my own money. But no German will cover his ass with it."

A new snag developed. Our Polish friend, Ludwik Golecki, got wind that he was on a list of those "wanted" by the Germans. Some from the list had been sent to Auschwitz. Ludwik had to go into hiding. He escaped to Warsaw, where he got himself a new identity document, in the name of Ludwik Golik. He was still sending merchandise to the store in Parczew. Mrs. Golecki was usually alone in the store now.

Helena was pregnant and couldn't help much. Two of the Goldreich sisters did some of the work: at the back of the store only.

Then the first great tragedy struck our family. One Monday morning in February 1942, I went over to my parents' place. Everything was as usual. My father had his prayer shawl on, and was in the middle of his morning prayers.

When he moved the shawl from his face, we looked at each other. From his expression, I guessed that his mind was preoccupied, not with his prayers, but with his thoughts about the precarious circumstances of the Jews. There was something in the way he looked at me that has remained with me forever.

I went over to him, kissed him and said, "Dad, I can't stay. I'll be back in the afternoon. There's a lot in the German newspapers I'd like to talk to you about." I left the house.

That same day, sometime around one o'clock in the afternoon, "the dog," Ili, approached my father on the street; a little later they were seen walking side by side into the backyard of a house where our family used to live. Someone ran to my parents' house and told my older brother that something was happening to our father. My brother ran to the backyard of our former house, where he saw "the dog" with his gun drawn, and heard him order my father to turn around. That proud Jew refused and looked the murderer straight in the face. Two shots followed. Father was dead. He died instantly.

Minutes later I arrived in my parents' house and saw my father's body. I looked at the stream of blood on his face. I could not believe that this man, who had been a beam of light to me in all my growing-up years, was dead. I didn't cry. How could I cry, being one mass of pain? I heard someone say, "'The dog' killed him." A spark flashed through my mind: revenge! I blacked out. About half an hour after the shooting, "the dog" came into our house and asked, "Is Mandelkern really dead? — But he was so big, so influential and so strong."

The German police ordered that my father's body be transferred to the cemetery immediately. Panic and disorientation gripped everybody in town. The interment didn't take place that same day. The family was worrying that stray dogs might desecrate his body. It was dark when my sister-in-law, Dula, not saying a word, slipped out of our house. Early next morning when the immediate family and the burial society arrived at the cemetery, we found Dula all bundled up, sitting on a stone near my father's body. She told us that she was watching Leib Mandelkern's body against animals the whole night long. Are there words strong enough to express the greatness of character of that seventeen-year-old girl? — alone, on a cold winter night in a cemetery, about 100 metres away from the German police station, fulfilling such a holy mission!

The family was in despair. My mother's eyes were overflowing with tears; but she couldn't bring out a sound. While sitting *shiva*, the period of mourning, I thought that if there was a God in this universe, he probably wanted to save my father from seeing what was about to happen to the people around him, to the people he had tried so hard to help.

The rabbi, who lived in Parczew and whom my father supported financially, came to the *shiva*. He commented on my father's refusal to turn around, his insistence on facing the killer's gun. "Leib Mandelkern figured it out, and very rightly, that this was now his only way to get even with the murderer. The face of that courageous Jew will always be like a thorn in the mind of that killer, always, right to the killer's last minutes of life."

The grief in town was universal. Jews and Gentiles wept openly. The Jews said that Leib Mandelkern's death was probably a sign of what was to come.

They were right.

The death of my father touched the human side of *Judenrat* members. They wanted to give us not only moral, but practical support. The new bosses, the ruling team of Kresh and Shulim Fuchs, approached me after our mourning days.

"Listen, Benjamin, you are working in the sawmill of Pohulanki, as a plain labourer. You'll be safer if you join the Jewish police. Once you put on a policeman's insignia, no German will touch you. Kresh and I have the power to take you into the police force immediately, and we are doing so, because your father did so much for the community. This is our thank you to him. You'll be safe."

As strange as it sounded to the team of Kresh and Shulim, I had no difficulty making up my mind what to tell them. Without hesitation, I answered, "No, Herr Kresh and Mr. Shulim, I don't want to be a policeman. I'll continue working in the sawmill. If my fate is to survive the war, I don't want to have it on my conscience that I ever put my hand on a fellow Jew and turned him over to the Germans. No, I don't want that. I'll continue working in Pohulanki."

The team looked at each other. Herr Kresh had on his face his typical smile, the smile so well polished in a German school somewhere. To this day, and for the rest of the days of my life, I have been grateful that I made that fateful decision in those dark days.

Chapter Six

Helena gave birth to a baby boy. We and the rest of the family felt the love parents always feel for their newborn child. But there was not the usual joy. The little boy came to this world just a few weeks after his grandfather was killed. The whole family was in deep mourning, still. We all did our best to muster smiles for the baby, but it was a great effort.

Every day after work, I stood over the baby's little bed and looked at him. What was I thinking? Would he make it? Would we make it with him?

Helena asked me: "Will he be circumcised?"

"I don't know. I don't think we should circumcise him."

"You mean, in case we have to give him up?"

"Yes."

"If I live, do you think I'll ever get him back?"

"Helena, dear, I don't know what to say. On my way back from work I was thinking that maybe both of us should go over to the rabbi and ask his advice in the matter. You know how highly my father, blessed be his memory, valued the advice of that spiritual leader."

Neither Helena nor I had ever, in our prewar life, thought about the meaning or importance or strength of the spiritual leader's advice. But now, circumstances touched the deep-rooted *pintele yid* (the inner mark of Jewishness) in us, and we wanted to do now what my dear father would have done in this grave situation.

We went to the rabbi. We told him about our indecision with regard to the circumcision of the baby. "Out of deep respect to the memory of my father, blessed be his memory, we would like to follow in the footsteps of our ancestors, but then, holy Rabbi, you know what circumstances are now...." We did not finish saying aloud what was on our minds.

Silence. The rabbi put his arms on the table he was sitting at, put down his head and hid his face in his hands. Long silence. Helena and I looked at each other, waiting in tension for the holy rabbi's words. He remained in this position, his head swaying slightly, as if a battle between invisible forces were being fought in his mind. He sighed deeply.

When he took away his hands, a changed face appeared, a face ravaged by inner soul-searching. "Benjamin, son of Jehuda, and Hinda, daughter of Shoel," his voice was low, very shaky but clear, "I have fought within myself. A big fight. I say that if you, Benjamin, and you, Hinda, do not have your son circumcised, you will be forgiven. In my argument with God, God lost His power to ever punish you for that. The devil is free in our society now, and to protect a Jewish life, a Jewish father and mother can take an exception from the covenant."

The rabbi stood up, put his arms on my shoulders and blessed me: "May the Almighty bless you and shelter you." He looked at Helena as if he were giving her the same blessing with his eyes. When we left the holy rabbi's place, Helena and I had decided not to circumcise the baby.

Then new doubts entered our minds. What if we had to give him away to a Gentile family and then never got him back, that is if we survived the war? We would suffer all our lives. Or if we didn't survive, our son might never know about his roots, he might even grow up to hate Jews. And what were our chances of surviving that inferno?

Helena's mother said: "My grandson is Jewish and he will be circumcised. Whatever our fate will be, his will be the same."

My mother: "I want the baby to be circumcised and be named Arya Jehuda, after my husband. All of us owe that to the memory of my husband."

The shock of my father's death had taken from Helena and me the strength to decide what we should do regarding our son. Like the rest of the family, we were confused. We decided to let events develop on their own. The circumcision took place. Our son was named Arya Jehuda. I saw my mother many times leaning over the baby and saying: "Dear Leibele, I love you. You must grow up to be a *mentch* like your *zeidi*." She then wiped her eyes.

Those inhabitants of Parczew who survived the Nazi hell will never forget the summer of 1942. It was past midnight when Gestapo officers, aided by the Wehrmacht, surrounded the town then went from house to house calling on all Jews to gather on the market square. "Any Jew not obeying the order will be shot dead on the spot," we were warned. The *Judenrat* members announced, repeatedly, that the Jewish population was being resettled in a different location.

Panic broke out. Nobody believed the announcements but the constant salvoes from German machine guns did not leave us much choice. We went to the market square. When God's sun appeared in the blue sky, the market was already full of people: young, old, mothers with young children at their hands or in their arms. People in anxiety calling each other. Soldiers beating the screaming people. A real inferno.

The officers ordered the Jewish police and the members of the *Judenrat* to be in the marketplace — to help organize the gathered masses in orderly groups. The Germans called the whole enterprise "the action," and organizing of the groups of people "the selection." Old people were selected separately, women and children separately, men separately. They announced over the loudspeakers that groups employed in different locations should group themselves separately. I took up a position among the sawmill workers.

German soldiers were hauling people out of their hiding places and beating them with rifle-butts. They marched the elderly away first, to the train station. I noticed in the marching line my grandfather Eli Lerner. He walked erect and seemed to be looking straight ahead. Poor grandfather, he suffered from cataracts in his eyes; he could not really see where he was going. He supported himself with a cane held in his right hand. And what was he holding under his left arm? What did Eli Lerner take, of all his possessions? Did he try to save something he might need on the road to his unknown destination? Rays of bright sunlight fell on the object Grandpa Eli was carrying and reflected the golden lettering TALITH (prayer shawl) on the blue velvet casing. He knew that he would die soon for his religion; and the *talith* was the only thing he needed now. It was the same *talith* he put over his head so many times all his life when he prayed to his God. Beside Grandpa Eli walked his wife, Grandma Pearl. She was holding her blind husband's arm and leading him. Grandpa Eli and Grandma Pearl were the only ones from my family I saw that morning.

The group I was in was ordered to march off to the sawmill in Pohulanki to work. They still needed us. There were only about twenty-five of us. The rest of our working unit did not come to the market. They were probably in hiding, or in confusion got mixed up with the big crowd.

Six armed soldiers guarded us on the march to Pohulanki. To confuse us, and to keep us in a state of panic, they made us walk fast, constantly shooting from their machine guns. When one of the workers appeared to be out of line, he was shot dead. The dead fellow worker was left in the field and nobody was even allowed to turn to see who it was. I heard right behind me a German yelling out: "*Schnell, du Hund einer!*" Before realizing that I was the one he was yelling at, I was hit with the rifle butt twice right between the shoulders. I leaped forward and avoided another swing of the rifle. I could just see the soldier attacking another man.

We reached the sawmill. I saw Karl Erlbacher, the assistant manager, running towards the gate. He signed a paper acknowledging receiving us and handed it over to the soldiers, who departed immediately, probably back to the city. We begged Karl to go to the city and get the rest of the workers. He sent us to work, took his bicycle and rode off. After a couple of hours we saw Karl coming back with about thirty men. Some of the men were not from our group at all, but Karl wanted to save them, claiming to the Gestapo that he needed them to run the mill.

We waited, trying to look as if we were working. Karl came into the yard, saw the way we were doing things, and did not say a bad word to us. He walked around, shaking his head. He was a German, but a decent human being. The day finally came to an end. Karl told us that everything was quiet now in Parczew, but if we wanted to stay overnight in Pohulanki we could.

We decided to go to town and see what had happened. The streets where most of the Jews lived were empty. I ran to my in-laws' place: nobody there. No Helena, no baby, no Dula, no in-laws. I ran to my mother's place. No mother, no brother Bunim, nor his wife and their four-year-old Kubush. Nor my oldest brother Moishele. They were all gone.

The look of the house deepened the tragedy. All the doors and windows were open. Everything in the house had been stolen. Literally nothing was left in the house, no clothing, no shoes, no furniture, no cutlery. I saw two of Kubush's broken toys. I ran out of the house. I saw silhouettes move in the windows of the Gentile neighbours; they were watching, probably in amazement at seeing me there. I ran to the neighbourhood that used to be 100 per cent Jewish. Maybe, I thought, I'll find someone there who knows exactly what happened to my family and the other Jews.

I found a group of about fifteen people. The first thing they told me was that my wife and our baby, my in-laws and Dula were right in the next house. I ran there and found them. They told me that they had all hidden in the underground shelter we'd built in the shack adjoining the house. They had come out of the "hole" two hours before, Dula coming up first to see whether the "action" was over. At that point, my brother Moishele's girlfriend and two Jewish policemen came into the house.

From them, I learned a few more details about what had happened to my family. My mother, my sister-in-law, little Kubush and my brother Bunim had been sitting together in one spot in the marketplace. Some members of the *Judenrat* tried to intervene with the Gestapo, but to no avail. They could have saved my brother by sending him off to work with one of the work groups, but Bunim refused to leave his wife, son, and mother. They had all been taken to the train station. My mother was shot in the arm during the march. My brother Moishele had been in hiding, but at noon, when he believed that everything was over, he came out and was grabbed by two Germans. He was marched to the station with a group of others the Germans found in other hiding-places. By the flickering light of a naphtha lamp we talked for the rest of the evening.

The following morning, I went back to work at the sawmill. I talked to the other workers, and we pieced together the events of the previous day. The Germans took between 2,000 and 3,000 Jews. Between 700 and 800 were left: some from the working groups, some the people who managed to hide. Was there anything we could do to find out what happened to the families that had been taken away? Had they been taken to another city? Could we send a Gentile to find out? Where was one to start?

Working in the office of the sawmill, I heard that a new group of Lithuanian guards had arrived. The departing guards came to the office for some papers, and they mentioned that the newly arrived guards had escorted a trainload of Jews to a camp. I decided to try to talk to the new guards, and to find out where the trainloads of Jews were being taken.

Armed with some paper folders, to look like a clerk, I went to the guards' quarters. They were all in black uniforms dressed up with German insignia. Their *Totkopf* ("death's-head") emblems said everything about the bearers. None of them wanted to talk about the Jews on the trains. Had they been ordered not to talk? Some of the guards just turned away from me, others gestured with their right hands as if to say, The Jews are gone for good. I offered, in an inconspicuous way, a bribe. Nothing. I found out nothing.

The same afternoon, a uniformed guard walked into the office. "Is the Frau manager in?"

"No."

"Good. Listen, don't offer anybody any bribes. There's nothing anybody can do for you. All the trainloads of Jews have been taken to death camps. They are gassed there and their bodies burned. This is the truth. Run away somewhere, because they'll take all of you to the death camps. And don't ever mention to anybody that I told you. If you do, I might pay for it with my head." He left the office.

I believed him at first. Then I started to have doubts. How could it be possible. Thousands of people gassed and burned? I shared my secret with a few of my co-workers. Some of them believed, others did not.

Chapter Seven

We came to work every day looking more like sleepwalkers than healthy young people. There was no discipline of any kind any more. Some workers had stopped coming. There were rumours that they had run to the woods and that partisan groups were forming there. I had been reassigned to the office, and the foreman of our group asked me to type up some new *Ausweise* (identity cards) for some of the Jews left in town so that they could work at the mill. Luckily, I found a pile of about fifty *Ausweise*, all stamped with the manager's name and ready to be used. I gave the foreman of our group this "treasure." The new workers were briefed on how to behave so that they would look familiar with the work and surroundings.

I was under strain, working in the office now. The manager had been replaced by his daughter Greta, who treated me kindly. But in my office I often unwillingly overheard conversations and witnessed situations that could have got me in trouble. Every day now two or three cars (Mercedes-Benzes, Opels and Daimlers, I hate them to this day) with high-ranking officers in them stopped in front of the office. Whenever I saw these Gestapo officers coming, I thought they were coming to get me. They never closed the door between Greta's office and my room. They used to tell Greta the news from the *Ostfront* (Eastern front), not caring at all that someone in the other office might hear. I found out this way about enormous casualties in lives, inefficiency of equipment in the bitter cold of the Russian winter, the falling morale in the army. I also found out from these conversations that Greta had lost her husband on the *Ostfront* eight months before.

I was scared. What if one of these officers visiting Greta asked her, Who is that young man in the other room? Does he understand German? If she told him that I was Jewish (she certainly wouldn't want to be caught hiding that fact), then he would finish me off in an instant.

A Jew, listening in to the bad news from the frontlines? Never, he has to go, and....

My fears were even bigger when a visiting officer started physically romancing Greta, not caring a bit about the open door to my office. I was afraid to move even a paper on the desk. When I saw them shutting the door, I ran outside thinking that one day I'd get it. What a character that Greta was! I could expect anything from her, good and bad, sweet and cruel. Her blond hair was always combed loose; she had big cheek bones, blue eyes, a high forehead, an aggressively shaped mouth — she was no beauty, but a riddle of a character.

Greta knew well that I was Jewish. Whenever she wanted something from me she called me by my first name. Unexpectedly, she would come over to my desk and start asking me questions: "Benjamin, are you married?"

"Yes."

"Any children?"

"A four-week-old baby boy."

"Has your wife enough food for herself and the baby? I'll give you some extra ration coupons. I'll give you some bars of soap and a warm sweater for you to use."

"Oh, thank you."

"Benjamin, maybe, for better protection, you should bring your wife to stay here. She would be safer here than in the city."

"Can she bring the baby with her?"

"Of course! I love babies."

Next day Greta shook her head in disbelief when I told her that my wife did not want to leave her parents and come to stay in the sawmill. Still, every few days Greta asked me whether I needed anything extra for my family. I didn't want to seem greedy; I asked her for very little.

"I'm going to town, can I go to see her? I'd like to see her and the baby." I couldn't believe my ears. This was supposed to be the wife of a former Gestapo man? I gave her the location where my wife was staying.

Greta told me the next day, "No, I had no time to look her up. Can you bring me a picture of her?"

"I will if I can find one. We lost all those things during the 'action' in Parczew."

It became an obsession of Greta's to get to know my wife. When I brought a photograph of my wife (I had none of my baby, never made one in those dreadful circumstances), Greta looked at it with concentration. "Is she blond?"

"Yes."

"And her eyes?"

"Blue."

"Benjamin, she seems to be a very pretty woman."

"Thank you. Yes, she is."

"Do you love her? Does she love you?"

"Very much. We have known each other since childhood."

"Benjamin, I hope you survive the war." Greta returned to her office and started her paper work.

The very same afternoon, after all her kindnesses in conversation with me, Greta walked into the office with a revolver in her hand. She put it in her handbag and came over to me. "Benjamin, I just shot and killed two Jewish boys."

I felt all my blood disappearing from my face.

Greta continued in a matter-of-fact tone. "I was out riding my horse when I noticed two boys coming out of the woods. They looked like brothers, ten and twelve years old, with earlocks. They looked very scared when I called them over. All these two boys could expect was misery and suffering. To save them from all that I shot them."

"Frau Greta, can I go and bury them?"

"I ordered Piotr, the watchman, to do that."

"Can I go out now?" I felt a tightening in my throat.

"Where do you want to go?"

"To find Piotr."

"You shouldn't go, Benjamin. Don't upset yourself, it is war."

"War against two Jewish boys?"

"You think it would be better for them first to suffer and then die?"

I felt tears coming to my eyes. Greta went away. I felt sick for the rest of the day. The same woman who showed me affection by providing me with extra food and other supplies, the same woman who was wishing me and my wife to survive the war, has murdered two Jewish boys of ten and twelve, in cold blood, calculating. "It's war," she said. To shoot two young boys? God Almighty, hide Your face in shame!

These two boys had not sinned! When I saw Helena after work, I didn't tell her about it.

Two days later, Frau Greta called out from her office: "Benjamin, put away your papers and come with me."

"Where to?"

"You should ask no questions."

I followed her outside. I didn't like the tone of her voice and I was sure she was up to something strange. She was walking fast and I was following her. Greta told me to take out a shovel from a shed nearby. A shovel? What was she planning? Would she order me to dig a hole for myself and then try to save me from misery, like those two boys? No, it couldn't be. She had not brought her handbag with the gun in it. Had she hidden the gun? Oh, no, Greta, wait a minute. It won't be as simple as that! I took a shovel from the shed, and kept myself a swing's length from Greta: I thought, If I see her reaching for the gun, I'll swing this shovel right at that blondie's neck.

"Call Piotr out of his house!"

When I called out the watchman, Greta went over to him and... boom. She slapped him right in the face. Before the poor guy realized what was happening to him, Greta hit him again. Greta turned to me: "Tell that *Schweinhund* that was for the mess he left near the flower bed this morning. Give him the shovel and tell him he has one hour to clean up everything or else I'll see him again. You can go back to the office now, Benjamin."

For how long would that monster be kind to me? I wondered.

A small number of Jews were left in Parczew after the first action. A new *Judenrat* was appointed. The original members, honest and concerned Jews who had tried so hard, and with so much self-denial, to help people in need, were gone — all but two: Shulim Fuchs and Boruch ("Butche") Reich. Fuchs, however, worked in collaboration with the new go-between, Rudi Kresh. There was not much Butche Reich, a man with a heart of gold, could do to help now.

The Jews realized now that it was only a matter of time before they were all taken to the place where the people from that big roundup had gone: Treblinka. People started to look for ways to hide. Some did so by finding hideout places in villages, others took to the forests to join the budding partisan groups. When several days passed and there was no news of my family, I knew it was useless to keep hoping. Only my in-laws, my wife and our baby and Dula, my wife's younger sister, were still together. We had to decide what to do with ourselves.

One possibility was Mr. Mrozowski, the storekeeper-client of the Ludwik Golecki store who had always been generous, and had assured Mrs. Golecki that he would be ready at any time to hide some of us in the village he lived in, in his own home. "I like these people," he told her. "I want to help. Tell Helena and her sister that they can count on me. All they'll have to pay for is their food."

Dula decided to accept his offer and, together with her boyfriend and two other couples, they went to Mr. Mrozowski's place. He inquired of Dula whether all these people had enough money or other possessions to pay for their stay in his place. Helena, however, was doubtful about Mrozowski's intentions.

Ludwik Golecki, who had been hiding in Warsaw under an assumed name, suggested that Helena come to Warsaw. Gienia, Helena's older sister, had found a hiding-place for her family on the Aryan side of Warsaw. Knowing what had happened to the Jews in Parczew, Ludwik advised Helena to come to Warsaw where he would help her find a hiding-place with a Polish family.

Travelling to Warsaw was dangerous. Someone might recognize Helena and denounce her to the Germans. Such things happened on the trains every day. The collaborators were of all ages, grownups and young kids alike. To the latter, denouncing Jews was a sport — and why not? After all, many of the Catholic clergy indoctrinated the faithful church-goers with the most vitriolic anti-Semitic feelings. They portrayed the Jews as eternal sinners who deserved their fate. So why should the faithful Catholics hesitate in denouncing Jews to the Germans?

We followed Ludwik's advice. Helena, dressed as a food-smuggling Polish farmwoman, equipped with baskets of food to be sold on the black market, got on the train to Warsaw. Her mission was to find a hiding place for the rest of our family on the Aryan side of Warsaw. Ludwik would help her by hiring and sending a truck to get us out of Parczew. Mrs. Golecki was the connecting link between her husband in Warsaw and us in Parczew.

Helena was reluctant to leave the baby, but there was no alternative. The only person who was against the plan was my mother-in-law. That daughter of a rabbi said to her husband: "Shoel, if you want to go to Warsaw, go. I'm not going. I don't want to eat *treife* (not kosher) food. I'll rather die as a true Jewess than live on *treife* food."

It did not work out as we had planned. Just two days after Helena left for Warsaw, the second "action" came. The Germans decided to put an end to the existence of the Jews in Parczew.

That morning, I was getting ready to leave for work. I just finished changing my son's diapers and had given him his formula when I noticed that the house was surrounded by Germans. They broke the door open, grabbed me and led me away.

I never saw my in-laws or my son again.

I was taken to the open place in front of the new synagogue, in what had recently been the Jewish part of town. It was a chilly morning, in the fall of 1942. So far, there were about three hundred of us. We sat cross-legged, surrounded by Germans with machine guns. The Gestapo were running wild. Every few minutes they brought over a few more Jews, pushing and beating them mercilessly. Just to keep their vigour high, some of these Gestapo heroes pulled bottles of alcohol out of their pockets, slurped them empty, then threw them away, and took off to continue the "hunting."

There were hardly any Jewish policemen now. The Germans didn't need or want them any more. No member of the *Judenrat* was in sight, but Butche Reich appeared before the assembled Jews. That tireless man, who had always tried to help in the worst of circumstances, waved his hand toward us. A faint hope sprang to life in us. Butche went over to a Gestapo officer. We heard him plead that he needed the rounded-up men for workers. The officer yelled at Butche, "Where are the damned Jews? You're hiding them, you pig!" He was kicking Butche Reich wildly.

"*Umdrehen* (turn around)!" the beast was yelling.

"*Aber, Herr...*"

"*Umdrehen!*"

Oh, God! Butche was turning around.

The German fired one shot from his revolver into the back of Butche's head. Never in my life, until that moment, had I ever imagined that a person's death could come so instantly. Butche fell to the ground faster than a rock dropped from a six-foot height.

We were taken to the market square where the Germans were holding more rounded-up Jews. The march to the train station began. It was not the fear of imminent death that overwhelmed me then, although I realized that this was my end; it was shame. I was ashamed of the terrible dehumanization of myself and the others! We marched in the middle of the street, surrounded by Germans with machine-guns. And on the sidewalks! When I lifted my head I could see the Poles, who had been educated, "enlightened," by the Catholic clergy, laughing at us. Young men and women I had gone to school with stood on the sidewalks and laughed right in my face.

What shame and degradation were being forced on me, in the last hours of my life! Suddenly I remembered the Polish officers I had seen walking to their unknown destination on the streets of Kovel three years before. Had I laughed at them? No, I had not. I sympathized with their suffering. They, too, were innocent people, weren't they?

By now, the day was hot. We were made to sit crosslegged on the ground as we waited for the train. The SS guards ordered us to empty our pockets of money, watches, everything. I had a pocket knife on me, a very special knife given to me by my father when I was eight years old. Whenever my father watched me working with it he expressed satisfaction that I liked it so much. "Watch that knife, take good care of it. You will have a souvenir, and it might help you out some day in a serious situation." I took the knife now and buried it in the sand underneath me, figuring I could grab it before getting up to be pushed into the train. Everything else I gave to the SS.

After several hours sitting in the scorching sun we heard the ominous whistle of the arriving train. The noise of the screeching wheels, the train stopping, the shouts of the SS. I still hear and see it now. The SS rolled the doors of the cattle cars open and the shoving, pushing, and beating started. I remembered to retrieve my knife, and to avoid being beaten I ran to the first open car.

When all the Jews were inside they rolled the heavy doors closed. The stench in the car was terrible, the floor was covered with excrement from previously transported victims. About forty men, from eighteen to forty years of age, were locked in together. The moment the door was closed pandemonium broke out. Men just went crazy.

Some cried, some screamed, others jumped wildly or banged the walls with their fists or heads. You couldn't tell what might happen next, whether the wild screaming would stop or whether they might start beating each other.

An hour passed. Then the train started to roll. Through two tiny windows you could see that it was already sundown. After we had travelled for about an hour some of the more daring tried to escape through the window openings. Whoever managed to slip out was shot at by the guards from special guard boxes at the ends of each car. The shooting went on for quite a while. I lost track of time. When the shooting started I called over my cousin, calmed him down as much as I could, and told him not to try to escape through the small hole. I considered it sure death — if not from the guards' shots then from falling from the moving train. I also told him that I would try to open the door and that we would jump out then, much later in the night. I took out my knife and started to cut away at the door, right above the latch. I figured to cut a hole, stick my hand through, unlatch the door from the outside, roll it open, and jump. If it wasn't padlocked.

My knife was very sharp, and I kept cutting and cutting. How long was I cutting? I don't know. I remember that I didn't want anyone to know what I was doing. I was afraid that they might start yelling and draw the attention of the guards. Most of my fellow passengers were asleep or lying indifferently in the dirt, resigned to dying in the next twelve hours.

It was probably midnight or later when I cut through the door. I put out my hand. The door was not locked. I unlatched it and moved it back maybe an inch. It worked.

I closed it again, called everyone, told them that I would soon pull the door wide open, and that everybody should jump out as quietly as possible so as not to awaken the damn guards, who must have been sleeping by then — there had been no shooting for quite a while. I remembered Ludwik Golecki once describing to me how professional thieves jumped off a speeding train. I gave instructions on how to jump — in the same direction as the running train — or even better, to lie down at the door opening, parallel to the tracks, and just roll off. I lay down and showed them how to do it.

The train was running, I guessed, at about 80 or 90 kilometres an hour. My cousin Bunim said he would jump first. I went second. After jumping I lost consciousness. When I came to I could still hear the *ta-ta-ta, ta-ta-ta* of the running train. I thought I must not have lost more than a few seconds. I saw people with lanterns along the tracks. To avoid being discovered and turned over to the Germans, I ran away from the track and climbed a big oak tree.

Chapter Eight

It was a cool night, and very quiet. What was I to do now? Suddenly I remembered my knife. Where was it? I felt my pockets; it was gone. I was heartbroken. Sitting in the crown of the tree I felt that my tragedy was complete. Hounded by my enemies, in a most hostile environment, there was nothing I could think of that might give me a chance to survive. I had lost even the last, minuscule, tangible link with my father and my childhood. My precious knife, the knife that had given me, and maybe others too, another chance at life. I concluded that I had lost my knife jumping from the moving train. I couldn't go back to the train tracks to look for it. I had apparently jumped near a station. From the tree I could see several figures walking along the tracks with lanterns.

Then other thoughts came into my head: "Maybe I dropped it climbing the tree...maybe I will still find it." Cold, exhausted, sitting in a tree in the dark, my mind worked hard to come up with an idea to save my life. Was I naïve? Maybe, but I decided to try. I remembered a saying of my father's: "As long as your pulse is beating, no matter how weakly, you still should have hope and try to make it."

Try, try, Benjamin. I had convinced myself that giving up would be wrong, but I realized that whatever I wanted to do, it had to be done without delay. I have to get down the tree while it is still dark, I told myself. Nobody must see me wandering around aimlessly in an open field. I tried to sort out my chaotic thoughts.

I sat in that tree for another two hours (so I thought). Cold, hungry, worn out. I thought about those people who had not escaped the train. My mind was racing with those thoughts and scenes of horror inside the cattle cars racing to the gas chambers. How had I kept my sanity long enough to escape?

I climbed down and started to look for my knife. It was still dark, so with my hands I touched every inch in the high grass around the tree trunk. "Oh, God, here it is! My only material possession, the only link with my past. My knife! My dear knife!"

Then I heard the noise of a horse-drawn wagon rolling along the highway. The sound of the rhythmic tapping of the horse was coming closer. I was sure that a Pole was riding that wagon because the Germans used cars only to move around. If I could only get a lift to wherever that rider was going! Nobody must see me walking in the middle of nowhere. I would have been very conspicuous: a young man, dressed just in trousers and jacket, the front buttons of which I lost somewhere, no cap on my head. No, I can't be seen in this state! I thought. I have to get close to a forest and make my way to Parczew where I know every road. I have to try something right now.

I went over to the road, straight to the man on the wagon. "*Niech bedzie pochwalony* (let His name be praised)," I said, using the commonest Christian greeting in Poland.

"Forever and ever," answered the driver.

"Can you give me a lift? Where are you going anyway?" I couldn't see the man's face. It was still dark.

Keeping a glowing cigarette in his mouth, he said: "*A to wsiadajcie* (get up on the wagon)." The way he said that indicated that he was a farmer.

One move and I was on the wagon, sitting on bags of grain. I kept turning and turning so the farmer wouldn't get a good look at my face. The sky in the east started to show a lighter colour. These farmers had a special gift for noticing anything suspicious-looking. He pulled on his cigarette and words came out of his mouth together with the smoke.

"You must be cold, take the *lachy* (rags) over there and cover yourself," he said, in a farmers' dialect.

"*Bog zaplac* (may God repay you for your kindness)," I answered and covered myself with some rags. In my way of speaking I tried now to be as close to farmer language as possible. I learned that from the Gentile neighbours of my farmer grandparents. "Are you going to the city to sell that grain?"

"Only one bag is for sale. The rest I have to deliver to the Germans. And they pay very little for it, the bastards." The way he talked showed he had confidence in me.

"Where are you from? What are you doing here in an open field at night? Are you coming from a woman or are you running away from something?"

I had to answer him. I laughed, "Coming from a woman, I like that. You sure know some good ones. Ha, ha, ha. But no, I'm not coming from a woman. I am running from the Germans. They caught other guys and me in Lukow, they put us on a train to be sent away to Germany to work there. I managed to escape. I want to get back to Lukow where I live." I lied so smoothly. I could tell all that story to the farmer because the Germans were often rounding up young Poles and sending them to Germany to work in ammunition factories or on farms.

"You're smarter than my son. They caught him about two months ago but he didn't run away. Maybe he couldn't. I got one letter from him already. He is working on a farm. This is my only son and since he is gone, I have to work all by myself. Very hard. Does your family live in Lukow?"

"Yes."

"Maybe you'd like to work for me?"

What should I say now? As a stranger in a village I would have to register in the community offices, but I had no "Aryan" papers at all. "Maybe I would go work for you but, you see, I have a girlfriend in Lukow and I want to marry her. If I'm away, she will find someone else instead of me."

"Hm."

"Are you going in to the city proper?"

"Yes. Maybe you shouldn't go there. The Germans are always around there. If they stop you and find out that you are a stranger, they'll arrest you and send you off to Germany."

"I think you're right. You know what? I see a house over there with a light in it. I'll go in there and ask how to get back to Lukow the best way."

" Let God lead you," he said in the customary farmer way.

I jumped off the wagon. "Thank you for the ride." I think the farmer believed my stories and he didn't recognize that I was Jewish.

The grass on the side of the highway was moist from the morning dew. I bent down, wetted my hands and wiped one hand on the other. I bent down again and with the dew I smoothed my face and hair. If I had only had a cap on my head, my hair would not have looked so messy. I combed my hair with my fingers. The only thing I had in mind now was to straighten my face, so that it wouldn't project any sign of being scared. I knocked on the door.

"*Otwarte* (open), come in."

I went inside. "*Dzien dobry* (good morning)."

The man and the woman, who looked to be in their mid-thirties, didn't seem to be surprised by the early-morning visitor. "Where does God lead one from, so early in the day?" In the Polish language, it's a very friendly way of asking.

"The Germans got me together with others in Lukow yesterday. They were shipping us to Germany, but I escaped. I'm going back to Lukow today."

"Mama," the man turned to his wife, "make some hot milk for the man, he looks to be cold."

"Oh, thank you very much, I really feel chilly." The man gave me some bread and butter and invited me to eat. "*Psia krew* (a Polish curse) — to Germany to work for them? Oh no, not me," I said, to sound high-spirited.

"Mama, I'm going out to the cows. I'll be right back."

I became suspicious. "Can I come with you? Maybe I can be helpful."

"No, no. You better eat, I'll be right back." The man returned shortly though it seemed to me to take a long time. I was very hungry.

I hadn't eaten or drunk for more than thirty hours now, but to look normal, I was eating at a controlled speed. "Your bread is delicious, do you bake your own?"

"Mama is a good baker. Stay with us for breakfast and you'll see what kind of cook she is."

"Thank you for inviting me but I want to get back to Lukow today. I better leave early."

"Don't rush. I think one of my neighbours is driving to Lukow later in the day. I'm sure he will gladly give you a lift." Turning to his wife now, the man said: "I can hear the baby waking up. Take a look in the bedroom, mama." The farmer watched me while I ate. When the mother came back she had the baby in her arms.

"What a beautiful baby. It must be a girl, you're dressing her in pink."

"Excuse me," the man interrupted, "I don't think it's good for you to stay here. You should leave now. In about one hour the Germans will come here to get milk, they come every morning, so you better go. You know what I mean."

He sounded scared. He had recognized who I was, but he would not denounce me, he was decent. He was afraid for his family's lives if he allowed me to stay. I got up from the chair not saying a word. "But before you go, wash your face and comb your hair. Your face is dirty. They will recognize you very easily if you go dirty like that. I'll give you a cap of mine to cover your head. Mama, warm up some water fast."

He took the baby from his wife. She prepared a basin of warm water. While I was washing myself, I felt sand coming off my face. I kept rinsing the dirt out of my hair. I dried myself and was ready to leave. The man gave me a cap and the lady put a few slices of buttered bread in a bag for me. "Let God be your guide."

I stepped outside. The sun was bright already. Where was I to go now? I realized that there was only one road for me: the road to the woods. Maybe I'd meet runaways like myself. I saw the line of forest edge about two or three kilometres away and started walking with the little paper bag in my hand. It was quiet. I didn't care a bit about the beauty of nature all around me.

No, I thought, I'm not giving up! I've had so many close calls already. I was saved either through somebody's help or through my own initiative. I would keep trying and maybe...I'd live to see the end of them. Oh, how I wished for that!

I kept walking, toward the forest. Slightly turning my head to the left and right, I tried to take as much as possible into my field of vision. The movements of my body had to be movements of self-assurance or they would betray my feelings. The bread bag in my hand started to bother me. I had to hold on to it but I felt it might restrict my movements. I took the bread out of the bag, divided it and put the pieces in the side pockets of my jacket.

Again, a slight turn of my head. Yes, there was somebody far away from me, on a horse. Was it a German? I kept walking towards the woods but I couldn't resist and turned my head towards the rider. Yes, he was galloping towards me. He was about 500 metres away from me. My heart began beating faster. I started to whistle a joyful popular song to show how carefree I was. I could hear the galloping horse a lot closer now. I turned my head. No, he was not German. He waved to me to stop. I did so, and waited.

"I've been looking for you for the last three hours."

"Oh, yes? Why? I think you have mistaken me for somebody else."

"No, I'm not mistaken. Your name is Benjamin and you jumped off the Jewish train."

"What do you want?" A whole scenario flashed through my mind: they caught the others who jumped off the train from the same cattle car I was in. Under torture, they told who else ran away and gave them my name.

"Listen," the stranger said, "I want to save your life. You have to believe me. You have a cousin, Bunim is his name; he was with you on the train, he jumped before you. I found him unconscious near the tracks. I was rubbing his temples. He revived and I took him to Siedlce, to the ghetto there. He gave me your name and asked me to look for you. Do you believe me now?"

"What do you want me to do now?"

"I'll take you to your cousin in the ghetto. That's all I can do for you. Follow me." We were walking towards the city. It was still early morning, bright and sunny. "Take my horse's reins and lead him. It'll look less suspicious if I walk beside you leading the horse."

We were passing more and more houses and buildings now. "You are leading me straight towards a big residential building of the kind usually occupied by Germans. Is that what you are going to do, turn me over to the Germans?"

"Jesus Maria! no!" He crossed himself. "If I was that kind of Pole I'd be out looking for you with an armed German beside me. I'm an honest Christian. You have to trust me." We walked in silence. "Listen, I'll bring you right to the ghetto line and when you see the barbed wire, be on the side of the horse towards the wires, spread them and jump right inside."

"How many Jews are there in the ghetto?"

"They talk of two thousand to three thousand. I don't know exactly. It's a small place and it's packed." Holding the reins in my hand, I walked with him down the middle of the street. The tall man, who refused to give me his name, pulled my sleeve: "Look, here is the ghetto, get ready."

We got to the fence. The man took his horse and walked off slowly. I was all ready to lift a wire-line to get in when I noticed three men
inside the ghetto positioning themselves as if to grab me. They were
gypsies with dark complexions and blood-shot eyes. I panicked and
jumped back from the barbed wire fence. I walked away along the
fence and about fifty metres from the place where I saw the gypsies I
could see only Jews behind the fence. I lifted a wire and went into the
ghetto.

Lots of people. Mostly older women and men. Were the young
people at work? Small children on the streets, but very few mothers. I
approached an old Jew and told him that I just came to the ghetto. "Is
there a *Judenrat* I can go to?"

He looked at me, lifted one hand toward his head and made a gesture suggesting that I was missing some marbles in my head by asking
him about the *Judenrat*.

"Wouldn't they help me?"

"Oh yes, they'll help. They'll send you off to work somewhere, you
are still strong. The Germans keep demanding more workers all the
time."

A man grabbed me at this very moment. He was crying. I didn't
recognize him; his face was all blue. It was Bunim. When we got over
the emotion of seeing each other again, cousin Bunim told me about
his ordeal.

"You remember, I asked you to let me jump from the train before
you? I was afraid that if you jumped first, I wouldn't have enough
courage to jump after you. When I jumped I fell with my face down
on the gravel around the tracks. I passed out. The next thing I knew, a
man was rubbing my head and I came to. He told me to follow him and
he brought me to the ghetto. I begged that man to look for you and
bring you here."

"Bunim, he did."

"He didn't want to take any money but I managed to give him ten
zlotys just the same. 'You might need the money to buy bread,' he said
to me. Benjamin, come with me, there are a few more guys here from
our cattle-car."

We found three more boys in one of the houses. Later the same day,
we found that there were fifteen of us in the ghetto. They all wanted to
know how I had managed to hide my knife from the Germans. "Do

you still have that knife?" they asked. When I showed it to them, one man after the other kissed the little saviour. They told me that no single person had remained in the railway car. We decided to stick together and plan what to do next.

Life in the ghetto was just terrible: no water to wash oneself, the public latrines — plain indescribable. Men, women, children all going there at the same time. We were not on the brink of indifference to everything around us, we were already indifferent. Food? To get hold of a few potatoes was an achievement.

I found out about the gypsies in the ghetto. There were a few hundred of them, and when a Jew from the outside arrived, the gypsies robbed him, taking away even the clothing he had on.

Every day, men left the ghetto to work. Some of them managed to smuggle in food on their return. We, the fifteen from the car, tried not to go to work. We were planning to break out and somehow get back to Parczew where we would go to the woods and join other Jews there.

The Germans came to the ghetto one morning. "They are going from house to house looking for men," the women reported. I ran into the nearest house. A woman offered to hide me by covering me in a bed, but there was no time to do it. The Germans were already coming up the stairs. "Hurry, run to the attic," the woman told me. In the foyer on the way to the attic steps I saw a big wicker trunk with no lid. I put it up in a standing position, got inside it and moved it with the open side facing the wall. Everything happened in a few seconds. The Germans burst into the room I had been in moments before and yelled at the woman: "*Manner hier*? (Any men here?)" Seeing nobody, the Germans left; they passed the trunk, with me in it. When everything was quiet again I moved the trunk and came out. My cousin Bunim told me that he had been hiding in an attic.

Some of our fifteen had some money they had managed to hide from the Germans when we were herded together at the train station in Parczew. They had it sewn into the waistbands of their trousers. We decided that all of us would chip in and try to hire a Gentile with a truck to smuggle us back to Parczew. Since I had no money at all, I promised to pay my part when we got back to Parczew. I counted on Mrs. Golecki for money.

We found a Pole who was willing to risk the contraband. The following morning, we gathered at the exit from the ghetto. As the workers left for their jobs, we walked out with them. Outside the barbed wire, the truck was waiting. Quickly, we jumped up into the open box. The driver covered us with empty cartons and old rags. Everything fast and quiet. It was a chilly November morning.

For two hours we jolted over rough roads on the hard boards of the truck. When we arrived in Parczew, we were lucky: nobody stopped us. The driver let us off on a side road near the town. Our group of fifteen split up, but Bunim and I decided to stick together. We were afraid to go into town in broad daylight; we chose to hide in the brush, away from the road. At dusk we went straight to the Jewish neighbourhood. Between the "left-overs" Bunim and I found two more cousins: Moishele Mandelkern, a son of one of my father's brothers, and Shlomo Lerner, a son of my mother's brother. The four cousins decided to stick together.

We were informed by our friends that some Jews were still working in the sawmill in Pohulanki. These workers didn't come to town any more, they slept and ate on the premises of the sawmill. We went to Pohulanki the next morning: there were only six Jews working, guarded by Ukrainians in uniform. Frau Greta wasn't in the office. Karl wasn't around either. I went to see the Polish accountant.

"The guards say the Jews won't be kept here for long. Take my advice and run from here while you still can," the accountant added.

We left the sawmill in a hurry. But where could we go? Moishele led us to a place of high brush. We were surrounded by a number of small artificial lakes where his father's employer used to breed fish. We sat down and ate the bread we brought with us from Parczew. The weather was sunny but cold. I wanted to wash myself in one of the little lakes because I was scratching constantly — I had brought lice from the ghetto in Siedlce.

"Don't do that, you'll freeze."

I didn't listen to them. They all followed me to the water. We took off our shirts, rolled up our pant legs and stepped in that ice-cold water. We cleaned our shirts before putting them on. Pneumonia? Inflammation of the lungs from staying in the icy water? We didn't even think about it. We jumped around for a while to warm up our blood.

We sat down and conferred about what to do next. Our conclusion was that we would all go to the woods. There was nothing else left for us to do. The sky clouded over. It felt as if snow was coming. Everybody agreed that we would have to leave the place before the snow came. We couldn't leave any footprints. "As soon it gets a touch darker, we'll leave."

Chapter Nine

There was a sound. Something was moving, nearby. Slowly, not making much noise, but something was moving there. Maybe an animal? We didn't speak above a whisper. And we listened. Yes, there was a sound of human footsteps and they were very near us. The underbrush was pushed aside. Three men with rifles on their shoulders stood before us.

"Don't be afraid. *My swoi* (we are of the same kind as you)."

"I thought that the Germans had found us," I said to the men.

"Oh, no, this is our territory. We won't let the Germans come in here." The three men took their rifles down off their shoulders and sat down. "My name is Kolka, these are my adjutants Wlodek and Wanka. We live in the woods and we organize the partisan groups. I'm the leader." They treated us to cigarettes. "Are you hungry?" Kolka asked.

"We ate some bread not long ago, we are not hungry yet," Shlomo answered.

"Wlodek, give them a drink."

We all took a sip from the bottle he offered us. It was *bimber*, moonshine. "Uh, strong stuff," I said.

"Is it? You better learn how to drink, there's no chocolate milk in the woods. What are you four planning to do?"

"We want to join the partisans. Can you help us?"

"Sure," the leader said, "we'll take you with us. There are a lot of Jews among the partisans. Are you from Parczew?"

"Yes, all four of us."

"There are many Jews from Parczew with us. I have photographs of some of them." Kolka took out a package from his pocket, unwrapped it and showed us a few pictures of a group of Jews we knew from Parczew.

"Why do you carry these pictures around with you?"

"We show them to people like you, who might be afraid to go to the woods and join us. When I show them pictures of people they know, I gain the confidence of the onlookers. You can take Kolka's word for it, right, boys?"

"Right, boss," his friends answered.

There was something in Kolka's voice I didn't like. Another round of cigarettes followed.

"Listen." Kolka turned to us. "We're going to the nearby village to get *prowiant* (food supplies) for our unit. We'll be back in about two hours. We'll take you back to the woods with us. You're lucky that we found you."

The three "partisans" got up, said goodbye and left us. All four of us had reservations about Kolka and his photographs, but considering the lack of alternatives, we decided to take a chance and accept their help.

It was only about a quarter of an hour later that our "benefactors" returned. They pointed their rifles at us and Kolka yelled:

"Get up. Put your hands over your heads. Quick, I said!"

They clicked the handles of their rifles as if they were loading them with bullets.

"Search them!" Kolka ordered Wanka.

Kolka and Wlodek pointed their rifles at us while Wanka went through our pockets one by one. He found about fifty zlotys on my cousin Bunim and...my pocket knife. He looked at that knife for a while as if he really liked it.

"Get undressed now," Kolka yelled out.

Yes, we will be executed now, I thought. My three cousins broke down and began to cry aloud. They undressed and cried. I did not cry. I knew that I was coming to my end. Another few moments and that would be it. No need to cry.

No, not so. When the four of us were completely naked, Wanka took all our clothes and shoes and bundled them up in two parcels.

Kolka said, "Go to one of the villages and ask the farmers to give you some clothing."

The "partisans" picked up their loot and left. We were shivering. We couldn't go anywhere yet; we were naked and it was still daylight. A light wet snow had started to fall.

"Jump up and down or you'll freeze to death," I ordered my cousins. They did as I said.

Cousin Bunim was the weakest of us. "I wish they had killed me. Why did I jump off the train in the first place?" he complained.

"Don't be stupid, you always have time to die," said cousin Shlomo.

"I'm going to go to Mr. Czarnecki's place," said Moishele. "He knows me well. But if he sees four Jews together, he'll throw us all out. Just me alone, maybe he'll help. Don't be angry with me for talking like this, I want to live." When it grew dark, Moishele kissed each one of us and, crying, he left.

"Listen, you two," I said. "I know a farmer in Milkow. It's only two kilometres away. Mr. Krasinski worked for my father for many years, he is a good man."

We started off. Three completely naked men running over cold, wet ground. The light wet snow kept falling. The tall Shlomo was first, I was second, Bunim last. Shlomo kept turning his head all the time to check on Bunim. When we reached Milkow, I took over the lead and we went straight to farmer Krasinski's house.

There was light in the house. I knocked on the door. The tall, thin Mr. Krasinski looked out the window, then, with his hands to his head in disbelief, opened the door of the house and called out: "Jesus Maria," he crossed himself. "Come inside, fast!"

The warmth from the wood-stove felt unreal after the events of the last twenty-four hours.

"*Syn* Leiby (Leibl's son), where have you come from? Jesus Maria, what happened?"

I told him the story of how we were robbed. Krasinski gave us bed-sheets to wrap ourselves in. The roughness of the home-spun flaxen sheets felt good.

"Where is your wife? What will she say when she sees us?"

"She is at a neighbour's. Don't worry, she'll do what I tell her to do. I'll make hot milk, you are all frozen."

We drank the hot milk, holding the cups with both hands, trying to absorb all the warmth possible.

"Panie Krasinski, you are the only one around here that we can ask for help. Let us stay in your barn tonight and all day tomorrow. Tomorrow evening we will leave."

"Boys, I want to help. I'm a Catholic. I want to help, but I'm afraid. You know how it is. Everybody around has eyes and ears. If just one person betrays us we'll all be finished."

"Panie Krasinski, let's go to the barn now, in case a neighbour happens to come in."

We went to the barn. Three white-covered ghosts and Mr. Krasinski. We climbed up into the hayloft. "I'll get you some rugs to cover yourselves with for the night."

When he returned, I asked him to go to Parczew the next day and tell Lola Golecki what had happened. The waiting time for the answer seemed endless. "Yes, boys. I will do it. Holy Mary will protect me." Mr. Krasinski left the barn.

The weather turned nasty. It was getting colder. Lying now under the rugs and curled up against each other to keep warmer, we could hear now the falling ice pellets knocking against the boards of the barn. Tired from what happened to us that day we slept well.

During the day, while Mr. Krasinski was in Parczew, we made plans. We decided to try Mr. Karpinski, the blacksmith who used to shoe my father's horses. We'd hide there, then try to make it to the hiding place Ludwik Golecki had told me about before he left Parczew.

Mr. Krasinski returned with clothing: underwear, shirts, pants, caps and overcoats. "Mrs. Golecki is a very good woman," Mr. Krasinski said, "when I told her what happened to you, she cried. She gave me all that clothing, and some food too. Bread, cheese, apples. A good woman."

We dressed ourselves and ate. "As soon as it gets dark you have to go. My wife is crying. She is afraid."

"Yes, Mr. Krasinski, we'll leave. We are very grateful for what you have done for us." When it was time to leave, the angel farmer gave us a loaf of home-baked bread and said: "*Bog z wami* (God with you)."

It took half an hour to reach Karpinski's house. The blacksmith answered the door. "*Syn* Leiby? Who are the other two?"

"My cousins."

"Come inside."

At that moment, Mrs. Karpinski came to the door. With one look at us, she started screaming: "I don't want them here. The Germans will kill us all. I don't want the Jews here, do you hear me?" she yelled at her husband.

"Woman," the smith said. "Let them in for one night only. They'll eat, have a rest and leave tomorrow."

"No, I said no! I don't want them here! I want to live!"

"Just for one night, nothing will happen."

"You let them in the house, and I'll go to the Gestapo right now. Do you hear me?"

We said goodbye and left Mr. Karpinski in a hurry and headed for Ludwik's hideout. Through sidestreets the three of us knew well, we sneaked into town. The hiding place was over a shed behind Ludwik's house, under a pitched straw roof. Before running away from the Gestapo to Warsaw, Ludwik had put in fresh straw, just in case he had to come back and hide. "Benjamin," Ludwik had said jokingly to me then, "maybe you'll have to hide. The place will be ready."

Ludwik arranged the place so that it was accessible either from inside the shed, by removing a concealed board in the roof, or from the outside, through a covered hole at the lower edge of the roof. The shed itself, usually used for storing farmer's tools, was connected to a larger building, a cow barn. The property belonged to three Golecki brothers but only one of them, Tomas, and his wife, Tomkowa, worked the little farm and tended the cows and pigs.

The cow barn and the shed bordered on the Catholic cemetery. There was no one in sight; we jumped the cemetery fence and climbed into the *kryjowka* (hiding place).

We lay down and talked in whispers. "We will stay here as long as possible. Then we go to the woods. Nothing else left to do."

Shlomo wanted to light a cigarette. We didn't let him. "With straw all around you'll burn the place down. No, Shlomo, no." We cuddled up against each other, covered ourselves with straw and tried to sleep.

Chapter Ten

N ext morning, we heard Tomas's wife and a helper come into the barn to milk and feed the cows. We could hear every word they said to each other. They talked about the Gestapo catching some Jews leaving town a day before. Not uttering a sound, we just looked at each other.

When the two women left the barn, we started to nibble on the bread Mr. Krasinski had given us the day before. In the circumstances, that bread tasted great. "What will we do for food when we will finish this?" Bunim wanted to know.

"Tonight I'll climb down and go to Mrs. Golecki. I'm sure she'll give us food," I said.

Most of the day we were quiet. There wasn't much to talk about. When it was quite dark I climbed down into the shed below, opened the door and went out into absolute quietness. Moving along the walls of the buildings, and then through open space, I came to the part of the house Lola lived in. One knock at the door. Lola opened it and...she embraced and kissed me a few times, as if she couldn't believe her own eyes.

"Jesus! Ben, how did you get here?" she asked in a normally loud voice.

I put a finger to my mouth and said: "Shh. Tomkowa might hear you."

"Where are you hiding? Still somewhere in town?"

"Not in town. I'm together with two cousins of mine. We're hiding about two kilometres from here."

"At the farmer's I gave the clothing to?"

"No, at a different place now. Thank you for the things you have sent us. Lola, I'm hungry."

Lola treated me with cream of wheat in hot milk. I ate fast. I had no time to waste. Then Lola, who always had trouble remembering things, told me some good news.

"Oh, yes, I almost forgot to tell you. I received a letter from Ludwik. He's asking about you. He is communicating with your wife and her sister. They all advise you to try to get to Warsaw. He gave an address to go to in Warsaw, but I left the letter in the store. Can you come tomorrow night? I'll bring the letter home so you can read it for yourself."

"I'll come back tomorrow, but don't forget to bring that letter. Lola dear, I need food for my cousins." Lola put quickly on the table everything she had in the house: bread, cheese, jam, butter and a piece of cooked meat. She packed everything in a bag. "Lola, give me also a knife. Oh yes, also two bottles of water to drink."

Good-hearted Lola was still looking around to see what else she could give me. "You remember, Ben, last Christmas and a Christmas before that? Ludwik was still home, you and your wife and the Goldreich sisters came for Christmas dinner," Lola started to cry. "And now look what's happened."

"Lola, I can't stay here. Somebody might see me. Listen. I'll try to come back tomorrow. I don't know when exactly I'll come. I want to ask you to get some warm underwear for me and my two cousins and warm overcoats if possible. We're planning to go to the woods and join the partisans. Pack up everything you can in one or two sacks. Don't forget Ludwik's letter."

Lola took out a piece of paper and started to write down a list of things to prepare. I couldn't tell her that we were hiding just steps away from the place we were standing now. I trusted her and knew she wouldn't object. But she had always been very talkative, and the truth might have slipped out. It hurt me, but I couldn't tell her. Lola kissed me goodnight and I left.

Shlomo and Bunim were happy to see me back. "What great food! And the water! What a woman that Lola is!"

I told my cousins what I had asked Mrs. Golecki to prepare for us for the next night. "I'm sure she'll do her best. She remembers what Helena and my family did for her and Ludwik. Now she wants to help me."

I also told my cousins about Ludwik's letter. We were all ready to go to sleep when Shlomo asked: "Benjamin, would you like to get to Warsaw and join your wife?"

"I don't know what to think about that. How could I get there even if I wanted to?"

None of us could sleep, but we didn't talk to each other. All of the next day we talked about whether to go to Warsaw or to the woods. "If you decide to go to Warsaw," said Shlomo, "there's a farmer I know I could try for Bunim and myself." Then Bunim mentioned a neighbour who was hiding the family's valuables — perhaps he could help. We talked on and off, all on the same subject. That evening, I went down to see Lola.

"First I want you to eat the hot meal I prepared for you, then I'll give you the food and clothing I have for you. And here's Ludwik's letter. I didn't forget anything this time."

I sat down at the table. Lola had even remembered to put down the blinds so nobody could see in. She set a plate of hot milk and potato-flour balls before me. With a spoon, I split the first potato ball into four bite-size pieces. I put the first bite in my mouth, and I liked the taste of it. But what was happening to me? I tried to swallow but the food was not going down my throat. The milk got through, but not the food. I was choking with each try. I tried again but no, nothing went down. I was frustrated: here I was sitting in front of a plate of goodies and...I couldn't eat; I couldn't swallow.

"What's wrong? Why don't you eat?," Lola asked.

"My throat is like locked, I can't swallow."

"Jesus Maria! That comes from eating dry food and not drinking enough. Your throat has shrunk. Let me help."

With a knife she cut the ball into tiny pieces. I tried to swallow them, one piece at a time. Slowly, with a lot of effort, it worked. I didn't want to stay there too long, but the eating was such a slow process, and how could I leave such good food? I was struggling. I looked at the plate and felt helpless. It was still full. Lola was glancing at her watch. I couldn't blame her for being afraid when I was in her house. She was risking her life. I ate as fast as I could. I was sorry when I had to make the decision to leave two potato balls. It would take too long to finish them.

Lola gave me the supplies she had prepared, and some clothing. I thanked her over and over. "Lola dear, can you make a bottle of hot milk? Wrap it first in a paper and then in a rag. That will be for my cousins, maybe it'll keep warm until the time I'll get to them." Lola prepared the hot milk in a bottle. Loaded with parcels, I kissed her goodbye.

"Will you come again?"

"I don't know."

"Ben, be careful. I am so afraid for both of us. It's Sunday tomorrow. I'll go to church, put something in the plate, and pray for you."

"Thank you, Lola." I was moved.

I returned to my two waiting cousins in the *kryjowka*. They were worried because it had taken me longer to get back than it had the evening before. We went over our plans that night and all during the following day. Shlomo and Bunim tried to convince me that with the help of Gienia, my wife and Ludwik, I stood a good chance of making it in Warsaw. I knew they weren't trying to get rid of me; on the contrary, I was sure they were wishing me the best. But I didn't believe that I could undertake that trip to Warsaw without some kind of identity card.

"On the other hand," I said, "if I go to the woods, I'll face different problems. There's a good chance that the 'partisans' will find out I come from a well-to-do home, and blackmail me suspecting that I have money and jewellery stashed away somewhere."

"Yes, you go to Warsaw," Shlomo said, "I'll take care of Bunim and myself."

We looked at each other. All of us had tears in our eyes. For a while we didn't speak. It was Bunim who broke the silence: "Benjamin, do you think we will ever see each other again if we break up now?"

We wept openly, wiping our eyes with the sleeves of our jackets. "Bunim...I don't know."

When it got dark outside, we kissed each other for the last time. "Don't worry about us, Benjamin, we'll make it," were the last words I heard brave Shlomo saying.

I left. I have never seen my two cousins again.

I leaned against a wall of the shed. New doubts crept into my mind. Where was I going? I would never get there. Whoever noticed me would denounce me. But the chances of survival in the woods were slim too. Should I go back up, or shouldn't I? I closed my eyes for a while. I started to feel cold.

I knocked at Lola's window. When she opened the door of her house, her eyes were full of fright. She crossed herself, probably to get some courage and divine help.

"Lola dear, I'll be here for two minutes only. I'm going to Warsaw. I have no money at all. Lend me fifty zlotys, I'll pay it back to Ludwik in Warsaw, I promise. Give it to me in small bills."

Lola looked for her purse in a hurry. She wanted me out of the house fast. She was scared. "Forty-two zlotys, that's all I have. Take it and go. No, wait, I'll give you two slices of bread with butter. And here's Ludwik's cap with ear-flaps. I forgot to give it to you before. And here's a warm scarf, take it too." Lola cried now. She kissed me and wished me the best.

It was dark, but still before the curfew hour. I saw people going by, everybody in a hurry. A slight rain mixed with wet snow was coming down. I turned in the direction of the train station. Once I reached the tracks, I changed direction again. I decided not to board the train in Parczew, where many people knew me. I didn't know how long I would have to wait for the train and I might meet someone eager to denounce the Jew. I decided to go to the next station, to Milanow, six kilometres away. And so I left Parczew. Would I ever see it again? Would I ever care to see it if I survived?

I walked and told myself that from now on I'd have to play a new, different game. I had to forget my real name, and change the expression on my face. My face couldn't show my inner worries or fright; my eyes should have the sparkle normal for young men. Nobody from the "other world" should be able to detect any uncertainty in my behaviour, even for a second.

The tracks ran between tall spruce trees. The rain turned to blowing sleet and ice. Shiny icicles appeared on the swaying trees. I kept walking. Six kilometres: why did it take so long? I started to hop faster on the wooden railway ties, skipping one now and then. Oops! I slipped and fell. It was nothing. I got up and jumped again. I felt something warm in the palm of my left hand. What could it be? I strained my eyes in the dark. There was a spot on my left hand. Was it blood? I licked my hand. Yes, it was blood; it tasted sweet. It wasn't a deep cut and the biting cold helped stop the bleeding.

I reached the Milanow station and went into the small building. The station clerk was sitting beside the kerosene lamp.

"*Dobry wieczor* (good evening). I see that you're reading a paper. Can you see the print with that little light from the lamp?" I asked for conversation's sake.

"It's hard, but it is much harder to sit and do nothing. The regulations don't allow a brighter light. It's wartime, my friend."

"When do you expect the Warsaw train to arrive?"

"The last message I received said 23.30. But it will be late as usual."

"What time is it now?"

"20.15"

"Should I buy the ticket now?"

"It makes no difference, now or later. The train comes from the east and if it's loaded with returning soldiers, they won't let you on, ticket or no ticket."

"Does that happen often?"

"It sure does."

I bought my ticket and decided it wasn't a good idea to stay there. I had more than three hours to wait and it was too cold and probably not too safe (for me) either. I asked the clerk if he knew of a place nearby where I could go and warm up.

"There are a few houses around the station. All friendly people. Try your luck."

I knocked at the first house, about 200 metres away from the station.

"Come in."

"Good evening. I wonder whether I can stay here for a little while. I'm waiting for the train to Warsaw and the waiting room is cold."

"Sure, you can wait here. Why freeze?" the woman said.

"Take off your coat and join the game," a man said.

"What game are you playing?"

"Simple stuff. Domino." Addressing one of the women, he said, "Kazia, give our guest some tea." He turned back to me: "Hang up your coat there in the corner and come to the table."

I hung up my cap but I had trouble with my overcoat. It felt like it weighed a ton and had the shape of a big cylinder. I couldn't hang that thing on the hook. The people in the house looked at me and my funny-looking coat and laughed.

"Put it standing on the floor near the stove. It'll dry out."

I did as I was told and sat down at the table. Halfway through drinking my tea, I looked at my coat. It started to collapse and lean to one side. Someone mentioned that the partisans had derailed a train near Lukow two nights before, and that was why there were more Germans than usual patrolling all the small stations on the way to Siedlce.

I looked at my coat. It had all fallen down now. "I should have spread out my coat, to dry it as much as possible."

"Use a chair near the stove, but not too close."

My coat was still heavy but at least it was pliable. Time was moving very slowly. We went on talking and playing, but I had the impression that the people in the house had had enough of that evening. The clock on the wall showed ten-thirty (22.30 train time). I thanked my hosts for their kindness, put on my almost dry coat and cap and said good night.

The train arrived shortly after eleven p.m. The conductor showed the few passengers to the cars reserved for civilians. No lights on the train. There were three other men in my compartment. A short whistle, and the train was on its way. What was I thinking about? I had a good chance to get to Warsaw, I knew, in about six or seven hours. A chance: one in how many? Who knew what the odds were? I tried to sleep. The others in the compartment seemed to be sleeping. But I couldn't.

After a half hour or so, I heard the brakes of the train; we stopped in the middle of nowhere. I could hear German voices. I was afraid even to open my eyes. I heard my neighbours getting up and going over to look out the windows. Turning and opening my eyes slightly, I could see them looking out into the dark.

"Two nights ago partisans unscrewed the tracks around here. The Gestapo are probably coming up the train now to check everybody out," one of the men said.

"They'll find somebody to question or just to send away to a labour camp in Germany. They do it all the time," another man answered.

Fear filled my mind: This is the end, I thought. I had no shred of any kind of document on me; I would be the first to be taken off the train. Interrogation? Torture? Bullet? Why hadn't I gone to the woods? What was happening now was only too predictable. Too late. All I could do now was try to control my fear. Whatever happened would happen. I stretched myself, hung down my head, and pretended to be asleep.

"*Ihren Ausweis, bitte* (your documents, please)." They were only two compartments away. Only one now. How should I behave and what should I say when they asked me for my *Ausweis*? I would search my pockets, then say that I must have left my documents in the work clothes I had on before taking the trip. Or maybe, I lost my *Ausweis*....

Three husky Gestapo men, each with a flashlight in his hands, came into our compartment. They checked the documents of my three co-passengers and returned them to their owners. I couldn't believe what happened next. The Germans left the compartment. They didn't ask me for my documents. I was shivering all over. I could still hear the German voices outside the train. And the train moved on.

Never in my life have I found a logical explanation for that event. Maybe they didn't notice me, or maybe each of the Germans thought that one of their two comrades had checked me out already. I was lucky, that's all.

A lot of people got on the train at Lukow. Looking at the big parcels they carried one could easily guess that they were smuggling food for the black market in Warsaw. They knew each other, and talked freely about their trade. The best prices — they told each other — were to be had near the Jewish ghetto. The Jews paid any price you asked them and if they had no money, they paid in beautiful clothing, or, even better, in jewellery.

We reached Siedlce about two in the morning. Here the Germans changed the route of our train. It would continue west, bypassing Warsaw. All Warsaw-bound travellers were to leave the train immediately. There was talk that the next train to Warsaw would arrive in Siedlce at noon the next day.

No smuggler or dealer in illegal goods wanted to stay such a long time in the waiting-room of the station. They were afraid of German police coming and confiscating their goods. Hefting their parcels, the smugglers left the station, all of them going in the same direction. Since my goal was not to be noticed by the police, I followed the crowd. But I was out of place — unlike me, they were all heavy-laden. I approached two women who were carrying more parcels than they could really handle.

"I'm going there too." (Where was that "there," I wondered). "I can help you carry your parcels," I said.

"Oh, *Bog zaplac* (may God repay you), young man."

I took two parcels from the ladies. Now I looked like one of the crowd. Together with the others, I walked into a room full of cigarette smoke and a terrible smell of alcohol. The warmth in the place was very comforting. The whole thing looked like a tavern set up exclusively for the Warsaw food traders. People sat at the counter drinking; others sat on the floor or against the walls. I found a free corner of the room, put down my coat and went over to the counter; I bought tea and a roll and returned to my place. As I ate I kept glancing around inconspicuously, hoping that I wouldn't see anyone who knew me from Parczew. At one point I imagined that one of the men was staring at me. I felt better when he stopped looking at me. Maybe I reminded him of someone he knew. I was thankful for the haziness in the room caused by the clouds of cigarette smoke.

A train for Warsaw was expected at three in the afternoon. Around two o'clock, I joined the crowd leaving for the station. The German police told the civilians to line up. The train was full. Only fifty new Warsaw-bound passengers would be permitted to board it.

The Germans were pushing people back, selecting one or two at a time and letting them on the train. I was singled out by a German policeman and allowed to board the train, probably because I had no luggage. That was luck. About twenty minutes later, the train moved ahead, but stopped a short distance from the station. A Polish conductor informed the passengers that we were waiting for clearance.

I looked out and recognized the place where, only a short while ago, I had leaped from the cattle train taking me to be gassed in Treblinka. So many things had happened since then. I had to remind myself to forget all that. I had to concentrate and behave differently now.

The train moved ahead and I fell asleep. Although it was only ninety kilometres from Siedlce to Warsaw, it was a long ride. The train stopped at all the small stations on the way to let military trains go through first. It was six-thirty the next morning before we arrived in Warsaw.

Chapter Eleven

E ast Station. I knew the place well. I didn't have to look around or ask anybody which way to go. If anyone had looked at me then, he would have seen a freely moving man, just one of the crowd, who had arrived with the others by train, and who, like the others, was rushing off to work.

For the last thirty-six hours I had been training my mind to regulate the expression on my face: no more melancholy in my eyes, no more strained muscles in the features of my face. Instead, my face had to project an image bordering on cheerfulness, but not too much of that either. As for my eyes, a gleam of a faint smile, just appropriate for my age. I felt that my inner self was splitting into two beings. One part of me had to overpower the other. The part of me getting bigger and stronger was the one pretending and playing a role. Many times I had to talk to my "old self" and ask for advice.

My goal now was a house on Twarda Street, occupied by a trusted Polish woman, the former housekeeper of Gienia, my wife's sister. The address of this place had been sent to me through Ludwik, along with a warning that, for safety reasons, I was not to write it down, but only to memorize it.

I went straight from the train station to the streetcar stop. It was early in the morning and the streetcars, packed with people collected on previous stops rushing off to work, didn't bother to stop. A number of people, who had been waiting, chose to walk to the city instead of waiting for the next streetcar. I decided to join them. Walking through Praga (a suburb of Warsaw) and then over the Kierbedza Bridge, I tried to keep up with the crowd of walkers. Somehow, I didn't look like the rest of the people. Everyone was carrying something in his hands: either parcels of goods to be sold or, at the very least, small brown paper bags probably containing a worker's lunch. I bought a newspaper from a vendor and put it under my arm. Maybe the newspaper would give me the look of a clerk, I thought.

I was sure that I remembered the address correctly, but I couldn't help thinking what would happen if my memory slipped and I knocked at the wrong door. I approached the house I was going to and I felt my heart, despite all my logical preparations for controlled behaviour, pounding almost audibly. I couldn't afford a moment of indecision; I went up to the third floor, not running, just walking up, and rang one of the doorbells. I recognized the man who opened the door. Thank God, it was the right man.

Pan Kazimierz recognized me too. He gave me some hot tea and then breakfast. He told me that his wife was working, that he would be going to work in the afternoon and said, "You're lucky I was home when you arrived." I agreed. "I'll let my wife know that you are here, she will get in touch with Gienia and your wife. I think they have a place for you to stay. You must understand that you can't stay here longer than a day or two at the most. We live close to the ghetto, and the Germans are snooping around all the time for Jews hiding in the neighbourhood. Believe me, I want to help — I'm a socialist, I'm a worker. But I am scared. I am ready to help out for a few days, but I can't do more than that."

"Panie Kazimierzu, I promise not to take advantage of your generosity. If Gienia and my wife have not found a place for me on the Aryan side, I'll go into the ghetto."

"No, you can't do that. That would mean the end of you. Gienia is very smart and brave, she'll come up with something. If not, I'll talk to my socialist friends who live further away from the ghetto."

I thanked him. Before leaving for work, Pan Kazimierz prepared food for me and then asked me to be very quiet when I stayed all alone in the house: "The neighbours shouldn't notice anything strange. They know that nobody is in our house when my wife and I are at work."

Pani Irena, Kazimierz's wife, arrived early in the evening. She had already talked to Gienia about my arrival, and my wife was supposed to come over either that night or the next at the latest: "Pani Gienia and your wife are smart, they live outside the ghetto. They have good looks and move around freely."

Helena did not come that evening. I slept that night in a regular bed. It seemed too good to be true. But what would happen if Gienia and my wife could not find a place for me to stay?

Helena came the next evening. We were a little shy with each other. We had so much to say; but for now we talked only about what had to be done right away.

"Tomorrow morning," Helena informed me, "you'll go to Sluzewiec. Here's the address; memorize it. You'll knock at the door of Mrs. Trochimczuk, you know her from Parczew. She'll give you the key to the apartment next door. You will stay there, for now anyway. You'll find food in the cupboards. Nobody lives there now, you'll be all alone. I have to go now, the curfew hour is soon. I'll try to come to you on the weekend and I'll tell you everything then about myself and Gienia."

We kissed goodbye. Next morning I left for Sluzewiec in the rush hour. I had to reach Mrs. Trochimczuk before she left for work. It was a very familiar route. Sluzewiec was the suburb where I had gone to university. I travelled that route for three years. I looked out the window of the streetcar now and every street, almost every building along the streets we were passing, looked so familiar. Still, everything belonged to a different era.

Stop thinking about the past, my new self told me, your problems might show on your face. Somebody hostile might notice it.

The street I was going to was two blocks past the university. One more streetcar stop. The house, a small apartment building, was the third from the corner. I noticed that the building on the corner had a sign indicating that it was occupied by a German police station. Two armed Germans were guarding the front gate. My new neighbours. I passed them with all the indifference I could muster. Glancing at them briefly, I could see that they had paid no attention to me. I looked for the apartment number Helena had given me, and knocked at the door.

"Good morning, Pani Felu."

Pale, Pani Fela wished me a good morning and handed over a key indicating at the same time a door down the hall. Then she disappeared behind her door and I went into "my apartment." It was a two-bedroom place. On the kitchen table was a note saying: "Don't turn on the lights. Don't make noise. Destroy note." In a kitchen cupboard I found potatoes, bread, jam and dry tea. The place looked to me to be ideal for my purpose.

In the evening of the first day of my stay I heard Mrs. Trochimczuk's door opening. I was surprised because I hadn't heard anybody walking up the stairs. Then I noticed a white piece of paper under the entrance door. Since I couldn't turn on the lights, I had to wait till next morning to read it. Mrs. Trochimczuk wrote, "I'll tap slightly on our common wall in the evening. Open your door and I will hand you a pot of soup. Destroy this note."

I followed instructions and received a pot of hot soup. With it came a bottle of oil and another note: "Use this oil to grease the hinges of your door, they squeak terribly, especially the entrance door. Destroy note."

Another day, Mrs. Trochimczuk handed me a *Kennkarte*, or identity document, which Ludwik had obtained for me. The name on it was Jan Piotrowski. It was a fake, not registered anywhere officially. A network of printers specialized in fabricating "authentic" personal documents. Not only "Aryan" Jews were customers for such documents, but "underground" Poles also had to change their names in a hurry. A false *Kennkarte* could buy a little time in a confrontation with the police. If you were lucky, they let you go. If not...well, that was the end.

During these lonely evenings waiting for the weekend and Helena's arrival, I had a feeling of temporary relief from being chased by the German hyenas. In these moments, images from the immediate past crowded my mind. I remembered a passage from the Book of Psalms, "By the rivers of Babylon...we wept when we remembered Zion," a lament uttered thousands of years ago after the destruction of the temple in Jerusalem.

I sat alone now, reminiscing about my dearest who had been so brutally taken from me. I felt the pain in me solidified my tears, and my eyes couldn't cry any more. The culmination of my pain came when the image of my son appeared before me. In my mind I saw now that little face as I had seen it for the last time. When he was born we still had hope that the beast would give up its pursuit of us and that we could eventually rebuild our lives.

In moments of extreme despair one hopes against hope that something positive, and even supernatural, will happen. We named the baby after my father. We thought that this way we would somehow continue and maintain the great spirit and strength of the man we had cherished. I asked myself: What happened to my baby? How did he perish? Did he suffer? Did he cry? If somehow I were to survive that inferno, those questions would remain with me all my life.

My mind worked without ceasing. Another image appeared before my eyes: the image of my father. What was he thinking in the last moments of his life when he looked at the revolver pointed at him? Did he think of those dearest to him, as it is said one does in the last moments of life? He was a man of superb dignity to his last breath. His refusal to turn away made a mockery of his assassin's show of force.

Wherever my mind turned was endless pain. Again, was it worth it? I had to find a purpose for living — if it was only to see with my own eyes the destruction of the beast.

Everything had happened so quickly there had never been any time to reflect, or to think about what had happened. My life then was like a building that was being destroyed by a wrecking ball. The five-ton ball hits the building and a big chunk of it comes apart. Before the dust from the first hit settles, there is a second blow, and a third, and so on and on until nothing is left of it. And so it was — before the dust settled from the first German assault, bang! the next one followed immediately, until the entire structure was destroyed. There was never time in between to think of anything; whatever I did, I did without thinking.

On Sunday morning, I positioned myself behind the curtain of the front window, and stared at the entrance gate in the wire mesh fence. I was waiting for Helena's arrival. There she was, holding a basket in her hands. She went first to Mrs. Trochimczuk's place, tapped the common wall to alert me and there she was in my apartment.

We embraced and kissed each other. I noticed right away that she had makeup on her face. It was the first time I had ever seen her wearing it. Her complexion was so fine, she never needed any before. "That's to cover my tiredness," she explained to me, although I had not said a word about it.

I started to ask questions. "I don't know where to begin," Helena said. Then she told me her story since she arrived in Warsaw.

"Just a few days after I left Parczew, Ludwik told me what happened to the rest of the Jews there."

She paused and we looked at each other. This was the first time we had had a chance to talk about these terrible things. Was she thinking about the loss of our son, and her parents? Her pain, like mine, must be terrible. As our eyes met, I thought she was going to ask me, "What happened to...?" No, she didn't ask, not then, or ever. It was as if we each lived in worlds filled with a different pain, and we didn't speak of our pain because we were afraid of hurting the other person even more.

"I didn't know whether you were alive, so I asked Ludwik to write to Lola and ask her to try to find out about you and tell you to do everything possible to come to Warsaw."

"How did you get this place?"

"It's a long story. When I came to Warsaw, I got in touch with Gienia. She couldn't do much for me because she was trying to find a hiding place for her family on the Aryan side of Warsaw. Then Ludwik advised me to go to Mrs. Trochimczuk, whom I, too, knew from the times in Parczew. Fela took me in with open arms. She was unbelievably kind. Both of us cried. I stayed with her for ten days. She was very nervous and scared but she didn't say anything to me. She knew that I had no place to go. But she felt better when Ludwik came over and gave me a new birth certificate. According to that document, my name is Krystina Bartkowska. People who used to know me as Helena still call me Helena — I'm sure it will be confusing for a while. I just hope I don't forget."

"It'll be hard for me to remember that change."

"Yes. It's hard for me to think of you as Jan."

She continued her story. "One day the woman from this apartment came into Mrs. Trochimczuk's place. This Pani Tarwid said to me: 'We can talk openly. I want to help. I believe Pani Trochimczuk is too nervous a person to handle this problem. Pani Trochimczuk knows me well enough to confirm my being honest. This apartment next door is my summer residence. I and my family live in Warsaw on Sienna Street. Pani Helena, I'm suggesting to you to come and live with us in the city. When asked, I'll tell my friends that I engaged you to help my boys with their schoolwork. Your "Aryan" looks are perfect. Please, come with me. I want to help you. If you decide to come to my place, you can come tomorrow.' After Fela assured me that Pani Tarwid is a very decent person, I decided to go to that family on Sienna Street and I am staying there now."

We had a small supper together, then Helena resumed telling her story. What I heard now was just a revelation: the Tarwids had three sons and their father Mieczyslaw Tarwid was the chief of the Blue police in Warsaw North. I turned pale when I heard that. The Blue police was a force created by the Germans, their uniforms were blue, hence their name. The Poles who joined the force were the most active in rounding up Jews and delivering them to the Germans. There were terrible accounts of Blue policemen blackmailing Jews, beating them and then turning them in. The brutality of the Blues had no limits. And now Helena was telling me that she was living in the house of Mr. Tarwid, who was chief of the Blue police in the northern district of Warsaw where the Jewish ghetto was located!

"You are staying at the home of the chief of the Blue police and I am now in his summer residence? This is a trap, Helena! We must leave this place immediately!"

Helena calmed me down and repeated a story she was told by Mrs. Tarwid. Before the war Mr. Tarwid served as military attaché in the Polish embassy in Paris, France. When the Germans invaded Poland they arrested a great number of Polish luminaries and sent them as hostages to the infamous Pawiak prison in Warsaw. The Germans were particularly after the former high officials and Mr. Tarwid was one of them. After a week or two the Germans approached some of the arrested and promised them freedom in return for their collaboration. The ones who refused were sent to Auschwitz. Some of the hostages, who knew each other, decided collectively to accept the German offer, believing that this way they'd have an opportunity to get cover for their eventual opposition underground activities. That was how Mr. Tarwid became chief of the Blues.

"Helena, and you believe all that?"

"I do. When I look at him, I see a decent man and I trust him."

As additional proof of the Tarwids' involvement in special activities, Helena told me now about a Mr. Kregielewski, nicknamed Tomas, who was living in the same house on Sienna Street. According to Mrs. Tarwid, Tomas was a chemical engineer who worked at a regular job in the daytime but two or three times a week he went out just before curfew to work for the underground making grenades. Helena believed firmly that Mr. Tarwid, too, was involved in underground activities.

"Helena, that story of yours sounds very convincing. Let's hope that we are not disappointed and have to pay for it."

"Let's hope."

I asked her about Dula. Helena told me that Dula, her boyfriend and two other couples were still hiding in Mrozowski's house in a village near Parczew. She had come to Warsaw twice and each time she brought supplies of food. During the first trip, Helena had to ask Mrs. Trochimczuk to let Dula stay in her apartment. Although she was frightened, Pani Fela agreed to Dula's staying temporarily at her place.

Helena told me about a frightening incident that had occurred during Dula's stay. On their way to Pani Fela's apartment, they got off the streetcar, and a Gestapo officer got off at the same place and followed them. They slowed down, hoping that the German would pass them. But no, he joined them. The two girls were scared, but not for long. The officer started to flirt with them. According to Helena, Dula was more skilful than she was. Dula laughed, giggled and charmed him with funny one-liners. When they reached the building Pani Fela lived in they tried to say goodbye to the man, but he insisted on going up to the apartment with them. Dula tried to convince him that this would be impossible, their landlady wouldn't allow a visit of that kind. The charmer insisted on going up with them, saying that he would talk to the landlady and that he was altogether very good and successful at talking to ladies, they could be sure of that.

When Mrs. Trochimczuk saw the girls come in with a Gestapo man, she couldn't bring herself to utter a complete sentence. They all sat down in the living room. Dula did most of the talking. She even argued with the German pointing out how unjust the Germans were to the people of Poland. Mrs. Trochimczuk kept leaving the room and coming back. She kept going to the toilet and...flushing it. Before he left, late that evening, the German assured the two girls that he would come back to visit them again soon, but he never did.

Helena also told me about Dula's second visit the week before. "This time Mr. Mrozowski came with her. It's always safer for a woman to travel in the company of a Gentile. Somebody to talk to. They brought a lot of good food with them to Sienna Street. Gienia picked up a part of it and paid for it to Mr. Mrozowski."

"That Dula sure has lots of guts."
"She really does. God bless her."

When Helena left Sluzewiec next morning, a new week of problems set in. I talked myself out of my doubts about the Tarwids, but loneliness overwhelmed me. It was terrible not to have anybody to say a word to. With all that free time, I reached for a book to read. When I reached the third page, I realized that the words on that page didn't connect to the words of the previous one. I couldn't make out what I was reading; my mind was not working. I looked at the print but I was seeing something else, pictures and images from the past: family, "actions," running, hiding....

I felt my head. Was it hot? Did I have a fever? Probably. I wetted a towel with cold water from the tap, put it around my head and sat down in an armchair. I dozed off. Then I realized that I had heard the entrance door being opened and I got scared. It was too late to hide. A woman entered whose looks fitted Helena's description of Mrs. Tarwid.

"Good morning," I said. "You must be Mrs. Tarwid."

"Good morning, Panie Janie. What's the matter, don't you feel well?"

"It's nothing serious. Just a headache."

She looked in her purse and took out from it a *kogutek* (a very popular powdered painkiller in prewar Poland) and gave it to me. "Take a *kogutek*, that should help."

Mrs. Tarwid gave me instructions on how to behave to avoid drawing anybody's attention to the fact that someone was staying here. "Just Mrs. Trochimczuk and the landlady, Mrs. Dutkiewicz, know about you. The three of us are involved with Helena's and your case. We will help." Before leaving for the city, Mrs. Tarwid gave me a few more *kogutek* pouches.

My headache eased a bit. Angels, real angels sent from heaven, I was thinking about all these people helping us. Mrs. Trochimczuk knew Helena and me from prewar times, but Mrs. Tarwid and Mrs. Dutkiewicz? Complete strangers. It was incredible. I tried reading again. No, it didn't work. I took a pencil and paper and started drawing random figures and shapes. That kept me interested for a while. I got up from the table I was sitting at and, not going too close to the windows, I started examining the houses in the neighbourhood. Mostly single villas. The people living in them must have been leading quite normal lives.

Everything outside these homes looked neat, the walkways were cleared of snow. Bundled-up, little kids were making snowmen. Yes, the world was going on. Just for some it was gone or going.

Mr. and Mrs. Tarwid came over the following Sunday. Mrs. Tarwid told me that Helena was staying in the city and helping out the boys with their schoolwork. She would come over later in the afternoon.

"This is my husband, Mr. Tarwid." A tall, broad-shouldered man; his face was proportionate, masculine; his eyes were those of a thinking person. When he talked, he looked at you as if he were assessing what kind of person you were. He never did it in an inquisitive way. He didn't talk much. He was the listening type. From his way of moving you could easily detect his military past. In total: a man of the *szlachta* (noble class). His looks and behaviour commanded respect. I liked Mr. Tarwid a lot, because in many ways he reminded me of my father. In the later months, I learned how noble a man Mr. Tarwid was.

Not long after the Tarwids had left, Helena came over. She had so much to tell about the way she was living now and how the Tarwids were treating her. Mrs. Tarwid's approach to her was like that of a mother. The three sons were told that they should consider Helena like an older sister. The most amazing thing was that family's moderate way of living. One would think that in those times of blackmail and corruption, a chief of the Blue police would live affluently, but no, the opposite was true. Meals were basic and simple, meat once or, at most, twice a week.

Mrs. Tarwid said to me once, "We are having problems not only with the Germans, but with a lot of our own people as well." When I asked her what she meant by that, she answered that when the right time came, she would have a lot to tell me.

While I was staying in the Sluzewiec apartment and Helena was at the Tarwids' in the city, I had the idea of looking up the Zaluski family. Perhaps they could help me financially. The Zaluskis had dealt with my father before the war and were always friendly with my family. I thought that since I knew the names of the Gentile fish-breeders my father used to deal with, and since I knew, too, that some of them owed money to my father, I would ask Mr. Zaluski whether he could be instrumental in collecting that money, which I needed so badly now. I knew that they lived in Sluzewiec, not far from the place where I was staying. I found their address in an old telephone book.

I talked my idea over with Helena during her next visit to me. Although both of us agreed that the idea had only a very slim chance of success, it was worth trying. We had nothing to lose and, as we had found out already, miracles did happen, now and then. "Maybe they won't help us, but they won't harm us, I'm very sure of that," I said. We decided to go to the Zaluskis together that very day. "Helena, your presence is important. Your blond looks are a great factor."

It was midday when I rang the bell to the Zaluskis' house. Using just our eyes, Helena and I asked each other whether we were doing the right thing. Could something unexpected and dangerous come up? Both of us felt tense about what might be ahead. We heard a voice through the intercom (it was a novelty then). "Come up." The ringing bell unlocked the entrance door. We walked up one flight of stairs and...Mr. Zaluski Senior was standing in the open door.

"Oh, my God, Pan Mandelkern!" he cried out in surprise. In one quick movement he embraced me and repeated: "Pan Mandelkern! Sofia, Sofia, come, quick!"

"*Matka najswietsza* (Holiest Mother)," Sofia wept, embracing me. "And who is this with you?"

"My wife, Helena."

"Is she Jewish, too?"

"Yes."

"Are you telling the truth? She does not look Jewish."

"Yes, she is."

The Zaluskis called their older son from an apartment downstairs. He came upstairs together with his Swiss wife, Liza. They too greeted us cordially. During the lunch they invited us to, Zaluski Senior wanted to know what happened to my family (he had already heard about my father's fate) and also, how Helena and I had remained safe till now. Liza Zaluski showed special interest in Helena.

"Mr. Zaluski, I would like to ask you a special favour. I assure you that I will understand if you refuse."

After hearing the details of the favour I was asking, Mr. Zaluski replied, "I know most of the people your father dealt with. I will certainly talk to them. Something positive is bound to come of it. But I strongly believe that you yourself should not try to talk to them; not all of them can be trusted. Please, leave it to me."

I was moved by all that cordiality. When we thanked the Zaluskis for their kindness and hospitality, my father's old friend had this to say: "Panie Mandelkern, I think it will be easier and safer if only your wife comes to us. I would like to see you, too, in our house, but we must not forget that your safety and ours is involved." Turning to my wife, he said, "Pani Mandelkern...."

"I had to assume a new name, remember that I'm now Krystina Bartkowska," Helena interrupted him.

"Well, Krystina, come back in about ten days. Maybe I'll have some results already. We are always home Sunday mornings."

Liza came over to my wife: "Pani Krystina, if you'll need my help, please tell me. I really mean what I'm saying to you."

We left the Zaluskis and walked back to my place. We both wondered where do these people get the courage to act as they did, to show so much interest in us and promise so much.

Chapter Twelve

One afternoon, Mrs. Tarwid came to Sluzewiec. She was usually calm and collected, but now she looked very upset. "Panie Jasiu, somebody denounced Krystina. I managed to get her out of the house in time. I don't know exactly what happened; the whole thing started in my husband's office, and I haven't spoken to him yet. I just came to tell you that you must leave this place. I'm afraid for the life of my family and of yours. I'm going now, that's all I wanted to tell you." Mrs. Tarwid's voice was breaking. With tears in her eyes, she said: "*Niech pana Bog prowadzi* (may God guide you). Goodbye."

Where was I to go? To leave the house and wander aimlessly in the streets would surely lead me straight into the arms of the Germans. Since Helena had managed to escape the trap, I thought, she would probably contact either Ludwik or Gienia and together they would plan for me too. Surely I would hear from them soon. Hours of agonized waiting passed; nothing. It was dark already; curfew time had arrived and still nothing. I should have walked over to the Zaluskis' before curfew, maybe they would have let me stay in their place for one day at least. Too late to think about that now. Where was Helena? Was she safe?

I couldn't bring myself to go to bed that night. Dozing off in a sitting position at a table, I had all kinds of nightmares. Next morning, not going too close to the window, I watched the gate at the front of the house. If I see the Gestapo coming, I'll jump down from the second storey, I thought, and whatever happens then, happens. I don't care any more. The end of me? It'll come sooner or later anyway.

Around midday Mrs. Trochimczuk came home and tapped on our common wall. A message appeared under the door. *Gienia wants you to go to the house on....*The address followed, then *memorize and* *destroy note*. Attached to the note was a little sketch outlining the location of the place. It was in Praga, on the other side of the Wisla River.

I washed my face and put on my "normal" expression. I memorized the address, checked the map, tore up the note and sketch, flushed the bits of paper down the toilet and left the house. At that moment Mrs. Trochimczuk opened her door and handed me a paper folder. Not saying a word she just motioned me to go. I understood that the folder was meant to give me the appearance of a person going to work somewhere. It was a standard trick in those times.

I took the streetcar to Praga. I knew the area well, and I approached the house confidently as if I'd been there many times before, just in case someone might look out a window and notice a man who seemed unsure of himself. I knocked on the door.

"Come in."

I stepped inside: "Good day."

The woman who answered my greeting was tall and corpulent. Her face looked motherly and I felt that I could trust her. The lady invited me to the living room and offered me tea. "My husband told me about your coming here. He will be home shortly, and so will my two boys. My name is Wanda Olszewska."

"I am Jan Piotrowski."

Pani Wanda excused herself saying she had some kitchen work to do. While waiting for Mr. Olszewski I started to read a newspaper that was lying on the table. On the first page I noticed a report about Poles being severely punished for helping Jews to escape from the Warsaw ghetto and then hiding them on the Aryan side. I put away the paper and started to think, Who is this Mr. Olszewski? Why would he agree to hide me? Was he a saint? I had no answer.

Mr. Olszewski came home. He was a tall, lean man, with a long narrow face, a high forehead, blond hair and blue eyes. "Everything is arranged for your staying here. I just want you to know a few things about our house."

When I asked Pan Waclaw who had made all the arrangements, he told me that a party comrade of his had been approached by a Mrs. Gienia and that I should trust him.

"Have you heard of my wife's whereabouts?"

"No. My friend told me only that she was denounced while staying in a place that is very sensitive to our cause. I suppose she will let you know where she is, or come to visit you."

Time was moving very slowly, especially since I hadn't heard a word from either Gienia or my wife. On the third day of my stay at the Olszewskis', Helena came over. Once again she was wearing make-up. At last I heard the story of the chain of events.

"I was in my room at the Tarwids' when the telephone rang. Mrs. Tarwid answered the phone, listened briefly and said: 'Miecio (diminutive for Mieczyslaw), someone is waiting for me, I'll call you back soon.'

"She ran to my room: 'Krystina, there's trouble, leave the house immediately.'

"'Pani majorowa, what has happened?'

"'I don't know yet. Leave the house right now.'

"I put on my coat and left in a hurry. Outside, on the street I noticed a German open vehicle approaching with two uniformed men in it. I suspected that they were going to the Tarwids'. I walked as calmly as I could in the opposite direction.

"I didn't know where to go. First I thought about going to Gienia's place, but that was too far away and, probably, their host wouldn't let me in. That could have also resulted in messing up Sewek's setup. I kept on walking and walking. The cold and dampness started to get to me. Suddenly I found myself on a street where a friend of Ludwik's was working. I walked into the store and introduced myself. The woman there promised to contact Ludwik, and a few hours later, he arrived."

Helena paused for a moment and sighed deeply. She gave me a long look. "Ben, we lost Dula."

I felt myself go numb. I could hardly concentrate on what she said next.

"Lola wrote that Mrozowski, the store-keeper, was demanding money from Dula's boyfriend and the other people hiding in his place. When Mrozowski found out that they had no money left, he denounced them to the Germans and they were taken away to the labour camp. Dula and her boyfriend managed to escape but they were recaptured and executed."

As Helena spoke, I felt as if I were witnessing that execution. Dula, that dear person, gone too!

"Lola was afraid that Mrozowski might know our whereabouts and denounce us too, so she sent word to Ludwik. Now he and Gienia have found me a place to stay."

We comforted each other as best we could, and planned what to do next. My stay at the Olszewskis' would be costly, and Helena knew that her own hiding place was temporary. We decided that Helena would have to try again the Zaluskis for help.

The following Sunday Helena came again and told me about her visit to the Zaluskis.

"While I was on the streetcar one thing was on my mind. Would Liza really help now, or was she just being polite when she spoke to me before? And could I blame her if she refused to help?

"When I arrived, Liza opened the door. She smiled politely and called her in-laws.

"'Good that you came,' Mr. Zaluski said. 'I have some good news. There's money waiting for you.'

"'Thank you so much,' I said. 'That money will come in handy now, since a lot in our situation changed since we were here last time.'

"'Has anything bad happened?'

"I told them that I had been denounced, that I had had to move, and that I could stay where I was for only a short time. Liza declared that she would go immediately to talk to a friend of hers. 'I will get something. If it doesn't work out with this friend, I'll talk to another one. I'll come up with a place for you to stay. If you have to leave your present place, come and stay with me for a few days. Can you come back tomorrow afternoon? I should have something for you by then.'

"The following day, she told me that she arranged a place for me to stay. 'I talked to a friend of mine. She is from Switzerland too. She is married to a Pole, and they have two young children. I told her about your problems, but I didn't tell her you were Jewish. My friend is willing to help. You know, Krystina, I really don't think I deceived her. I, my husband and my in-laws all believe that somewhere in your past there was a Gentile in your family's blood — and that explains your looks.'

"'If there was one, I don't know about it. My parents were always talking about rabbis in the family. They never mentioned any Gentile ancestors, unless....' Here both of us started laughing.

"'Let's forget your Gentile ancestors for now, ' Liza said. 'I am happy because I believe you'll feel comfortable in my friend's house.'

"'I just don't know how to thank you for your interest in me.'

"'We'll put that part off until after the war. Krystina, I'm a believer and I'll keep praying for you. If I can contribute to the saving of your life, I'll consider that my highest reward.'

"Jasiu," Helena said, "I'm now at Mrs. Malicka's place — only three blocks from the Zaluskis. So far, so good. I keep my fingers crossed."

A few days later, using Mrs. Trochimczuk as an intermediary, Mrs. Tarwid got in touch with Helena. The meeting took place at the house of a trusted friend of Mrs. Tarwid's.

"Jasiu, she said I was on her mind all the time. 'Tell me everything about yourself, ' she said. 'Maybe I can be of some help. My boys keep asking about you and Pan Major talks about you every day.'

"I told Mrs. Tarwid about everything that happened since I had to run away from Sienna Street. Then I asked her, 'Pani majorowa, do you know exactly what happened that morning?'

"'To begin with,' Mrs. Tarwid replied, 'I have to say that "luck" is too weak a word to explain how our lives were saved. It was a miracle, a real miracle.'

"She told me the story. Two Gestapo men walked into Mr. Tarwid's office and, with no preamble, one said to him: 'It's been reported that a Jewess is hiding in your house.'

"Tarwid laughed out loud. 'You aren't serious, are you, Lieutenant Bruhl?'

"'*Jawohl*, I'm very serious.'

"The other officer joined in: 'Officer Tarwid, maybe you don't know she is Jewish. Some of them are very good at camouflaging.'

"'There's nobody in the house but my wife and my children, I assure you. I know what happens in my house.'

"'Maybe the Jewess comes in as temporary help and you, working in the office, never see her.'

"'I can't afford to pay for help.'

"'A Jewess would work for a meal, nothing more. Chief Tarwid, you realize the danger to your family and yourself if you are found to be hiding or helping a Jewess. We have known you long enough to trust you, but your wife? Maybe she's hiding something from you. Talk it over with her. We'll come back tomorrow morning. If you co-operate and we get the Jewess, nothing will happen to you, I assure you. Nobody else will even know about it.'

"'I'll talk to my wife, Herr Bruhl.'

"'Heil Hitler. See you tomorrow.'

"Tarwid suspected a trick. The minute the Germans left his office, he called his wife on the phone and told her to take his shoes to the shoemaker. That was their password for danger, decided on when I first went to stay with them.

"A few minutes after I ran out of the house, the Germans arrived. These few minutes were just long enough for Mrs. Tarwid to grab my few things and put them among hers. She threw a few pieces of her boys' clothing into my room.

"The bastards looked over every room in the house. She treated them to tea. While they were sitting at the table and drinking, one of them said, 'You know, Mrs. Tarwid, your hands show that you do a lot of housework.'

"'Well,' she answered, 'three sons and a husband are enough to keep one busy around the clock.'

"They laughed. When she asked the reason for their visit, they said only, 'Your husband will explain it to you.'

"Half an hour later she called her husband and told him that his shoes were in good shape, they didn't need to be repaired. He understood the message.

"I sat speechless listening to Mrs. Tarwid. When I sighed at the end of the story, Mrs. Tarwid stroked my head in a motherly way. She told me her husband felt even though he and she weren't practising believers, they should go to church and say a thank you prayer for the unbelievable miracle that had happened to all of us.

"The Gestapo didn't come back to Mr. Tarwid's office next day and they never looked for you at the summer apartment in Sluzewiec. Before we parted, Mrs. Tarwid said: 'Dear Krystina, if there's anything we can be helpful with, just let us know. The war will not go on forever. If we help each other in these gruesome times, we'll stand a better chance of survival.'"

Helena and I had been incredibly lucky. As for the Tarwids, I don't think I can comprehend their heroic strength of character or the greatness of their deeds. And they did it all for people they had known only a few months.

Chapter Thirteen

When Helena (Krystina now) went to the Zaluskis hoping that they might help her find a place to stay, Mr. Zaluski had told her he had money for us. One of my father's debtors, Mr. Jan Zaorski, was giving us 1,000 zlotys.

It seemed strange to me that Mr. Zaorski would pay back money he owed to my father. It was pure generosity; after all, it was obvious that you didn't have to pay debts to people who didn't exist — who no longer had a right to exist. And on top of that, I remembered him expressing anti-Jewish views when we shared a compartment on the train to Warsaw once before the war. He had been discussing Jews with a clergyman, and I reacted to their talk by saying a few loud nasty words and leaving the compartment. And now the same Mr. Zaorski was stretching out a helping hand to me. It was hard to understand.

Mr. Zaorski had left the money with his brother-in-law, Dr. Sobieranski. I put on my best face and took the streetcar from Praga to the centre of Warsaw. Although the city-centre was usually heavily patrolled by the German police, I didn't see any just now. Still, without turning my head, I kept glancing to the side. I passed through the big entrance gate.

The concierge was looking out of his cubicle. "*Do kogo, prosze* (whom are you going to see, please?)" he asked.

"Dr. Sobieranski," I said in a self-assured voice.

"Thank you."

Oh, brother! One speck of suspicion, and that concierge would have denounced me immediately. Most of them were extremely co-operative with the Germans. I rang the doctor's doorbell. A white-uniformed young lady opened the door. There was one patient before me, a woman reading a book. Good, as long she didn't look at me. When my turn came and I walked into the doctor's office, I told him immediately who I was.

He was surprised but said immediately, "Remove your jacket and shirt, I'll examine you. In case the nurse walks in, you understand." While poking my back, the doctor was talking to me: "My brother-in-law left this for you." He went over to his desk, took out an envelope and gave it to me. "Jan asked me to tell you to come back in four weeks for more money. He wants to know how you are making out so far."

"I'm staying with very good people."

"So, you are not in a bunker? Good." When the doctor heard the door being opened, he said, "Your right lung is quite a bit congested. That's probably left over from your cold."

The uniformed girl was standing in the opened door: "Doctor?"

"I'll be free in a few minutes. Wait outside, please." To me, when she had gone, he added, "Come back in approximately four weeks. Here are some *koguteks* and a few bandages, just in case. God be with you. Goodbye."

I dressed quickly and left his office.

I stayed at the Olszewskis' for almost two months. Pan Waclaw kept me informed about the current news. The Germans were having big problems on the Eastern front. The English had parachuted some weapons — not many, but every little bit helped. Underground commandos had executed a few Blues who were routinely helping the Germans in the manhunts that now took place frequently in the streets of Warsaw. Helena came to the Olszewskis' to see me once every two or three weeks, usually on Sundays. The Malickis were treating her well. Now and then Liza dropped in to see her.

One evening, Mr. Olszewski moved aside a chest of drawers that was standing in a corner, to show me a secret trap-door. He explained that beneath the door was a hole, a hiding-place in case of an emergency. "It's built in such a way that tapping or poking will never make a sound of emptiness underneath."

"Has anyone ever hidden down there?" I asked.

"Yes. We had two Jewish couples staying here, one at a time."

"Where are they now?"

"They are safe outside Warsaw. Our underground organization does everything to help. We are in constant touch with the ghetto. A group of Jewish fighters is preparing an uprising there. We are helping them to stockpile arms and ammunition."

I told Mr. Olszewski how hard it was for me to believe that Poles were helping out Jews, and in such an organized way.

"I can understand your reaction. But the Poles in our socialist movement don't see any difference between Jew and non-Jew. The church is spreading hatred, to keep control of the faithful. It's an old trick of theirs and we know about it."

"Aren't the hate-mongers in the majority?"

"It's hard to fight them, but we do our best. The Germans won't last forever. There are signs already of their coming downfall."

Mr. Olszewski told me about the danger the underground faced from the Blue police, but trusted people — I assume he meant officials like Major Tarwid — placed in their midst alleviated the problem to a great degree. At the same time, the Blues, supported by the Germans, were placing moles among the ranks of the underground. "We fight them. Our secret press often reports the execution of these traitors." Pan Olszewski explained why he accepted payment for my staying in his place. "Most of what you give me goes to the underground, you are helping us help you."

I had greater confidence in Mr. Olszewski after our talk. Once or twice a week now, my host gave me underground literature and news to read. "This should lift your spirits a bit." I often lay awake at night thinking about Mr. Olszewski. Where did such people come from? I wondered. The chief of the Gestapo in Warsaw had placed posters all over the city, threatening the death penalty for anyone who helped the Jews in any way. How many Olszewskis were out there in Polish society? "Since we only live once," Mr. Olszewski had said to me, "why not try for the profoundest satisfaction possible — defending the life and dignity of man?"

Holy words in a sea of hate.

A new picture of Polish society was taking shape in my mind. In the wake of the Nazis' anti-Jewish brutality, the anti-Semitically poisoned majority was having a field day. On the other hand, islands of dissent were emerging. People like Mr. Olszewski, socialists, had opposed fascism all their lives. Now, they did what they could, working underground, to help the most oppressed. Another group consisted of Poles who had understood that once the Germans were finished with the

Jews, they would in all likelihood decide that the elimination of the Slavs was next on the master race's agenda. Although these Poles may have been anti-Semitic, it made sense to them not to collaborate with the Germans against the Jews. Then there were the Poles, like the Zaluskis, who had known Jews before the war and considered them no different from other people.

Now and then Mr. Olszewski left the house right after dinner and returned after curfew-hour. Although he never told me, I assumed he was doing "underground" work. He told me then about the bitter fights with different Polish political factions and about German manhunts and the colleagues he had lost. The German military situation on the Eastern front was said to be more and more precarious. At the same time, the situation of the Jews in the Warsaw ghetto was tragic. Mr. Olszewski said it was no longer possible to smuggle in food, and that thousands upon thousands of Jews were dying either of starvation, cold and sickness in the ghetto, or in the death camps.

"Panie Olszewski, do you think that the Jews behind the walls are in a position to fight the Germans?"

"I don't think so. We are trying to get the organized fighters out of the ghetto to join our ranks, but they refuse to leave. They say it would mean deserting their brethren. These fighters, men and women alike, are brave people. They have been distributing leaflets in the ghetto, telling the Jews, *Don't die with the Torah in your hands. Die with weapons in your hands.*"

As the days went by, Mrs. Olszewski's behaviour changed visibly. She had seemed full of life and energy when I first arrived but now she complained of headaches, lack of appetite and sleepless nights. One evening, Mr. Olszewski called me into a separate room, and going straight to the point, told me that his wife was growing more sick with fear every day of my stay. She was concerned for the lives of her two sons. No amount of explaining and reasoning had any effect on her. Pan Waclaw understood my position, but he asked me to find a new place for myself within a week or ten days.

"Mr. Olszewski, I'll talk to my wife the next time she comes. I understand the situation — no matter what the consequences may be for me, I'll leave here as soon as I can."

My wife turned to Mrs. Tarwid for help. Once again, those kind people stretched out a helping hand to us. Pan Tarwid was sure that the case of a Jewess staying in his home was closed. I was once again in their summer apartment in Sluzewiec.

I returned to Sluzewiec and immediately went "public," but kept a low profile at the same time. Of the five tenants (besides the Tarwids) in the building, two knew I was Jewish. Mrs. Trochimczuk knew, and so did the landlady, Mrs. Dutkiewicz. The other three tenants were informed by the landlady that the Tarwids had hired a man to do the gardening, and that he would be staying in their apartment. According to Mrs. Trochimczuk and Mrs. Dutkiewicz, the other three tenants were nice people, "But who knows what they think of Jews?" I had to be careful, and act like a real gardener.

The Tarwids' garden plot of good black soil was about three-quarters of a kilometre from the house; it measured 200 by 200 metres. There was a tool shed in the centre of the lot. I devoted myself to growing vegetables. Every morning I went out to work, and to enhance my professional look, I carried gardening implements with me: one time a small wicker basket, a big one the next time, large paper bags, jute bags, pails of liquid fertilizer, and so on. When I finished my work, I went home to a quiet evening at the apartment: a reasonable combination of being seen and not being seen. I hoped that no one would get too curious about me.

The whole Tarwid family used to come out to Sluzewiec on the weekends. We worked together outside. When he had the time, Mr. Tarwid liked to come over during the week too. He told me about the execution of Jews and Poles in the Pawiak prison; the executed Poles were mostly members of the underground. He told me about the death camps, about the tricks the Gestapo used to fool the Jews: giving them bread and marmalade at the *Umschlagsplatz* (place of processing) for the duration of the forthcoming journey to the new "working places."

Major Tarwid complained about the behaviour of the Jews. "I realize that they are physically exhausted, but why do they not make a single move and choke at least a few Germans to death? After they've been taken to the *Umschlagsplatz* it is impossible that they don't know what will happen to them next." Mr. Tarwid was angry. He would turn over a pail, sit down on it and talk: "I'm getting information that there's an underground organization in the ghetto. They're supposed to come out in the open and fight the Germans. I know for a fact that our *pod-*

ziemie (underground) is supplying them with weapons and ammunition. What are they waiting for? I'm not a Jew, but a Christian and Polish patriot. It hurts me to see what is happening, and to see no reaction at all. Not a single drop of that poisoned German blood spilled. As a human being, I feel degraded."

One date I will always remember. It was April 19, 1943. At about four p.m., Major Tarwid came to the garden plot where I was working. First he looked around, then he called me over close to the shed.

"Panie Janie, I've got big news. We'll pretend we're working and I'll tell you. It's a big day in the ghetto. The Jews have begun the fight against the Germans. Some say it's too late, but they are doing their best to defend Jewish honour and their dignity, the dignity of man over the ferocity of the beast. I am happy now. The Gestapo called me in to witness the action. Panie Janie, I am happy. No, don't cry. Be proud of them! The Germans tried to enter the ghetto in a tank and two armoured vehicles, but they were met with a salvo of shots. Eight or ten Germans were killed instantly. Think of it: brutal, armed Germans killed by almost defenceless Jews! Oh, what a feeling it was to see that! That's the best possible propaganda to bolster the underground."

"Did the Germans get into the ghetto?"

"No, they retreated in panic. They never expected Jewish resistance. When the Germans regrouped, they started to shell the ghetto with artillery fire. We will see what happens. It's not an even fight, far from it, but at last German blood has been spilled by Jews."

The ghetto uprising lasted over four weeks. I waited impatiently for the major to come out to Sluzewiec every day and tell me the news of that tragic, hopeless fight. And Mr. Tarwid always had a lot to tell me, since he was actively involved with the underground collaboration with the Jewish fighters.

On the fourth or fifth day of the uprising, I was working in the garden, and I saw two uniformed Germans approaching on horseback. My first thought was that they were coming to get me. Somebody had denounced me. I hunched over and continued working, at the same time watching out of the corner of my eye as the two riders came closer. Yes, they were coming in my direction. Should I run and try to hide between the buildings, about half a kilometre from the garden? No, I wouldn't run! Maybe they just want to ask directions. If I ran, they — being on horseback — would certainly catch me and then....No, I wouldn't run, but if I heard *Hande hoch* (hands up), then I'd run and that would be that. It was bound to happen anyway, sooner or later. I glanced again, toward the riders. They had turned in the direction of the big house with the white fence around it. Yes, that was where they were going. About fifteen minutes later I saw the two Germans mounting their horses and leaving.

At the same time a woman came out from the big house screaming, waving her hands in despair. She came running straight to me. She cried out loudly: *"Die haben ihn todgeschlagen* (they killed him)!"

I understood that someone in her family had been killed. Calmly now, I asked the woman (in Polish, because I didn't want her to know that I understood German), "What has happened? Has someone been killed?"

Lamenting loudly, she said, in Polish now, *"Te Zydy* (those Jews) from the ghetto killed my son, my only son is dead, killed by Jews! Oh, *mein lieber Gott, mein einziger Sohn is tode* (Dear God, my only son is dead)." She turned around and, still screaming, ran back to her house.

What did I think about all that then? I had no pity in my heart for that woman. I thought of my baby son, and other Jewish sons and daughters who had been so brutally killed, for no reason at all. That German mother called to her God in despair. I called mine and begged him, "Allow me to live to see their sons being killed. I know that our dead can never come back, but I want revenge, revenge for the lost ones, revenge for the shame and degradation inflicted upon us. Dear God, if You are there to hear me, give us justice, I want revenge. Please, Almighty God!"

I told Major Tarwid about the woman's son having been killed by Jewish bullets from the ghetto. "I know that *Volksdeutsch* family," he said. "Good, let them start finding out what the pain of losing a son means. They have had a foretaste of it on the *Ostfront*, but it is not enough. Nowhere near enough."

The uprising in the ghetto was not over. One evening, the residents of the apartment building I was staying in gathered to watch the flames of the burning ghetto. One man laughed aloud and said, "The bedbugs are on fire. The Germans are doing a great job." Nobody in the group reacted one way or another to that remark.

Finally, it was over. Mr. Tarwid told me about the tragic end of the ghetto uprising, how only a very few escaped, through the sewers. "Panie Janie, as a military man I have to say military defeat is tragic, but defeat after fighting a battle for human dignity is in itself a great moral victory, a victory that will be remembered by history as a lesson for the future and as an eternal monument to the heroic fighters."

In my grief and sorrow, I said to him, "I ask myself, again and again, where are the big democracies of the West? Where are all the volunteers who joined ranks and went to Spain a few years ago to fight tyranny? Why are there no volunteers now to press their governments to intervene on behalf of the innocent Jews? Nothing has been done to help us. What is left for us? All we can do is pray for someone like Samson to bring down the temple together with our enemies. Then the whole world will burn and turn into ashes, just as we have burned to ashes. Do you think it is painful for me to say that? Not any more."

Both of us were silent. "Panie Janie," the major spoke again. "There's a part of our Polish society, a very small part unfortunately, which understands your feelings. These people also understand the real aims of the Germans and the Russians when it comes to the question of Poland. Now, take my case: under the threat of death I took a position as the chief of the Blue police. I work in the underground and try to save Jews and Poles. I risk my life and my family's lives every minute of the day. But when the Germans are defeated and if I survive the war, the new regime, (which will surely be dominated by Fascist Russia), will be after me for serving in the Blue police. One way or the other, I have no future. After the war, my sons will have no father."

I felt that there was something I had to say to that man now. "There will be people after the war who will tell about the real Mr. Tarwid."

The major lifted his head, looked at me and said, "That's not how things work out in Fascist regimes."

What a sad conversation that was.

Chapter Fourteen

When Helena came to see me, I told her how hard it was to be alone, with nobody to talk to. She was among people all the time; she could talk and listen to them. But she told me that was no better. Mrs. Malicka, at whose house she was staying, didn't know she was Jewish. She had to be on guard all the time, and even more so when Mrs. Malicka's friends dropped in. They were openly wondering who the good-looking help was. Helena had heard one of them remark that hired help usually had a rougher face. I was forced to admit that, in that respect, my wife had it harder than I.

"I think," Helena said, "that I should leave that house before it's too late. I wonder what Mrs. Tarwid would say to that."

Pani Mieczyslawa's advice was clear. "Krystina, you're right. You must definitely leave that place. I know that segment of our society well and I don't trust them. I'll talk to Mrs. Dutkiewicz, our landlady, and I'll get back to you."

The next Sunday, Helena-Krystina was visiting me on her day off. Mrs. Dutkiewicz, the landlady, came up to the apartment and told us she met Mrs. Zgierski in church. They talked about Krystina, the "underground" girl, who had had to leave her home town and hide in Warsaw. Mrs. Zgierski agreed to engage her as a governess to her little boy, but she couldn't provide her with permanent accommodation. The governess would have to rent a room somewhere.

The following day, Helena went to see Mrs. Zaluski, Jr., who said she knew an older lady who had a big house. "She has one girl tenant already. I'll talk to her today. Something will work out."

And so it did. That was how "Krystina" came to rent a room from Mrs. Lukaszewicz at number 42 Wilcza Street. Liza confided Krystina's real identity to the new landlady. Mrs. Lukaszewicz and

Krystina developed a real friendship. "Watch out for that other girl tenant, she's a real loudmouth," the lady warned.

All during the time I stayed in Sluzewiec, I was very conscious of my appearance. How did I look to a stranger? Did I appear to be a genuine working man, or just someone hanging around? I tried my utmost to look and play the first role. Sometimes I had doubts, other times I thought that I was doing fine. I felt I was being the right man when, carrying a rake and a cultivator, I was stopped by two ladies and asked if I would have the time to take care of their gardens, not far away from the place we were standing. I answered politely that since I was already attending two large gardens, I simply had no free time left. Thank you.

My food at that time was of a very modest nature. There was sometimes a knock on the wall from Mrs. Trochimczuk's apartment, signalling that I should open my door and take a pot of soup she had prepared for me.

But when "Krystina" dropped in on a Sunday, she always managed to make "something out of nothing" and that "something" tasted great. Once she made *kopytka*, dumplings consisting of (more) potatoes and (less) flour. That was a treat and I asked my wife for the recipe. During the week I tried to make *kopytka* myself. I don't know what I did wrong but my dumplings had the density of rocks. There was no question of throwing them out, I had to eat them. I cut the little "pebbles" into small pieces and down they went. My culinary effort was rewarded with a stomach ache, which I cured by drinking boiling water for two days.

Each time she visited, Krystina brought me news about what was happening in the heart of Warsaw. Once, she told me that she had met Karl, the German policeman from Parczew, on the street. He noticed her and smiled. She smiled back, but walked quickly away in a panic. She realized later that Karl probably had no bad intentions and might be glad to see her alive, but she did not want to take any chances.

One Sunday, the Tarwids arrived in Sluzewiec and acted busier than usual. He was helping out in the garden, trying to arrange everything neatly, and Mrs. Tarwid was busy in the apartment. Soon enough I found out that their friends from years ago would be coming for a visit the same afternoon. The visitors knew that a man with an underground background was taking care of their garden, but they were never informed who I really was. "Who knows what anyone thinks about you know who in times like these," the major remarked. "Pan Waclaw was formerly a high official in the prewar Ministry of Defence. Pan Andrzej is a former judge and Pan Henryk is a colleague of mine from when I worked in Paris."

The three guests came straight to the garden. Each one greeted Mrs. Tarwid by kissing her hand. All of them looked to be around the same age, in their fifties or older. Mr. Tarwid introduced me briefly, saying that I was the man who did such a splendid job of gardening. Apparently, the classy visitors did not care about the "hired hand" and they paid no attention to his presence.

It was quite easy to tell who was who. The one with the know-it-all expression on his face had to be from the defence department. The judge was probably the man who propped both his arms on the table and kept looking around just the way a judge does in court. The diplomat listened attentively when the others spoke, and used very colourful words and had an ironic manner. Since I was eager to eavesdrop on their conversation, I tried to keep myself busy not too far from the place where they were sitting. I was sure that they would eventually talk about the *you know who*.

"I brought a bottle of whisky," the official said. "Let's have a drink."

"I can't see anything wrong with that motion," the judge answered.

The official opened the basket he had brought along, and took out a bottle with no label on it (moonshine?). While filling glasses he had also found in his basket, he asked who should make the toast.

"Andrzej, you make the toast," suggested the diplomat, turning to the judge.

On the judge's suggestion, Mr. Tarwid invited me to have a drink with them.

"To the good health of the Tarwid family and may our country soon be free."

"Amen," all answered.

I downed my drink, thanked them, and returned to my work.

"Panie Janie, come back," the official called after me. "The toast was for two very good causes, so we will have another shot."

"Motion approved," the judge said, smiling broadly. I joined in the second drink. Everyone seemed to be in a more talkative mood. I thanked them again for the good cheer and, not far away, I waited to listen again. They talked about common friends who had been arrested, some when they were caught doing "underground" work, others for no reason at all.

"The Germans will pay for all that. Our boys will not let themselves be slaughtered. Every day there are a few grenades here and there. The Germans are afraid, and they are putting up heavy security guards in their neighbourhoods. We will not be like the Jews. We will fight and the Germans will have to respect us."

"You make it sound very simple, Waclaw," said the former diplomat.

"As for the Jews," the judge broke in, "I don't think there was much they could have done in their own defence. The Germans were ruthless and, I am very ashamed to say it, many of our own people helped the Germans in their devilish work. When I think about what I have seen with my own eyes, I feel deeply ashamed."

Humming a legionnaire's tune (would a Jewish boy hum that kind of a song? I did it for a cover-up), I moved closer to the table trying to catch every word of the conversation.

The official, Waclaw: "As for the Jews, I don't think I'll miss them much."

Judge: "Before the war I had my reservations about Jews. I belonged to the *Endecja* (the ultra-nationalist party), but now I see everything in a different light. Should the Germans become the masters of Europe, they will treat us Slavs the same way they treated the Jews."

The former diplomat: "Luckily, the political situation and the military, too, seem to be turning against the Germans now."

"I still don't think I'll miss the Jews. I only miss my Jewish doctor. My wife and I had so much confidence in him. He was a good diagnostician. Poor Dr. Mitler, they killed him in the Pawiak."

"During my work on the bench I met many Jews. It's true that many times I felt disgust toward them but I also met many outstanding lawyers — Jews who were brilliant commentators on the law."

"Would you want to see the Jews back?"

"Yes. Because in retrospect, and in light of the Nazi philosophies and their cruelties, I conclude that our own Polish anti-Semitism, of which I was a part, was a sort of an easy way out — looking for scapegoats. To my understanding now, our anti-Semitism was more our fault than the fault of the Jews." The judge sounded serious.

The diplomat expressed an inclination to share the judge's opinion.

Waclaw said, "Miecio, what do you think?"

"What the Germans have done and continue to do is bad and cruel," said Tarwid. "No member of the human race deserves what they did to the Jews. Besides that, my opinion is that Jews have no more faults, or virtues for that matter, than the rest of humankind on this planet."

"Well said, Miecio," the friend from Paris said.

Still pretending to be busy with my work, I listened to that depressing conversation about a people of which only the ashes remained.

The former defence official sounded perplexed when he asked, "So all three of you really think that in my view of the Jews I represent a minority?"

Judge: "Waclaw, at this table you are a minority, but out there, among the masses of the Polish people, I'm afraid you represent a majority. I honestly think the deeply rooted Polish anti-Semitism is a *hanba* (a strong Polish word for shame) in our Catholic, not Christian, but Catholic upbringing."

Waclaw: "Andrzej, you make it sound as if we are Catholic pagans."

Henryk: "Waclaw, I think you've hit the nail right on the head."

A silence followed that serious discussion. It was broken when Waclaw suggested another round of alcohol. I was glad not to be asked to join this time. The new conversation was about the health of different people. I went off to work in a different spot, far from the table with the guests.

I had gone to Dr. Sobieranski three times. Each time he had 1,000 zlotys for me, given to him by Jan Zaorski. On my way to Hoza Street I wondered if I would make it safely there and back. Many times during the trip I became suddenly afraid, and felt the blood leave my face. But the suntan I had acquired from working outside helped cover the pallor of my face in those moments of fear. Before leaving the house for a trip through hostile surroundings I put on my mask of normality and kept it on till the moment I put the key in the keyhole of my door, and what immense relief I felt then!

The only document I carried around was the *Kennkarte* Ludwik had obtained for me, made out to Jan Piotrowski. Then the authorities issued an order that each person had to get a new *Kennkarte*. We had to go in person to city hall, bringing along our birth certificates. *Anyone caught not having a renewed Kennkarte will be arrested automatically* — the proclamation posters were warning.

I had to get a genuine birth certificate, and Krystina needed a new one — but where would we get them? From Ludwik, where else? He brought two "authentic" certificates. Krystina's was made out in the same name as before — Krystina Bartkowska. But for more "authenticity" she also received a middle name — Lydia.

My certificate, by mistake, was made out to Jan Mankowski and not to Jan Piotrowski, the name I had in my faked *Kennkarte*. I too received a middle name: Witold. The change in names made no difference to me since the Jan Piotrowski document was not registered anywhere. So a totally new name was all right for me.

The clerk at city hall, before issuing a new *Kennkarte*, checked in the official registry books whether the name on the birth certificate was registered at the address given by the respective applicant. To get Krystina's name, and my name, in the official residents' registry was not too difficult for Ludwik's connections. Krystina's street, Wiejska, sounded familiar, but mine, Kaliska Street, I had never heard of. But what difference did it make? The problem now was to get through the personal appearance in the police department of city hall.

Moving around in the streets of Warsaw in those months was extremely dangerous for a young man. The Polish underground forces organized daring attacks against the Germans and in reprisal the Germans staged "round-ups" in different parts of the city. A quiet residential neighbourhood turned unexpectedly to hell within minutes. The tension in the city was particularly high in August and September 1943, after a successful bank robbery, executed with utmost precision by the underground. In response the authorities increased the number of police patrols throughout the city.

I had no alternative, and so I put on my "mask of indifference" and took the streetcar to city hall. German sentries were walking up and down the long line-up in front of the building. "Single line-up" was their only order to the waiting people. Once inside the building I felt very nervous because German policemen were walking along the line giving everybody an inquisitive look.

Are they after...? a thought flashed through my mind.

At that moment I felt somebody pulling at my trouser leg. I turned around. It was a baby (sent by God Himself), a two- or two-and-a-half-year-old boy. He was holding on to his mother's skirt with one hand, and with the other the little angel had grabbed my trousers. I realized that this baby was giving me a golden opportunity to hide my face from the crowd, and especially from the police. I started to play with the toddler.

"*Bist du der Vater?* (Are you the father?)"

I straightened up. There was a German policeman asking me that question. "I don't know," I answered in Polish.

Everybody around laughed, the German included. "*Ah, du Lump* (Oh, you bum)," the *Volksdeutsch* policeman said and walked up the line.

The birth certificate ready in my hand, I reached the clerk's desk.

"Your name and address, please."

"Jan Witold Mankowski, Kaliska Street 16."

It must have been the mention of the street name that made the clerk look up at me — which was enough to give me a scare. He opened the voluminous registry book, ran his index finger down a few pages, then stopped. "Put both your index fingers on the ink pad, yes, good. Press the right finger here and the left one here. Good." He actually pressed my two fingers on the new *Kennkarte* and looked at me again. Handing me over the new treasure, he said, "That's all, thank you."

I remembered to walk out of that city hall building in the most natural way. I breathed easier when I reached the house in Sluzewiec.

Ludwik explained to me later that the clerks, who were our "own" boys from the underground, had been told to expect some special applicants at certain addresses. "When the clerk heard the address from you, he looked up to see how Jewish you looked," Ludwik said. I was now in possession of a genuine, duly registered *Kennkarte*, signed by the chief of police of Warsaw himself. The document stated that I was born in a place near Cracow (a place I had never heard of before that day), and that I was a tailor by profession.

Krystina had also got her *Kennkarte* without trouble. I have kept those two documents to this day, as souvenirs.

Chapter Fifteen

I always looked forward to Sunday. I was alone most of the time, and by the end of the week I was anxious for the Tarwids and Krystina to come out to Sluzewiec, to have their company and hear what was going on in the wide world. That particular Sunday turned out quite differently from what I expected.

The Tarwids came at about eleven a.m. When Krystina arrived, in the late afternoon, I noticed a change in her. Although she took part in our talks about everything, I detected a certain apprehension in her behaviour. It was not until the Tarwids left for their city residence that Krystina literally fell on me and started to cry.

I embraced her, hugged her and tried to make her talk. My first thought was that her employer had found out that she was Jewish and told her to go. And then I thought that maybe someone had recognized her and she had to run away. There were so many things that could have gone wrong, I didn't know what to think of first. And here was Krystina crying and not saying a word, just as if she had lost her voice and her ability to speak. I felt that both of us were completely helpless. I held her in my arms, wiping away her tears, kissing her head and face with all the love I had for her in my heart.

It took quite a while for the rapid beat of her heart to grow slower and her sobs less frequent. She started to talk. "My dear Ben, oh, no, I forgot, my dear Jasiu, I don't think I can take it any longer, I am completely exhausted physically, and what is worse, I can't cope with it any longer morally."

"My dear Krystina," I said, "I love you. Rest your head, lean on me and just relax. You can tell me everything a little later. Just try to relax. Look in my eyes. Oh, good, I think I see a little smile." And when she looked in my eyes, I kissed her gently. She kissed me too. We looked at each other, as if we could in that moment gather strength to help each other.

After a few moments of silence, I said, "Now, my dear, tell me what happened. What made you cry? I'll hold your hands in mine and you tell me everything."

Krystina sighed deeply. "As you know, Mrs. Dutkiewicz recommended me to Mrs. Zgierski as a governess, not as a cleaning woman. But yesterday, Mrs. Zgierski told me to scrub and wash the floors in her house. The tone of her voice as she was ordering me around was just impossible to take, and believe me I tried very hard to keep myself in control. I couldn't sleep all night long, I just kept crying. This morning Mrs. Zgierski told me to polish the whole family's shoes and do it fast, she said, because everyone was going to church. After the church service, they had guests for lunch and as I brought dishes to the table, all I could hear them talking about was Jews, Jews and Jews again. The derogatory remarks and laughter had no end. And all that from the people who belong to the elite of the Polish society! All this time they were addressing each other "Count so" and "Countess so-and-so." No. Jasiu dear, I just can't take it. I don't feel I can go back to that house." Krystina fell silent.

"Dear Krysiu," I said slowly, "I realize what you are going through. I understand now why you were crying, but you have to endure. Some day everything will change and we will be free again."

"How? That is impossible," Krystina said.

Both of us were silent now.

After a while Krystina spoke again, "Look, Jasiu, Mrs. Dutkiewicz never told Mrs. Zgierski that I was Jewish. If Mrs. Zgierski had the slightest suspicion of who I am really, she would denounce me immediately. She is a pathological anti-Semite. You can't imagine how they were talking about Jews at that lunch today. All the ten or eleven people present gave *credit* to the Germans for liquidating the Jews. The most vitriolic opinions were voiced by the Catholic priest of the church the Zgierskis attend. He sat at the head of the table as the guest of honour. All those faces were just beaming with satisfaction when that representative of brotherly love was commenting on the Jews."

"But look, not everyone is like Mrs. Zgierski and her company. Just think what the Tarwids, Mrs. Dutkiewicz, Mrs. Trochimczuk, Ludwik, the Zaluskis, the Zaorskis, Dr. Sobieranski — what all of them did and still are doing for us. All of them know we are Jewish. There are more people like them. I admit that they are just a fraction of Polish society, but they risk their own lives to help others. All we should do now is try to endure and maybe some day...."

"Yes, but realize that if I make even the slightest slip Mrs. Zgierski will turn me over to the Germans. She would do it with the greatest satisfaction."

"Krysiu dear, you'll never slip. I know you. You will never slip-say or slip-do anything that might give you away."

"I don't know. I feel that my inner strength is all gone."

"Krysiu, you've mixed with the Gentile world all your life, as a child, in school, and later at work. Your behaviour, your way of expressing yourself — all that will never give you away. Your looks are great. Your pretty, symmetrical face, your long, blond hair, deep blue eyes! You are my dear *schikse*! Think of all these assets of yours!" I tried to cheer her up.

"Tell me, Jasiu, what is the use in playing that game? I don't care any more for my life and if...they find out about me, they would torture me to death. So why....Why not commit...?"

"Oh, no." I interrupted. "No suicide. I have thought of all that, our situation I mean, many times. I decided never to commit suicide. I want to live and survive this hell. I want to survive and see with my own eyes the downfall of these damned beasts. But I also decided that if I ever get caught, I'll run, try to escape and be shot dead. I'll never be tortured to death. And I want you, Krysiu, to think the same way. I want to live, but not alone. I love you and both of us have to survive together."

I couldn't speak for a moment. Krystina, her hands in mine, was silent now. After a while: "Jasiu, dear, your wish seems just that, a wish, an impossible dream. I have no hope."

"Krystina, it's a dream now. But don't say its impossible. Look, I read every single word in *Das Reich*, the official mouthpiece of the Nazi inner circle. I read all the lines and between the lines. And believe me, there are big cracks in the 'invincible German war machine.' Even their own Goebbels, asking for more effort from his compatriots, is admitting there are cracks."

"Let's say it's true. But we won't live to see their collapse. Every day the newspapers report Jews being flushed out of their hiding-places. The German authorities print warnings in the press that anyone hiding a Jew will be shot dead. What is the point in going on with life in these hopeless circumstances?"

Silence fell again. There was not much to say. My mind was full of chaotic thoughts. And then, "No, Krystina, I don't want to give up. Maybe it will take six months or, who knows, maybe even longer, but they'll lose the war. I want to live and I want to see it. After that, after seeing their collapse, I really don't care what happens to me. Do you understand?"

"I understand very well. But I don't care any more whether I ever see their downfall. I am exhausted. You go on. It's different for me."

"No, Krysiu, you and I are one. The downfall of that beast will have a meaning to me only if we both live to see it, you and I together. Promise me that you will try."

"Do you know that you are asking me to go back to floor-scrubbing and shoe-polishing and other things like that? And above all to that abusive language about Jews? I didn't want to tell you what I witnessed on my way here. But I can't keep it in me any longer. On the streetcar, at one of the stops, two Gestapo men got into the streetcar with two Jewish boys. They looked to be in their early teens. Their faces were pale and scared. All the passengers in the streetcar were looking at them, some of them even laughing. One man said that he recognized them. 'They were selling cigarettes on the corner,' he said. Someone else, in the seat next to me, said to his wife, 'This is the end of them.' Now, do you want me to go through the same thing as these two boys?"

I let go of my wife's hands, turned around, and went over to the table in the middle of the room. I sat down in one of the chairs, with my back to my wife. I sat as if frozen, but I felt tears coming to my eyes. And then I felt my Krystina's arms around me. She said softly, "I shouldn't have told you about the two boys, I know. Forgive me. My dear Benush, no, Jasiu, if you want so much to live, I'll help you. I promise to get myself together and fight all the odds. Kiss me. I love you. That is all we have now."

We embraced each other strongly. When we started to talk again, I told her how the week had been since we last saw each other. I told her about my success in gardening on the Tarwids' land. I told her all the news from the German weekly *Das Reich*.

We were still talking about our problems, about the bad news coming from all sides, when Krystina suddenly said: "You know, I have often thought that I should carry around, concealed, a sprayer bottle filled with vitriolic acid to spray the face and eyes of the German Gestapo beast who captures me. That way I will die knowing that he will suffer all his life. His family, too, will have the right souvenir from the slain Jewess."

"Krysiu, you certainly are thinking the right way. But neither you nor I should do a thing like that."

"I'm surprised to hear you say that. You always advocate fighting back."

"You're right. But when I think about it now — how we would be caught and tortured, and how we might reveal the names of innocent people like Mrs. Tarwid, who would lose her life, I'm having second thoughts. I really don't know how I would act if I was personally attacked."

Exhausted from all the talking about our precarious situation, Krystina and I decided to go to sleep. What awoke us turned the next few hours into a nightmare. We heard a very intense knocking at the gate of the wire-mesh fence surrounding our small apartment building. The gate was usually kept closed after the curfew hour. Krystina and I, hiding behind the curtain, looked out the window and saw two German gendarmes at the gate.

We moved away from the window and embraced each other. In the most controlled voice, Krystina said, "Now, that's it. Let's say goodbye to each other. Remember, when they take us out of the building, you run one way and I'll run the other."

"No, Helena, both of us will run in the same direction. That way they'll shoot and kill us at the same time."

"No, Benush, we must run in opposite directions. And in zig-zags. We'll have a better chance to be missed."

"It won't work. They have machine guns."

"Then we will just run. And that's it."

We were locked in an embrace. We were not crying. The deep fear of our inescapable fate stopped our tears. But both of us were shaking uncontrollably. We waited for the knock or kick of the heavy boots at our door. All my being was concentrated on listening. For a moment I thought I heard the sound of heavy footsteps on the stairs. Helena and I didn't say a word to each other. We listened, we waited.

In a rapid move, Helena took her head off my shoulder and whispered, "I'll stand near the door. You hide in a cupboard or under the bed. When they see me, they'll just take me away. Maybe they will be satisfied with their prey and look no further. You will be saved."

"Oh, no. We go together."

"Listen, Ben. You are strong, so I want you to live. I am tired and exhausted. I can't anymore."

"*No.*"

We were talking to each other now and thinking of each other as Helena and Ben. In these last moments of our lives, we didn't need our assumed names, Jan and Krystina. No more need to pretend to be someone else. We stood in silence. Nobody had come for us yet, not yet. Then we thought we heard voices, laughter, a door slamming.

I dared to look at the clock on the wall. "Helena," I said, "I think half an hour has gone by. What is taking them so long?"

"Please, Benush, don't talk. I feel as if I were moving away to a different, far, far-away world."

An hour passed, an hour and a half, and nobody came for us. "Ben, they're in the building. If they had left, we would have heard the slamming of the gate. They're sure of themselves and their prey, they're probably talking to the tenants."

Nobody came. In the early hours of the next morning we started to believe that the two Germans had left the building without our hearing them leave. We had to get ourselves together and resume our normal routine. Krystina had to go back to her governess job at the Zgierskis', and she usually left in the morning with Mrs. Trochimczuk to avoid suspicion.

When Mrs. Trochimczuk came for Krystina, she asked whether we had heard the German officers coming into the building the evening before. She said, "My first thought was that they had come to get you. I fell on my knees and prayed and cried. I was shaking all over and crying. But then Mrs. Dutkiewicz came up and told me that the Germans were looking for a lost pig that escaped from their station next door. That pig was supposed to be their next day's meal. When she told me, we both knelt down again and thanked God that you were safe."

Chapter Sixteen

It was a dull morning in the late fall of 1943. When I looked out the window of "my" apartment in Sluzewiec, I could still see patches left over from a heavy fog during the night. There was not much work left to do in the garden: just the fall clean-up. I had my usual meagre (low-calorie) breakfast and left for work.

Everything in the garden was wet and muddy. I decided to leave the work until the sun was out and had dried the place up a bit. After all, I had to think about my clothes and shoes. I couldn't overwork them indefinitely. Who knew then how long the war would last? My entire wardrobe was the clothes I wore day in and day out.

Instead of starting with the removal of the wet vegetable stems and roots, I went to the shed to clean the dry garden tools and storage baskets. I unlocked the door to the shed, but when I tried to open it, I couldn't do it. Something was in the way. I bent down to push away the undergrowth, but it wasn't that that was blocking the door. A bundled-up parcel was there on the ground, all covered with leaves and vegetable stems.

Oh, I thought, a stranger, taking advantage of the night-time fog left something here. I was curious to find out what the parcel contained, but war experience had taught me to act with caution at all times. Maybe someone was watching me. First I moved away from the find, very casually, and looked around to make sure that nobody was there to see what I was doing. The coast was clear. I went over to take a close look at the parcel.

I couldn't believe it! It was a German uniform, all bundled up. And what else was there? Something shining. I looked closer. It was a rifle, sticking out of the leaves that had been heaped over it.

Shocked by my discovery, I went into the shed to "have a conference with myself." What was I to think about all that? Had a soldier been murdered and then stripped to fake a desertion? Was the murdered soldier buried nearby? I left the shed and looked as far as I could for freshly dug-up earth. I found nothing. Ah, I'm probably complicating the matter too much, I told myself. All that's happened is that a German soldier has defected from his unit and changed to civilian clothing. With that conclusion in mind, I took the parcel inside the shed. If I didn't find any bloodstains, I decided, I could assume it was really a case of defection. I checked the jacket, trousers, cap and shoes. Everything was clean.

Now an idea came to my mind: the uniform would undergo a transformation. It would be reincarnated by Jan Witold Mankowski, whose *Kennkarte* claimed him to be a professional tailor, into a made-to-measure suit. Yes, that was what I would do. I repacked the bundle, put it in a basket and covered it with old rags, ready to be carried to the apartment for its transformation.

The shoes? No, I couldn't use German military shoes. It didn't say in my *Kennkarte* that I was a shoemaker (I tried to have fun now) so I couldn't give the shoes a civilian look. I decided to bury them. I took a sharp spade and dug a hole in the shed, packed the German shoes in a jute bag and into the hole they went, all covered with earth. Maybe I'd find a use for them later; after all, things might change, they said the picnic of the German military machine was over.

What was I to do with the rifle? I couldn't leave it uncovered, outside in the wet. I would tell the major about it. I took it into the shed. It was a Mauser, but shorter than the one I had used for practice in the paramilitary camp after my high-school years. Inside the shed I checked whether it was loaded. No, it was not. But wait, maybe my Hans, or whatever his name was, left some ammunition too. I checked the ground outside and, lo and behold, there was a small container of bullets. I wrapped the rifle and the small pack of ammunition in two jute bags, put everything against a wall of the shed and put lots of gardening junk on top. Major Tarwid could make good use of my find.

When Major Tarwid came out to Sluzewiec, I told him about my find and my plan to transform the uniform for my personal use.

"I'll ask Mrs. Tarwid to get some brown dye. That's the best colour for that green uniform material. I'll be back tomorrow to collect the rifle. It will go straight to the arsenal of the underground fighters. It may eventually shoot a few Nazis — that will be to your credit, Panie Jasiu."

"I wish I could see it in action against these bastards."

"It might happen one day soon," the major said.

Mrs. Tarwid brought a few pouches of brown dye and advised me to open all the seams of the uniform and then, using a big pot, boil the whole thing in the dye solution. "The word for the job is precision," Mrs. Tarwid said. The cloth looked good after boiling in three consecutive solutions. No blotches.

Next I had to change the design from a military cut to a civilian one. Would I — the *Kennkarte* tailor — succeed? Except for occasionally sewing a button on a shirt, I had never handled a needle and thread. But I was badly in need of a "new" suit now, so I had no choice but to test my skills.

The most important component of the suit, the jacket, fitted me quite well. I started my work with the trousers. Everything I did was hand-crafted, the most artistic kind of tailoring. I used the hand-cranked sewing machine Mrs. Tarwid kept in her apartment only when I had to make a straight seam. I broke quite a few needles, since that military material was too thick for the regular household machine. Using pins extensively, I put pleats in the trousers, widened the legs as far as the material permitted, put on cuffs of the fashionable width, ironed the finished product to sharp creases and *presto!* a pair of trousers by the famous designer Jan Mankowski.

I put them on and stood in the front of the mirror. Everything was good and looked right, but I had forgotten about the buttons in the fly department. No big problem, except that I couldn't use the German military metal buttons. I found the right colour buttons (zippers weren't commonly used then) among the old rags in the house, and I checked my looks in the mirror again. From the waist down I looked like a new person, almost elegant.

While working away on the trousers, I thought a lot about that soldier — Hans, I called him. To defect in such circumstances — when the law could so easily reach and prosecute him — it took courage to do that. Maybe Hans had found out that he was about to be transferred to the *Ostfront*, which meant never returning home alive. With the best of luck he might return half-frozen or wounded or both. Then, I thought, maybe Hans found a Polish girlfriend to provide him with food, shelter and clothing until the whole thing blew over.

While I was patiently pushing the needle and thread through that hard military material, still another thought came to me: maybe Hans had a trace of Jewish blood in his veins. The press, controlled by Goebbels (minister for propaganda) had reported many cases of "impure" Germans penetrating the army and party. Had the "impure" Hans run away for that reason?

Hans, if I could only have met you and talked to you! We had many things in common, don't you think? You hated them; so did I. You were chased by them; so was I. You did nothing wrong; neither did I. I was thinking a lot about Hans.

Transforming the jacket required lots of work. The sewn-on pockets had to be replaced with lined ones inside. The front buttons had to be removed and only two buttonholes made. Ah, the lapels! that was something else. I made some dummy samples, transferred the paper outlines to the material and then, when I was satisfied with the looks, I switched to pinning and sewing.

I don't know why, but all the time I was working on the jacket I had the impression that my friend Hans was right beside and watching me so I wouldn't make a mistake in the transformation of his garment. A silent dialogue went on between us.

"Hans, are you angry with me for ruining your uniform?"

"Angry? Not at all. On the contrary, I'll be happy when you feel warm wearing that suit."

"Hans, why did you run away? Isn't that treason?"

"Oh, no. No treason at all. They, the Nazis, are the ones who commit treason every day of their lives."

"Tell me the truth, did you ever kill a Jew?"

"Honestly, no. I was in a firing squad once, but I lifted my rifle above the heads of the lined up Jews. Fully conscious what I was doing, I missed."

"You are really telling the truth?"

"Yes, and I have peace of mind."

"Hans, will we survive Hitler and his war?"

"Some of us will. We can't give up trying to be among the survivors."

That silent, imaginary talk with Hans made me feel positive about the future. For now, anyway. The jacket turned out very well. The Tarwids and my wife gave me a lot of compliments on my good work. I wore the suit right up to the time of my liberation, in January 1945. The rifle most probably found its way to the hands of a fighter during the Polish uprising against the Germans in August of 1944.

"Hans, you must have been a decent person. Good things come only from decent people."

Late fall, 1943. The gardening work was all done. I stayed on in the Tarwids' apartment in Sluzewiec. I was lucky to have a place to stay, but on the other hand I was desperate, being completely alone all week and sometimes longer. The Tarwids didn't come out on weekends any more. Like other Jews and Poles who were free to move around, Krystina was constantly doing courier work, carrying messages and money to people in hiding. Now and then she had to skip a Sunday and could not come to see me. It was just devastating not to have anybody to talk to for a whole week or two. And when Krystina did come, she was too tired from her work to be interested in talking. All she wanted was to rest and sleep.

These occasional meetings between us were sometimes loaded with bitterness. "Krystina, would you prefer not to come and see me any more?"

Silence. "Listen, Jasiu, I know that I'm wrong, but I can't help it. I'm completely indifferent to everything around me. Leave me alone and don't make me talk. No amount of your explanations can help me."

I left her and went into the kitchen, where I sat down at the table. I was depressed and worried. Krystina was breaking down. Was there anything I could or should do to help? And how could I help when she refused to listen to me?

I was waiting for Krystina to come to the kitchen and speak to me. It seemed a long time before she came, her face all covered with tears. "I'm sorry for the way I acted. Did you really think that I don't want to see you? Please, understand me. The tension of the last two weeks just got to me. My work — and then Gienia!"

She was too upset to continue. I didn't know whether to ask questions or just wait for her to resume.

Krystina rushed on. "My work at the Zgierskis' place is getting harder all the time. The little boy is sick and that made things even worse. I had to stay overnight with him several times. He requires constant attention — I've had no sleep and I'm exhausted."

Then she told me what had happened to her sister. Gienia and her boy Witek were staying in Milanowek, a prewar resort place, near Warsaw. They lived in a rented apartment by themselves, while her husband Sewek hid in Warsaw. Early one morning, when Witek was playing somewhere outside, Gienia noticed two Gestapo officers getting out of their car in front of the house. Realizing that she had been denounced and that they were coming to get her, she quickly unlocked her entrance door and ran to the corner of the room where a Christian icon hung on the wall. She knelt, pretending to pray.

The Gestapo knocked at the door. Gienia did not answer. They knocked again, and still she did not move to let them in. The Germans walked inside, and seeing a woman at her prayers, didn't interrupt. Pretending that she had finished praying, Gienia got up from her knees and acted surprised at seeing the officers. She excused herself for not having heard her visitors before. They understood; she was praying. They asked the religiously devout woman whether she could help them with some information. "I'll certainly try," Gienia told them.

The officers explained that according to information they had received, a Jewish woman with a boy of around seven or eight years of age lived in one of the houses around here. "Have you maybe noticed these two? They would be new here."

"Yes, I saw a new woman here but she has two children, a boy and a girl. That woman looked to me to be Jewish."

"When did you see her last time?"

"Ilm, I would say ten days or two weeks ago. She always acted scared. I haven't seen her the last few days."

The officers thanked her for the information and apologized for interrupting her morning prayers. When the Germans took off in their car, Gienia put on a sweater and a light coat, and ran out of the house. She found Witek and both of them left immediately for Warsaw.

" Brave Gienia. And a miracle too."

"Jasiu, sooner or later we will run out of miracles. Every day a Jew is running out of miracles. The same thing awaits us."

"Krysiu, let's not give up."

"I may be resigned and hopeless, but you are certainly naïve."

We looked at each other as if searching for the courage to change the subject and forget everything that was going on.

The winter of 1943-1944 was approaching fast. Polish underground forces increased their activities against the German authorities, who were spreading terror all over the city. Round-ups and executions were the order of the day.

I was thinking how hard it would be to sit all alone in the apartment in Sluzewiec when, unexpectedly, Mrs. Tarwid came over to the apartment. "Panie Jasiu, I have some bad news. We have to make some changes. We managed to arrange a new setup for you so you mustn't worry."

"Has something happened to Krystina?"

"Not at all. She is safe."

Mrs. Tarwid told me what had happened. Mr. Kregielewski, the electrical engineer who lived with the Tarwids and was very active in the underground, had been arrested. Mr. Tarwid learned that the man had been taken to Szucha Avenue, the headquarters of the Gestapo. Under torture, he might reveal his connection with the Tarwids.

"Mr. Tarwid is preparing for the worst: a search in the house on Sienna Street and possibly a search here too. The Gestapo might even dig up the old suspicion that a Jewess was hiding in our place. All we can do now is wait and see."

I had to leave Sluzewiec. Krystina and Mrs. Tarwid arranged for me to stay with Krystina in the room she had rented from Mrs. Lukaszewicz on Wilcza Street. I packed up my few belongings in three bundles, feeling like the eternal wandering Jew.

"Panie Jasiu, you mustn't carry anything. I'll take one parcel now and bring the others over to you later in the week. I want you to look like somebody going home from work."

I put on my good suit (the former German uniform), my overcoat and cap, and left the house for the streetcar stop. Mrs. Tarwid was following me. It was already dark. When the streetcar arrived, I let Mrs. Tarwid get in first. I adjusted my expression and followed her. We were riding along Marszalkowska Street, the route I knew so well from before. Would I ever travel along that street again as a free man? I shouldn't have been thinking about that then.

Wilcza Street. Mrs. Tarwid and I walked beside each other now. For the sake of talking she was telling me what she would make for supper that night. I tried to keep the conversation going. We reached the place: 42 Wilcza Street, apartment number 1, on the ground floor. Mrs. Lukaszewicz, the landlady, showed us to Krystina's room. Mrs. Tarwid left after a short while.

Krystina came in just before curfew. She closed the inside wooden shutters and switched on the lights. "I brought you something to eat. I had supper at the Zgierskis', so it's all for you." After a while she added: "Think about it, I'll be seeing you every evening now, isn't that great? I'll keep complaining and you'll keep trying to make me feel good...."

Krystina introduced me to Mrs. Lukaszewicz and then to the layout of the new place. The landlady was a woman in her early sixties, widowed since 1930. She looked very neat and tidy. She said that she didn't want me to smoke cigarettes, for my own sake. If the smell of the smoke lingered in the house, someone might come in and wonder who was smoking there. Another few *do's* and *don'ts* and Mrs. Lukaszewicz left us alone. Krystina told me that it wasn't hard at all to persuade Mrs. Lukaszewicz to take me as an additional "tenant." Mrs. Tarwid was very helpful. "I know what I'm getting into, but I want to help," the landlady said.

"I don't know yet what the new rent will be, but I'm sure Mrs. Lukaszewicz will be reasonable. We both have to remember that there's another girl tenant here, Marjanna. She is a real bitch, she is always fighting with her boyfriend, who visits her very often. Under no circumstances should that pair find out about your staying here or who we really are."

Krystina took a pencil and paper and drew a sketch of the layout of the house. Marjanna had a separate entrance from the vestibule, the other door led to the rest of the house. From the centrally located dining room, Krystina explained, one could hear every word of the conversations between Marjanna and her friend.

"If you say something to Mrs. Lukaszewicz loudly, Marjanna might hear you. You have to be careful."

"What if I sneeze accidentally?"

"I have no answer to that kind of question. Just remember what's at stake. What else can I tell you?"

A new phase in my way of living. I was hiding now. When I moved around in my room or had to go the washroom, I did it on tiptoe, as quietly as possible. Every evening Krystina told me the news she had heard that day at the Zgierskis' house. And that winter of 1943-1944 was an eventful one in the streets of Warsaw. The underground of the A.K. (Home Army) was attacking German military units. The Germans responded ruthlessly. Besides the increased number of round-ups and arrests, the Germans imposed a tax on the residents of Warsaw. Tensions kept growing.

From the newspapers Krystina brought home sometimes, I found out that the Russians had stopped their westward offensive. That gave the German administration more courage to be bestial in their treatment of the enslaved people. The situation seemed to have become hopeless again and that was depressing.

One evening, Marjanna had a fight with her boyfriend. I couldn't hear what he was asking her, but she answered, screaming, "If you want all that, you'll have to give me more money."

"More money? That's what you want?"

"Yes, that's what I want! All my girlfriends are getting lots of money from their boys!"

"Here's more money!"

He probably slapped her, because she yelled out, "Ouch, you son of a whore...." I could hear another slap now and noise of flying objects. Marjanna screamed, "Let go, you....All your friends will know about that...."

"I couldn't care less. You want more money? Where am I supposed to get it?"

"Do what your friends are doing, they know some rich Jews in hiding and...."

"What? That's what you want me to do? Become a *schmalzovnik*? Blackmail helpless people?"

Slap. Loud screaming... "Wait, I'll teach you a lesson for all that beating me, you...."

"You want to teach me new ways how to make money? You listen to me, you sh—. I'm a gambler, I'll steal or rob, but never, I say never will I blackmail or expose a Jew to the bastard Germans, like those *schmalzovniks* you're talking about. Get that in your sh—y head."

"Oh, what a gentleman boyfriend I have!"

"Maybe not a gentleman, but for sure not a beast. You want proof? Here...."

Smack. Scream. "That's enough for today," he said.

"Where are you going? Come back, I've got something for you...."

"Keep it!"

A bang of the outside door. Marjanna was now talking to herself. Mrs. Lukaszewicz tiptoed into my room and asked whether I heard what was going on behind the wall, in Marjanna's room. I nodded my head and said, "She is terrible."

"She is a real bitch and I'm afraid of her."

Chapter Seventeen

For the first months of 1944, I sat in the house on Wilcza Street just like a prisoner. The cell was of a good size and with conveniences, but still a cell. I kept wondering, would they find me in this cell or would they just overlook this prisoner? It had happened once before, on the train to Warsaw. Could it happen again?

German roundups were now taking place all over Warsaw. City blocks were being sealed off, men and women were arrested with no questions asked. We had had some hope when the Russians were on the move. There was a standstill on the front now. We couldn't figure out what had happened. Had the Russians run out of steam? Or was it, as some rumours had it, a political power play by the Russians against their Western allies? Whatever the reason for the stalemate on the front, we in Warsaw were its victims. There were public hangings now. The Germans let their victims dangle from the gallows for days, just to prove to the rebellious civilians who was boss in this city. Pictures of the executions were printed in the papers daily. New rumours abounded every day about an imminent uprising of the A.K. against the oppressor. Nothing of the sort happened.

I tried to read a book Krystina had brought. *Gone With The Wind*. Very good reading. I was thinking how differently a war was conducted in those years of the nineteenth century. In America, the North and the South fought each other, but only on the battlefield. Civilians suffered inconveniences when an army crossed their territory — but mass killings of the aged, of women and children? Never. Soldiers even had the freedom to carry on fancy romances. The basic dignity of man was respected. And now, one hundred years later? Mass-killing took place in the name of creating a super race, an idea that found many followers among ordinary criminals and pseudo-scientists who longed to make themselves famous.

When these thoughts entered my mind, all the letters in the book I was reading ran together and formed an illegible mass. I had to close the book. I was tiptoeing across the room thinking, Will this ever change? I wish so much to see with my own eyes the downfall of the beast! Will I? I don't know whether I still believe in anything, but oh, God Almighty, fulfil my prayer, please. If I am to die at a young age, at least let me die one hour after the collapse of the Nazis. This is an old prayer of mine, show how great You are and make it happen!

The only times I ever left the place were to get money from my Polish benefactors or go to the barber once every six weeks. I had to do this in order not to look like as if I came from the woods, with overgrown long hair on my head. My appearance had to be "regular" in case I had to flee the hiding-place in a hurry.

When I was sneaking out of the building I first had to make sure (with the help of Mrs. Lukaszewicz) that the concierge was not in his watch-cubicle checking on who was entering and leaving the building. When I returned, I used different tricks to find out when he was absent from his post. One time I would go inside the large arched entrance and pretend that I had to fix my shoelaces; other times, in winter, I would rearrange my scarf around my neck — all the time keeping an eye on the concierge's window. I manoeuvred always in such a way that he wouldn't see my face, always trying to be ingenious and to look "normal." And I prayed. I couldn't do anything else.

My dear Krystina used to go out to work every morning and return "home" just before the curfew. She told me how, on her way back to me, she would often be overwhelmed by the fear that when she got back I would be gone. "I think to myself that you must have been detected by the Gestapo and taken away. Probably they have beaten you, and the landlady too. Maybe they are still there and waiting for me. But I have no choice but try to build up a little hope and strength and go home. I fight back my tears and walk and walk, afraid at the same time that someone will notice my frustration and become suspicious that I am Jewish, and in his or her zeal of co-operation with the 'good' Germans, denounce me. It happens every day. They talk about it in the streetcars and write about it in the papers. When I get here and find you alive I attribute the miracle to my constant, silent prayers." Many times when Krystina returned home, she embraced me and cried silently. "Benush," she whispered, "if it weren't for my deep love for you I would break down. I'm so exhausted!"

One evening the curfew time was coming closer and closer and Krystina was not back yet. I was getting upset. Fifteen minutes left, ten minutes, five minutes. Then it was seven o'clock: curfew time. I could hear the gates to the building being locked by the concierge. Krystina didn't return home. I didn't know of her having any courier missions that day — usually I knew about them in advance. She was supposed to come straight home from work.

I was sure she had been caught and was now in the final hours of her life. My mind was working in one direction only. They would torture her to find out about more Jews. I was sure that, out of devotion and love, Krystina would never reveal anybody's whereabouts. She would not betray them — not the Krystina I knew. After the tortures they would shoot her.

Oh, God, why?

The hours dragged on. Eight o'clock, nine o'clock. My dear Krystina is being tortured now, I thought. I wish it was already over for both of us. There is no hope for anything good to happen anyway.

Suddenly, sitting in the darkness of the room, I heard a truck stop in front of the building. It had to be a German vehicle, there were no other vehicles but German. Now I could hear the voices of the Germans jumping down from the truck. The noise of their cleated boots was like spikes driven into my head. My mind was working fast now: the Gestapo had found out, from Krystina's documents, where she lives. Now they were coming to check the place out. My end was coming. Krystina dear, I addressed her silently, we will both die the same night.

I moved towards the window and looked out from behind the shutters. I saw the truck full of soldiers. Four of them, with their rifles in a military position, raised their right hands and yelled out "Heil Hitler." Then the truck took off with the rest of the soldiers. The foursome started to walk the street. I realized that these soldiers had nothing to do with me. It was just a routine drop-off of night patrols.

Maybe, I thought now, Krystina had not been caught? Was it possible? But if she had to go somewhere unexpectedly, she would have let me know somehow. She would realize how worried I would be by her not returning home in time. No, something was wrong for sure.

I sat through the whole night at the table in my room. I figured that if I was to be captured, I would rather be dressed and ready. The less time it took the better. Every time I heard German voices outside, either from a passing patrol or from gendarme-motorcyclists, I couldn't help thinking that they were coming to get me.

It was a long night. The curfew lifted at seven in the morning. I heard Polish voices in the street. People were going to work. Their lives were resuming their normal daily routine. But what about Krystina and me? Where was she? Was she still alive? How much of my miserable existence was left to me?

Just a few minutes before eight o'clock, Krystina walked in. I thought I was dreaming. "Krystina," I yelled. We embraced each other. Krystina cried.

"My dear, I couldn't get home last night, I had a terrible ordeal. I know what you must have been thinking. Listen, I have to be at work by nine o'clock; I have to leave now. I'll tell you what happened when I come home tonight. I can only tell you that all of us are very lucky, for now at least."

"All of us?"

"I have to go now." She washed her face with cold water, arranged her hair, covered the lines under her eyes with powder and left. When she came back that evening, and after our quick modest supper together, she unwound slowly and told me what happened the evening before.

"When I left work, I met Gienia and Ludwik. He had picked up some money for Seweryn, and Gienia asked me to deliver it. I asked Ludwik to walk me to Seweryn's hiding-place. I always feel safer when I walk in someone's company. Once we reached the building Ludwik said goodbye, because he lived far away and had to make it back before curfew time.

"I walked into the building and knocked at Seweryn's door. A stranger opened the door. I realized instantly that there was trouble. The stranger took me by my hand, pulled me gently inside and closed the door. Inside the room there was another man who had a pistol in his hand. Seweryn was sitting on the floor in one corner of the room, his hands joined in the back. In another corner was Seweryn's older brother, Henryk, also on the floor and his hands tied behind him too.

"The two strangers looked to be in their late twenties, and were well dressed. The one who opened the door had a very aristocratic look in his face, the other was a rough type. They spoke excellent cultivated Polish. I realized by now that they were not Germans, but two Polish *schmalzovniks*.

"'Who are you?' the 'aristocrat' asked me. He did all the talking, the other one threw in a word now and then.

"Something inside me told me to act tough. There was not much to gain any other way, so why not try something different? 'I'll tell you who I am, but first you have to tell me who the two of you are and what you want here.'

"He pulled his identity card, with the Gestapo insignia on it, out of his pocket. 'We are from the Gestapo and we came here for these two Jews. What's your name? I can tell you aren't Jewish. You are a natural blond and you have blue eyes. Is one of the two Jews a lover of yours? Which one is it, the younger one or the other? They must be rich if a girl like you comes to them, right?'

"'Listen, you better shut up. I can tell you are not Germans but their ass-licking Poles, the worst kind there is. You're a disgrace to the nice language you are speaking.'

"'Don't be too smart. You too will come with us to the Gestapo. You didn't tell me your name yet, smartie.'

"'My first name is Krystina and I'm Jewish. This one is my brother-in-law. The other one is his brother.'

"'So all three of you will come with us. But I don't believe you are Jewish. Your looks, your courage and your language aren't the qualities I see among the Jews every day.'

"'So you are working full time denouncing Jews to the Gestapo? What a profession for a young Polish man!'

"'Enough,' he yelled at me. 'We'll let you go, but these two have to come with us unless....'

"'Unless what?'

"'Unless they can pay us right now 1,000 zlotys apiece.'

"'What?' I screamed now. 'You *schmalzovniks* — you call yourselves Poles? Your way of speaking shows that you have had a good education behind you. What great Polish poet — Mickiewicz, Sienkiewicz or Zeromski — gave you the idea for your profession?'

"'Listen, Krystina. I don't want to know what you do for a living and it's not your business to teach us what to do. Is that clear to you? Now, curfew hour is approaching, and for your own good, you'd better get out of here.'

"'Oh, no. I won't go until I've told you exactly what I think of you. And don't interrupt while I'm talking. You should be ashamed to call yourselves Polish. I'm sure neither of you even served in the Polish army. Two brothers of mine served in the army when the war broke out, they were fighting the invading Germans. I don't even know where they are now. But the two of you, two Poles with an upbringing in Polish schools, are co-operating with the Germans who are and have been our oppressors for hundreds of years. That's the history of our Poland; I know from school and I'm sure you learned about it too.'

"'Stop,' yelled the one with the revolver in his hand.

"'No, I will not stop. You want to take us to the Gestapo? Remember, they will kill us but my words will follow you around as long you live. And who knows, maybe the Germans will kill you too. After all, you belong to the lower Slavic race.'"

Krystina stopped talking. She was shaking all over, as if she were reliving last night's events.

"Can you continue?" I asked gently.

After a deep sigh, Krystina continued. "After a short pause I said to them, 'All right, you want 2,000 zlotys from them, but I know that they don't have any money on them, you can search them if you want to. I brought 1,000 zlotys with me and here it is.'

"The 'aristocrat' went over to his comrade and they talked to each other for a while. I couldn't hear a word of their conversation. Then he came over to me and said: 'We are doing this for you, not for them,' he pointed to Seweryn and Henryk. 'We want to prove to you that we are human. We don't even want to take your money. We are leaving right now.'

"'No,' I said, 'you won't leave before you give me your word of honour, I mean your true Polish word of honour, that you will not do any harm to us.'

"'We are giving you our word of honour that we won't harm you or those two. But you have to promise me that you will leave this place the first thing in the morning. The two brothers have to get out of this location before noon tomorrow, that is if they still want to live.'

"'I will go for sure, but they have no place to go.'

"'Look, it's up to them. I want you to know that there are more like us in this game. It's a routine to exchange names of Jews and their hiding-places, so each of us gets the opportunity to blackmail the rich Jews. When there's no more money to be extorted, well, you know what happens.'

"The two guys shook my hand to confirm their promise. The 'aristocrat,' on his way to the exit, turned to me and said: 'Krystina, I hope the war will be over soon. When the Germans are defeated I'd like to have the opportunity to meet you again. Goodbye.'

"Yes, my dear, that's the story of last night's events. I talked to Gienia already. Seweryn and Henryk are in a new hiding-place."

Later that evening, I asked my wife, "Krysiu, dear, where did you get the courage to act as you did? I mean the way you talked to these *schmalzovniks*?"

"I have no answer to that question. I can only say it happened. How? I don't know. What I said to them and what came out of it defies any explanation."

Krystina and I looked at each other. I was thinking, Can miracles really happen? How many will it take us to survive this hell?

I opened the wooden shutters one morning and there they were. Two armoured cars, two paddy wagons and German police armed with machine guns blocking the arch entrance of the building right across from the building I was in. Within minutes a group of men and women appeared in the archway and were pushed into the waiting paddy wagons. Shouts in German, a short salvo of machine-gun fire in the air and all the vehicles disappeared.

When my landlady ventured to go outside our concierge told her that the Germans arrived across the road at about five in the morning and searched all the apartments in the building. They arrested eighteen men and women. The afternoon of the same day, Mrs. Lukaszewicz told me that she couldn't stop thinking about what had happened that morning across the road. If it had happened in our building, she would have been arrested for having me in her house. "I am very upset and I want you to look for another place to stay. I can't live under such a strain. Your wife can stay here."

It took two days of Gienia's outstanding efforts and a new place was found for me to stay. It was in the suburb of Praga, at a shoemaker's house. Gienia's husband, Sewek, and his brother Henryk had been staying there since the incident with the *schmalzovniks*. The tiny house was located on a small street. The shoemaker, Mr. Muszynski, and his redheaded wife were a good team. Both of them talked a lot. While he was a sort of homegrown philosopher who expressed his political views very authoritatively and in colourful, often vulgar language, his wife, Pani Stacha liked to tell us what a good cook she was and how good or bad her neighbours were.

Physically, Mr. Muszynski reminded me of Charlie Chaplin. Short, with a tiny moustache, black short-cut hair combed with a part. His black shiny eyes always seemed about to tell or ask you something. Making comments on the politics of the times, he used his arms and fingers to give more body to his explanations. He never stood still as he talked. He enjoyed his audience of three grownup men who very seldom disagreed with him openly. Why shatter the man's heartfelt beliefs?

Mr. Muszynski's workshop had all the equipment a shoemaker used in those times. There were piles of old shoes lying around, apparently waiting to be repaired, but in reality they were stage-dressing, meant to give the occasional customer the impression that the shoemaker was loaded with work that was his only way of earning an income. Although he always had his working apron on, he never actually worked much. The three "tenants" were paying him very well for their room and board. He was worth every cent of it: the Muszynskis were providing not only shelter and food, the two most precious commodities a hunted Jew could dream of then, but they also tried to make us feel good. They knew that by sheltering us they were risking their lives, but they believed in their good fortune. Mr. Muszynski prided himself on being a lifelong member of the Polish Socialist Party and, as he said "we have to f—k the *Schwabs* (Germans) wherever we can. Helping the Jews is another way of fighting these f—ing fascists."

We had been living like that for some weeks when the shoemaker brought the news that the Russians had started a new offensive and that they were pushing the "f—ing" Germans back all over the place. "The Germans are kaput," he boasted, "and our boys are getting ready to give the *Schwabs* a piece of our mind. Our government in London is sending us military supplies via air-drops."

June 6th, 1944. Mr. Muszynski, holding a newspaper in his hand, told us that the Allies had landed in Normandy. "Now the *Schwabs* are being f—ed front and back" (here the shoemaker used both his arms and body to illustrate the military action on both fronts), "that was what I was waiting for."

At night we could hear Russian planes bombarding German positions. Every day the news talked of the Germans retreating, and we, the miracle-hungry individuals clinging to life, were inclined to think that our oppressor was about to collapse. But nothing drastic was happening and the Gestapo were still boss in Warsaw. My situation was getting harder to take; I had no more money to pay my way. Krystina decided to talk to Mrs. Lukaszewicz and the good old lady agreed to take me back to her apartment on Wilcza Street. The rent there was relatively low. An added bonus to my renewed staying on Wilcza was the fact that Marjanna, the bitchy other tenant at Mrs. Lukaszewicz's, had moved out.

It was the beginning of July 1944. Warsaw was teeming with all kinds of activities by the Germans and the Polish underground as well. The German newspapers carried proclamations every day. The illegal papers reported successful attacks against the authorities and called on the Polish population to get ready for the big moment, the day of the *Powstanie* (Uprising) against the occupiers. Every night now we heard the noise of the Russian planes and saw the beams of the German searchlights.

One day, Krystina and I were in the house when Ludwik came over and suggested that the three of us go out to the main streets of the city, where something out of the ordinary was taking place. "Jan, nothing to be afraid of any more," Ludwik added.

When we reached Marszalkowska Street, we couldn't believe our eyes. The sidewalks on both sides of the street were packed with Polish onlookers. What a scene it was right in front of us! The German army was retreating from the east to the west. Hundreds of trucks loaded with once seemingly invincible soldiers were moving westward. These trucks could only move slowly, because the street was full of German soldiers on foot and German civilians dragging little carriages with their belongings. The blondies had scarves on their heads to keep their once proudly waving hair in place. Mothers, pure Aryan mothers, were pulling pure Aryan offspring. The screaming of the women brought to mind different memories, the memories of our Jewish families driven so mercilessly to the gas chambers by these very Germans. And why did they do it to us? I had to cover my face because I felt tears coming from my eyes. If only more of us could see what was so justly happening to that master race now!

Dear God, You were answering my prayers. I was witnessing their downfall with my own eyes. Thank You, Almighty. But it was not enough. I wanted more revenge for the shameful death of our parents, brothers, sisters and innocent babies. Silently I prayed, dear Almighty, more revenge, please!

My satisfaction with what I was seeing kept growing. German women tried to climb on the trucks loaded with soldiers, but they were thrown brutally down by their German brethren. The women and children cried and cursed the soldiers. There was complete chaos and disarray. And the looks of the soldiers? They were dirty, sweating; they wore expressions of resignation and fear at the same time. There were no officers in sight. Had they pulled off their military insignia, for fear of being mobbed by their own people?

The Polish onlookers were laughing and mocking them. "Hey, Karl and Hans, if you ever see Adolf, don't forget to give him regards from the Polish people!" A woman laughed about that message and added, "Yes, tell him to come to my house for a painting job!"

Krystina came up with a suggestion, "Listen, I have eighteen zlotys on me. Let's buy some bread and kielbasa and celebrate this great moment."

We applauded the idea and went to the store. We couldn't get much for eighteen zlotys, but with our purchase packed in a newspaper, we went to Wilcza Street. The sandy, scratchy bread we knew well, but that kielbasa, wow, that was really a treat.

We divided a ten-inch-long piece in three equal parts and started to eat. In the absence of champagne, we toasted each other with glasses of boiled water.

We went back to the streets in the afternoon. There were no more masses of people. Light artillery weapons and armoured vehicles rolled by. Eyewitnesses from other parts of the city were claiming that they had seen Gestapo units leaving Warsaw, and that we should expect it to become a no-man's-land. There was talk about the Polish underground forming an administration. Rumours and more rumours.

In the evening of the same day I had another surprise, a surprise of a very different kind. Krystina told me that she thought she was pregnant. She looked at me searchingly, waiting for my reaction. I was surprised and didn't know what to say. I kissed her affectionately. Without giving me a chance to speak, she went on, "Don't ask me to try an abortion. I won't do it. Whatever happens will happen to me and my baby. It's about three weeks since I started to feel different. I held back from telling you about it."

"It will be a lucky baby and it will bring us freedom," I said.

"It could also be a false alarm. The constant tension might be the reason for that."

I gently stroked Krystina's hair.

The following day, the German police patrols were all over the city again, just as if what we had seen a day before was only a mistake of ours, a mirage, something unreal. So, it wasn't yet the end of our misery. I still hadn't seen the end of that damned Third Reich. The thought that Krystina might be pregnant made the return of the old reality harder to take. Krystina confided her unusual physical condition to Mrs. Zaluski Jr., whose doctor confirmed the pregnancy.

Each day seemed so long and hopeless again. And boom! July 20, 1944. Great news. Hitler *assassinated*! Mrs. Lukaszewicz brought the news to me. I kissed her. I believed the news, but then doubts surfaced. Maybe it was just a rumour? Was that possible? Could it be true? If it were true, it would mean a complete turn-around in the situation. I asked my landlady to try to get some more information about what had happened. She brought an "extra," a newspaper flyer. What a disappointment! There had been an attempt on Hitler's life, but he got away with light scratches. He had just made a statement on the radio about the incident, the "extra" informed us, to the effect that the guilty had been caught and would be dealt with properly.

When Krystina returned home that day, she told me that she heard people at the Zgierskis' saying that the Germans would now increase their repression of the Polish people, just to keep them frightened. And then she confided, "Jasiu, I'm worried. It's a few days since I last heard from Gienia. None of the Polish friends I contacted have heard from her either. What will we do if something bad has happened to her?" Unfortunately, Krystina's fears proved to be well-founded. Gienia disappeared without a trace. We have never been able to find out what happened to her.

The Russian troops were in Praga, that is, on the eastern side of the Wisla River. Despite all the military action around Warsaw, the Germans managed to keep up the appearance of being in control of the situation. Although I was certain that liberation was around the corner, I was very much afraid that the Germans might move that corner away from me. Nothing I could do but keep hoping for more miracles, and that we would not be trapped at the last moment.

Apparently the Germans were expecting a Russian attack. They issued a proclamation calling for 100,000 Poles to show up for trench-digging. "We have to fight our common enemy," the Germans said in their proclamation. Nobody trusted the hated enemy and no Poles, except for a small number of aged people, showed up in response to that call. The military trucks were left empty at the designated gathering place. The consensus was that the Germans were planning to round up all the young men and send them to Germany because they were afraid of the upcoming rebellion, which everybody was talking about. The Germans were right.

Chapter Eighteen

The long-expected Uprising finally took place. Looking out my window I saw people rushing in all directions. Within minutes the street was deserted. I could hear only sporadic rifle-fire. Nothing of great magnitude was visible. I was hoping that Krystina would still be able to get home. If something great and dramatic was about to happen, I thought, it would be better for us to be together, especially since we knew for sure now that she was pregnant. I thought, too, that the uprising would get immediate support from the Russians who were only a few kilometres away. If that were to happen, the end of German rule would be very near, and our baby would be born free. But events proved once again that history has its own twists, which make or break the lives of individuals.

Krystina did not come home. I asked myself whether she was trapped somewhere. Was she safe? She would surely do everything possible to join me. Waiting for her was agonizing. But day after day passed and she did not return. I could only hope that she had found a safe place to stay in all that chaos.

Wilcza Street was ominously quiet the first afternoon of the uprising. There wasn't much activity the next day either. I could only assume that something was going on somewhere since no German patrols were visible any more, and no German military trucks or motorcycles either. Should I go out of the house and see for myself what was going on? Should I join the partisan forces?

Mrs. Lukaszewicz, my landlady, found out from people in the courtyard that fierce fighting was going on in certain parts of the city, especially in Zoliborz and the Old City. The closest fighting to us was in the vicinity of Marszalkowska and St. Krzyska Streets. "Panie Jasiu," Mrs. Lukaszewicz said, "You should wait a day or two and then join. Nothing seems to be very well organized yet. All the concierges are keeping the gates closed. If you make one open move, our concierge will start asking who you are and what you are doing in this building. I think you should wait."

It made sense. At night we heard the noise of aircraft and heavy shelling. I presumed that German anti-aircraft guns were shooting at Russian bombers. The fourth day of the uprising came and there was still no military action in our block. Then, that same day, all residents were told that a block committee had been formed and that its first task was to go from apartment to apartment and register all men and women. I told my landlady that I would register. I would tell them that I had come to the house to meet my fiancée, and because of what was going on I had not been able to get back to my place. In case she was asked, I wanted the landlady to confirm that she knew me and that what I was saying was true.

Day five. Three men walked into my room, two of them with rifles over their shoulders. The third man, short and very bald, aged around forty or forty-five, turned to me. "Do you live here?"

I said no, and told him my story about visiting my girlfriend here.

"When did you come here?"

"About noon on the day the uprising started."

One of the other men blurted out, "*Golembiarz*." A *golembiarz* was a person who ran from roof to roof giving signs to the Germans about the movements of the uprising. I did not react.

"Where is your girlfriend?"

"She is working in Mokotow (a suburb) and she never made it back home. Could you possibly tell me whether Mokotow is cut off from us or is there a way to get there?"

"Do you really need that information?" He looked surprised by my question.

"Yes. I would like to reach my girlfriend."

"We'll see about that later. Would you give me your identity card, please."

I handed him my document. He looked at it and asked   here Kaliska Street was, the street shown on my *Kennkarte*. I told him where it was. "Any other documents?"

"No."

"No *Arbeitsbescheinigung* (certificate from work)?"

"I have more documents, but they are in my house on Kaliska Street. I forgot to bring them with me." I lied, not showing a trace of intimidation under their questioning. I would have told them the truth if I could, but how could I trust them?

"How can you forget your documents? If the Germans stopped you and you didn't have your documents with you, they would arrest you, or send you off to Germany immediately."

"*Golembiarz*," said the other man again.

"Listen, Mr. Mankowski," said my interrogator, "you are a suspicious individual: you have no documents; you didn't report to any of our units offering your help against the enemy. I have my ideas about you. In the name of the power vested in me by our Home Army I arrest you." I protested vigorously, declaring that I was as good a Pole as anybody else. "You'll be taken to a military unit and they'll decide what to do with you."

"Follow me," said one armed man, "and no tricks. I'll shoot if you try anything." I protested again but to no avail. I was now between the two armed men. The interrogator took away my *Kennkarte* and he was the last one to follow us. All the people present in the courtyard of the building I was taken from were watching us with great curiosity. I heard remarks like "They caught a *Golembiarz*, I wish they'd let me get my hands on him," or "Ha, don't worry, he won't be working for the *Schwabs* any more."

I didn't know where they were taking me. I was walking between the two armed men pondering whether I should end the game by divulging that I was Jewish and not a *Golembiarz*. Out of fear that I might be in the hands of the ultra-nationalists, I decided to put off telling the truth. Yes, I would tell the truth, but only when they put me against the wall for belonging to the fifth column. Only then would I play my last card. And if that didn't help, then...then nothing, finished. Somehow I didn't believe that would happen to me.

When I was first led down to a basement, it flashed through my mind that something bad was imminent, but then I heard, "Bend down, some passages are very low." I was being led somewhere through underground passages. It seemed that the whole neighbourhood was connected by corridors made by knocking out basement walls. The man in front of me had a lit candle in one of his hands now. We emerged in a courtyard that was, as I found out later, at 13 Poznanska Street, the site of the district's police station from before the war. The sight in that courtyard was just incomprehensible, a sight straight out of prewar Poland.

There was a long wooden table, covered with a fabric in the two national colours, white and red. Sitting at the table were a number of Polish officers of all ranks. Their uniforms were padded to give the wearers a well-built look. The medals on their chests shone in the mid-morning sun. Their four-cornered hats, tipped slightly to one side, looked as if they were fresh from the manufacturer. A general sat at the head of the table. When I looked at this elegant ensemble, I figured that nothing bad could happen to me. I should be able to talk myself out of my problems.

One of the officers nodded to my bald interrogator to step forward and present his case. I was presented as a suspected spy since I didn't have clear enough identity papers, I hadn't taken part in the uprising, and had been found in a place where I was not registered as a tenant.

The officer, with the rank of a major, stepped before me and, looking in my *Kennkarte*, asked, "Your name?"

"Jan Mankowski."

"Why do you have no other documents?"

I repeated the story I had told my first interrogator. I don't know why but I felt very comfortable giving my answers. I felt the self-assurance in my voice. The truth I would tell only when I had to.

The major said, "We are in the fifth day of the uprising and you didn't come forward to help. Who are you? What kind of Pole are you?"

"I am as good a Pole as anybody else. Let me explain...."

"I have no time for explanations. Can you give me names of people who know you?"

"Yes." I gave the names and addresses of the Tarwids, the Zaluskis and Dr. Sobieranski.

"We cannot reach these people now," the officer said. The major looked at me for a few seconds and then he looked at my *Kennkarte* again. Could he be suspecting me of being...? No, I was sure he would not conclude that from my way of talking or from my behaviour. My talk showed guts and fearlessness. "Listen, Mankowski," the major broke into my thoughts. "I don't know whether you are telling me the whole truth about yourself. In times of war we usually solve these *zagadki* (puzzles) with a bullet. But there's innocence in your eyes, and I don't want to have on my conscience the life of an innocent man."

The major turned to the bald man who brought me here. "*Obywatelu* (citizen), take Mankowski back and assign him to work on the barricades. Keep an eye on him."

The residents on Wilcza Street were surprised at my return. One of them said now, "By his looks I knew he wasn't a *Golembiarz.*"

Acting on the order of the major, I was assigned by the block committee to the barricade-building squad. With bare hands we tore apart the pavements and sidewalks, using the cement blocks to erect barricades across the roads to prevent German tanks from coming into the region. We also used, for that purpose, the bricks from the basement walls. It was amazing how everybody did his or her best at the work. We had a common goal: to get rid of the Germans and free Warsaw. The shooting, which often seemed very close, didn't interrupt our work.

At this point we didn't know exactly how far away the German positions were, but it did not matter to us. Enthusiasm for our goal kept us going. There was no reliable communication between the working and fighting units and we had to rely on rumours for news about events. Some of the news was very exciting. We heard about successful fights in different parts of the city, about the capturing of key buildings not far from us. All that gave us courage. I was happy now because, finally, I was feeling like a free man — moving from place to place, talking to people — with a purpose: the work I was doing. Soon, soon I would be completely free, find my Krystina and together we would rebuild our lives from the ashes.

That excitement of mine was hampered by a lack of food. I was going around hungry, literally starving. Mrs. Lukaszewicz shared with me whatever she could afford, but that was not much. The block committee tried to help out with bread and drinks but, because of the shortages, the quantities were very limited. I was told that a few houses away another committee had set up a public kitchen and was dispensing soup to the needy. I got a little pot from my landlady and went to the address I had been given. And yes, they really were giving out soup! I took up maybe the one-hundredth position in the line of waiting people. I felt pain in my stomach from hunger and the people were moving so slowly! I had no choice but to wait.

I noticed an elegantly dressed woman walking along the line-up. She stopped and looked at me for a while, and then said: "Please, come with me."

"Why? I don't want to lose my place."

"It does not matter, please come."

At first I was suspicious, but then I thought that goodness was written all over her face and that there was nothing to be afraid of. I followed her to an apartment on the second floor. We entered a big dining room. The furniture matched well, the cabinets with the dinnerware and glassware looked elegant. The look of this place and the reality I had known for the last few years were an unreal contrast.

"*Niech pan usiadzie* (Please sit down). I'll be back in a few minutes," the mysterious lady said, and disappeared.

Intrigued and shy at the same time, I sat down at the big table, putting the small pot on the floor right beside me. The lady walked in with a tray in her hands. What was going on? Was I dreaming? She placed real cutlery before me, then bread and a plate of soup.

"Please, eat, I'll be back soon." She left the room again.

I was too hungry to meditate any more. I ate. It was a thick cabbage soup with chunks of meat in it (real beef, where did she get it?). I realized that I was eating fast. I slowed down. The slices of bread I put in my pockets for later. When the lady returned to the room, she brought a dessert-plate full of apple sauce. She sat down opposite me.

"How do you feel now?"

"Full and happy, thank you."

"That's good. Come back tomorrow, between one and one-thirty p.m. I'll keep this door unlocked so you can walk right in. I'll be waiting for you. I have to go now."

I thanked her and said goodbye. The next day I was there at the stated time. The lady was waiting and again she served me a good meal. My curiosity took over and when I finished eating, I asked "*Prosze Pani* (please, lady), why are you are treating me so royally? You saw me for the first time only yesterday."

"Hm. I'll tell you. I looked at you when you were standing in line. I can't explain it, but I had the impression that you were not only hungry but that you had other problems as well. I just wanted to make you feel better, so I took you out of the waiting line."

She recognized that I was Jewish. Maybe she was Jewish too.

"You are a very kind person," I managed to say.

"Come back tomorrow at the same time."

I did not go back to the public kitchen the next day. While working on the barricades, I met a professor from my university days, who told me to join the A.K. (Home Army). He wrote me a letter of reference, then warned me, "Don't tell anybody that you are Jewish. Unfortunately a big part of our movement is very anti-Semitic. I hope you end up in a unit with a decent commanding officer. Even then be careful. Officers go and come. Good luck."

I went immediately to the given address. A uniformed soldier looked at my note and gave it to an officer.

"Are you familiar with the use of a rifle?"

"Yes, I was in cadets at school and at military camp."

"Good. Right now we don't have enough rifles. We expect to get some from air drops and captured German depots. You'll get one then. For now I'll assign you to a transportation group. The officer will explain the operation that you will be taking part in."

A new note and a new address. The officer I was referred to was a young man of twenty-eight to thirty, with a very amiable expression on his face. He explained to me that the task of the unit I was joining was to supply the fighting army with all kinds of military needs. Every night we'd be going out to different parts of the city, sneaking into German military warehouses and stealing whatever was useful to our cause. The boys would introduce me to the job in a practical way. Our base was at 13 Poznanska Street, the same place where, a few days ago, the good-hearted major had second thoughts about solving with a bullet the problem of my possibly being a *Golembiarz*.

I was happy now to become a part of the action. Our group consisted of more than thirty boys. Every evening the group, divided in two parts, went off in different directions. We walked through interconnected basements and crawled through city sewers. Many times we had to take a risk and run out on open streets.

To get the most from us, the army introduced an incentive system. The first twenty kilograms of food hauled in belonged to the army; anything over that belonged to the soldier who brought it in. It was hard to pull these loads, most of the time crawling through the sewers and basement-corridors, but every young man wanted extras for himself, so he pulled the loot and sweated. When we returned to our base, we looked like chimney-sweeps, dirty from the mud and dust of the underground trails.

The food we brought in was of many different kinds: beans, rice, canned foods, pressed chicory, liquids of all kinds, anything and everything that could be used by an undernourished army of *powstancy* (uprisers). My first surplus (more than twenty kilos) was sugar and potatoes. I took it over to the lady from the public kitchen, the lady who had fed me so generously when I was hungry. When I told her how I got hold of that precious stuff, she kissed me and said, "My instinct was right again. You are a good person. *Bog zaplac* (God bless you)."

I did my utmost to get as much as possible over the twenty-kilo mark. It certainly felt good to be able to return to the building and not care whether the concierge was sitting, or not sitting, in his cubicle. There were so many strangers around in those days that nobody paid any special attention to me. Mrs. Lukaszewicz was delighted. When I brought home a bag of wheat grain, she ground it in a little coffee mill and baked bread. True, the bread was full of chaff, but with tea it was a meal.

After a few nights of work in the transport unit, I accumulated more food than Mrs. Lukaszewicz and I could possibly use. I decided to distribute it among the residents of the building I was living in. That project was a success. Every morning now when I returned home, people from the building formed a line and I gave them whatever I had brought as surplus. I usually took a helper and instructed him to give preference to the aged and to children. It was painful to watch when there was not enough to give out to everybody, but there were no complaints. The people left out one morning were compensated next time. I felt good about my work.

One day a man came over to me with a proposition. He was lightly grey-haired, around fifty years old, and had a respectable-looking face. "I live in this building. I have a wife and two grownup daughters. I'm always short of food. If you'll sell me some extra food, I'll pay for it with Russian rubles, I mean Russian gold coins. When the war is over these gold rubles will be of high value. I'll be thankful to you now and after the war is over you'll be thankful to me."

I didn't know what to say. Should I take up this offer or not? The man was ready to strike a deal, he was jingling a few coins in his hand. Then, as if someone else was talking through me, I said, "Panie..."

"Lipowicz is my name."

"Panie Lipowicz, I can't do it. Maybe I'll be sorry, but I can't do it."

" I understand. You know, one thinks of one's family, so I tried, but I understand."

"Boys, I need eight volunteers tonight for a special job," our officer would say to us in the morning when we returned from our nightly expedition. I always raised my hand to volunteer. I didn't consider my willingness to be heroism on my part. I just wanted to be useful. I didn't care about the risks involved because I was all alone, had nobody to care for me and nobody to care for. Being a remnant from a big clan and doubting many times that Krystina and I would ever see each other again, why should I not do something that might help eliminate at least one of the beasts who caused my miseries? Whenever our officer called for volunteers, I raised my hand.

What kind of assignments did the volunteers get? Very important, very risky ones. We were given addresses of places where the Germans had mechanical shops. Via basements and sewers we had to get there and steal bottles of oxygen and acetylene. We needed these gases for welding and for manufacturing hand grenades. Usually, two of us harnessed together dragged one such bottle through mud at a hush-hush noise level. When we came back to our base we were hardly recognizable but very proud of our achievement. When we couldn't find the item we set out for, we took whatever was available, a box of tools, a set of drills, files and similarly useful things. The slogan was never to return empty-handed.

After one of the night raids I came home, unloaded my extra supplies, told Mrs. Lukaszewicz what a good haul we had that night and went to bed for a nap. I woke up about an hour later. I felt horribly ill. I was soaking wet with sweat, the bed felt like a puddle. Drops were rolling down my face. I managed to call in the landlady and told her what was happening to me. My good old lady brought in a few towels and started to dry me out. Then she started to laugh. Looking at her made me angry. Why was she laughing when I felt so terrible? It looked to me as if she wanted to say something but, laughing so much, she couldn't get the words out.

Finally, she blurted, "It's the syrup that has made you ill, Panie Janie."

The night before, our officer told us to take big jute bags for the upcoming trip. We would be going to the warehouses of a brewery where there were stockpiles of grain, sugar and other foodstuffs. "Take big bags with you and spare no effort because we need food for our boys and the general population as well," the officer said.

Inside the brewery we found lots of different food supplies. Loading my bags, I noticed huge wooden barrels resting on special stands. I tapped one of the barrels. The deaf-like sound of the knock indicated that it was full. I looked for a tap in the barrel but there was none. A cork, maybe? Yes, there was one, but it was right at the top, below the rim. There was no way I could turn the heavy barrel. I found a steel bar and after a few strong knocks I managed to spring a hole in the barrel. A thick liquid started to come out. I tasted it. Great, it was raspberry syrup, the same delicious kind we used in our house for mixing with carbonated water on hot summer days. I put my mouth against the stream of that heavenly liquid and drank as much as I could. I called the others and showed them the sweet fountain. I found a few empty bottles and filled them with syrup to take home.

It was the syrup I had drunk in the brewery that had made me so sick. I perspired heavily for twenty-four hours. And my landlady kept on laughing at me. "Can I treat you with some good syrup?" she teased me.

The Poles observe all ceremonies where religion is concerned. It did not matter that the shooting seemed to be right around the corner, that artillery fire and bombing filled the air — at the set time, people were gathering for mass. An altar was usually set up in a courtyard or in the large arched entrance to a building. To give the greatest number of people the opportunity to pray collectively and receive the priest's blessing, a different courtyard was chosen every time for the service.

Men, women and children fell into a trance, singing in unison the liturgical songs. There were always a few young people, dressed in religious regalia, helping out the priest as he performed the service. They handed him different religious accessories and then, at the proper moment, they took them away. Everything was done with precision and these helpers knew exactly what to do.

It was "natural" that all the residents of the block attended the mass. Unless on a military mission, I went to the service too. I followed all the movements the others made, kneeling and crossing myself at the right moments. When the mighty sound of the national religious hymn "*Boze cos Polske*" ("God who protected Poland for ages") filled the air, I would sing loudly, I knew the words and the tune well. Everything then was so emotional I always made sure that my neighbours heard me singing and saying *amen* when the occasion called for it.

One morning, when I returned from my night shift, Mr. Kusak, the concierge, said to me: "Mr. Mankowski, I have pleasant news for you. In appreciation of your helping out with food supplies, some tenants have suggested that we offer you the honour of helping the priest with today's mass."

I smelled trouble...."Yes, Mr. Kusak. That's an honour, indeed. I'll be ready," I answered with no hesitation. "What time will mass take place? Noon, as usual? I'll still manage to get a few hours' sleep."

I went to my room. I felt sweat coming on my forehead. What could I do now? I couldn't say no to Mr. Kusak, that would have been an insult and a very, very improper thing to do in that Christian environment. But what did I know about the mass ceremony? The rabbi never did teach that little Jewish boy those things. Neither was I ever interested to know the procedure of a Catholic mass. To improvise? The worshippers would notice it immediately. Gossiping would start right after the service and there would go my secret....

I decided to take a rest and think about the "honour" later. When I got up, I went up to Mr. Kusak just before the service and told him that I was very sorry but I would not be able to attend the mass at all: I had just received a message to show up with my army unit for a trench-digging job.

I left the building and met a friend from my unit. We talked for a while, exchanging views and news. When we said *czesc* (goodbye) to each other and parted, we set off in opposite directions. Two or three seconds later I heard a sharp *swoosh* just around my ears. I ducked automatically. I turned my head and there was my friend lying on the ground, just a few steps from where we had been standing and talking moments before.

He was dead. A stray bullet had killed him. Was it a German bullet or one of ours, firing a shot for the fun of it? It made no difference. A comrade of mine, in his early twenties, was dead. He was buried in a small square, just like the other victims of those times, for later reburial in a real cemetery. A small marker was placed on the new grave. I was wondering why fate did not allow us to talk for a minute longer. That fatal bullet would probably have missed both of us. Although I had in the past few years seen many innocent people die, it still shattered my mind and spirit every time it happened.

Chapter Nineteen

ouriers from different parts of the city reported bitter fighting and large numbers of casualties. Some of the groups, once employed only for the transportation of food or other goods, were now switched to military operations behind the lines, mostly emergency trench-digging. The group I belonged to went out at different times of day or night to dig trenches or to put out fires caused by the German artillery shelling or bombing. Our task was to keep the fires from spreading and to protect the city as much as possible. Every day it became more obvious that the enemy was determined to wipe Warsaw off the map. Preventing the fires from spreading meant being exposed to all the horrors of war.

We were on constant alert. We received an order to depart immediately to a location near the corner of Marszalkowska Street and Jerozolimska Avenue. Two buildings there were on fire. These buildings were completely engulfed in flames and nothing could be done to save them. We had to concentrate on saving the neighbouring houses. First we evacuated the people, then we attempted to save their belongings. Anything that could easily catch fire we threw out through the windows into the courtyard.

Three boys and I came up to an apartment on the fourth floor of a building. The people from that place had probably just left because everything in the house was still in order. I opened the door to the living room. Everything still so elegant, so much in contrast with the reality of the moment. One did not feel like disturbing the preserved harmony by starting to remove things. But the noise of shelling coming from outside left us no choice but to carry out the instructions and try to save whatever it was still possible to save. Smoke from the neighbouring buildings was coming in through the open windows and with each shell flying by we could feel the building sway.

As I carried things to be thrown out to the courtyard, a different noise came to my attention. I listened. No, no mistake, that was a bird chirping, as if it was calling for attention. I turned toward the sound and there...there was a cage, with a canary inside. Seeing a human being, the canary jumped around vigorously and did some more chirping. I leaped forward, grabbed the cage, brought it over to the open window and let the bird go. Everything happened in seconds.

Through with the work on the fourth floor, the four of us moved down to the apartment below, on the third floor. This place was messy, but everything spread out on the floors bore signs of affluence. The owners seemed to have been selecting things to take with them when they left. Looking at the elegant leftovers one couldn't help thinking how worthless they were now. Rich people had lived here. Where had they gone? In one corner I spotted a row of men's shoes, all clean and polished to a shine. Trenchcoats, hats, shirts, ladies' leather bags, a fur coat. The usefulness of these things had gone. Out the windows they went!

"Everybody down, staircase on fire. Quick. Staircase on *fire*." That was our group leader calling from the courtyard.

"*Chlopcy* (guys)," one of our foursome called out, "throw rugs over your heads." How cool and intelligent he was! When I was running down the stairs, some of the banisters were already on fire. I jumped over a few small flames, and I was on the ground floor. Out of the little entrance hall, I ran to the courtyard and....

What happened? It was only seconds later when I got up off the pavement, about twenty feet away from the staircase exit. I was still dizzy from the shock when I heard a call, "*Ratunku, ratunku* (help, help)." I turned in the direction of the screaming person. That screaming man had had both his legs blown off. More people came running and the poor man was taken away on a stretcher. What had happened to him? — a German projectile had hit the building we were in. The force of the explosion threw me away into a shielded corner of the courtyard. The poor man was probably hit by a ricocheting fragment of the exploding shell. Some others suffered minor scratches.

Although I had always been aware that some factions of the A.K. were extremely anti-Semitic and that a Jew trapped by them would meet the same fate as he would in the hands of the Gestapo, still when it happened right before my eyes, I was devastated.

A few units gathered at our usual meeting-place one morning. We were waiting for the officer's order telling us where we would go trench-digging. The boys in one of the groups were extremely noisy. When I got closer to the rowdy bunch, I heard laughter and all kinds of remarks.

"*Nu*, Moishe, do you know how to dig a trench?"

"Moishe, tell us how you fooled the Germans until now?"

"Moishe wants to be a hero, he came to help us."

The subject of all these derogatory remarks was a portly man of around fifty years of age. He tried to get away from his cruel companions but they kept following him, pushing him "accidentally." Not a word of protest from anyone. The whistle of an officer who came out of his quarters interrupted the harassing of the Jew. The units were sent off to the designated areas.

The next morning, one member of the group the Jew had been with the day before was happy to let us know that "Moishe will not be coming with us today, or ever, for that matter. We took care of him. He was surprisingly flammable."

I was shaken and depressed. The A.K. was full of these killers. That they were Poles and not Germans made no difference. I was thinking the whole day of how these "patriots" had cruelly murdered a man whose only crime was that he was Jewish. I thought of what that man probably went through since he first hid from the Germans. Now all he had wanted was to help fight the tyrants. What an end!

The military situation of the uprising was deteriorating swiftly. The fighters, under heavy fire from the Germans, had to give up the Old City at the beginning of September 1944. The loss of life was high, and the devastation of that historic part of Warsaw just terrible.

Since the city centre was under the control of the Home Army, people from the Old City came under cover of night to the centre via the sewers. Reorganizing its forces, the military had begun building a new line of defence along Jerozolimska Avenue, which was a dividing line between north and south. The long, wide avenue was completely in our hands, but the Germans had their firm positions at both ends of it and were able to fire along it. That corridor of constant fire made it practically impossible for the A.K. to coordinate the military efforts of the northern and southern parts of the city centre.

Half of our unit, eighteen boys, was assigned to go out at seven in the morning for trench-digging along the southern side of Jerozolimska Avenue. The other half of our group was to take over at 1:00 p.m. Our officer changed the order at the last minute. The morning group, of which I was a member, would now go in the afternoon. The other part of our group went in the morning instead. Why the change? We didn't think about it — it was of no relevance.

Around 11:30 that morning we were told that a tragedy had occurred. All the boys from the morning group had been killed by a round of German artillery fire. The part of the unit I was in, plus an additional unit, went out to the place of tragedy to pick up the bodies of our comrades. It seemed to have been a direct hit; the recovered bodies were hardly identifiable. Our tragic mission completed, we talked about what had happened that morning, when the orders were switched. "It could have been our remains being collected for that mass burial." A very inexplicable turn of events.

The month of September was a time of hope and fear for the population and the Home Army. We lived on rumours. The girl couriers brought in news from different parts of the city. The slightest success story brought out feelings of pride and hope; when the news of the next hour or day was bad, the general mood sank into discouragement. I recall listening one afternoon to a radio broadcast from London, England, on an illegal radio that somebody had pulled out of hiding. Prime Minister Churchill was talking in the English Parliament. An interpreter was translating the speech into Polish. Churchill roared, in his deep voice, that while he stood there, England's brave pilots were flying over Warsaw, dropping military supplies to England's heroic friends and allies. "We will never, never disappoint our fighting allies," said Churchill.

I ran out of the house to catch a glimpse of the numerous formations of planes Churchill had mentioned. There were none. People said that two airplanes had flown over and dropped a few bags. The bags seemed to have fallen behind German lines.

People in Warsaw were disappointed and bitter. Nobody could understand why the West couldn't influence the Russians, who were only one or two kilometres away, to help their beleaguered Polish allies.

Our unit received an emergency call to go to a certain building to put out a fire. When we reached the place, we found other units working there already. No flames were visible. The basement of the building was full of anthracite (coal) and it was this anthracite that had caught fire. The task was to isolate the glowing coal, try to extinguish it and thus prevent the buildup of gases that could trigger an explosion and destroy the building, which was strategically located, and was needed for cover and defence.

The boys formed a chain right up to the opening to the basement. Pails of water were passed from hand to hand to one man inside the basement to splash over the glowing coal. Another man stood outside the opening and counted to ten. Ten pails of water were the most the person inside could handle. After that he was replaced by another comrade. Some of the firefighters had to get out of the basement before the full count of ten. I could make it only to eight. The fire consumed the oxygen from one's lungs, and one had to run for fresh air. At the count of seven I felt dizzy and my lungs were contracting. We worked tirelessly until we managed to isolate the danger and forestall an explosion.

The Germans were using *ryczace krowy* ("screaming cows") more and more. These were missiles fired with the power of compressed air. We always had twenty-odd seconds before a missile of that kind exploded. We would hear four loud crankings from the projectile firing unit, followed by a roar and the impact of that huge "cow." As soon as the cranking started, people, gripped by panic, ran to the shelters for protection. Even in the basement you could feel the solid building above you vibrating strongly because of the power of the missile.

Amazing as it may seem, people did get used to the bombardment. Many reasoned that it did not make sense at all to go down to shelters during an air attack, because a direct hit would bring down the building over the "hole" and there would be no chance of getting out from under all that rubble. So why suffer while still alive, crammed together with others?

The morale of the population was getting lower and lower. Grumbling was widespread. People asked bitterly why the exiled Polish government in London did nothing to help. Didn't they care? Why were the Russians, who were so close, not helping the besieged?

Some other people figured that they had the answer: the Polish government in England didn't have enough clout with the Allies in the West and the Allies cared only for their own skin. The Russians didn't want to help because the Home Army was too nationalistic, demonstrating its anti-Soviet attitude openly. Stalin's adopted policy was now: "Let these romantics stew in their own juices." None of the states fighting the Germans seemed to care that the civilian population of Warsaw was being crushed.

You also heard people present a different scenario: "Let's say we surrender to the Germans. The Russians will then start an offensive and chase the Germans right to Berlin. What's in it for us? That will just be like changing the German boot for a Russian one. Neither of these boots will bring any comfort, just another kind of oppression."

I couldn't help thinking of what might happen to me in all that turmoil. If the uprising failed and we surrendered to the Germans, what would I, a Jew, do? What about my pregnant wife? How was she managing now? Where would I hide when all my benefactors from before the uprising were gone? Would I be lucky and find them again? They probably were ruined people by now. A feeling of helplessness and uncertainty engulfed me with those thoughts.

The territory held by the Home Army was getting smaller and smaller. Just a small part of the city centre was left. The Russians were staying put on the east side of the Wisla River. Facing complete destruction of the city and with only unarmed, physically exhausted fighters, Commander-in-Chief General Bor-Komorowski resorted to the white flag and surrendered to the Germans.

When the proclamation of surrender was read to us, we wept. We had known for a week that surrender was inevitable, but we didn't want to believe that it would actually happen. Any minute, we tried to believe, might bring a miracle. The men from all A.K. units gathered to hear the conditions of the surrender.

"Hey, fellows, this man is a Jew!" I heard someone calling out. I looked up in the direction the voice was coming from and there was a man, standing about fifteen feet away from me, pointing his right hand at me. I felt blood coming to my face. I saw that man for the first time. He was my age and one head taller than I.

"All right, *chlopcy*, I'll finish this one," he shouted. I was expecting the worst now. In a haze I saw him running towards me. When he was close to me, I jumped and with all the force I could muster punched him right in the head. I must have hit him right on the temple, because that tall muscular man just fell to the ground. He got up swiftly and attempted again to hit me. Just wild now, I gave him another punch and down he went again.

I heard a burst of laughter around me. The boys were now laughing. The big hero, apparently embarrassed by the laughter, didn't want to give up. He got on his feet and tried to get me. In an effort to separate us, a few boys held him down, and a few others grabbed me. The officer was called from his office. We, the attacker and I, were still shouting insults at each other when the officer approached us.

"Young man, what unit do you belong to?"

"I'm from Wola. What difference does that make? He is a Jew." He pointed at me. "And I'll kill him before the Germans pull out of here. I will...."

The group of boys I had been working with for almost two months now were surprised by the stranger's "discovery." I had the feeling that some of my comrades were on the stranger's side, but the others openly expressed their respect for me. "If Mankowski is really Jewish, he certainly deserves credit for delivering a good punch." A salvo of laughter followed that remark.

"Quiet, boys," the officer said, "Mankowski belongs to our group and it makes no difference whether he is Jewish or not."

"*Prawda* (true)," some of the guys said.

The officer turned to me. "Mankowski, tell me, are you really a *Zydek*?"

I was furious at this insulting way of describing a Jew. "No, Panie poruczniku (lieutenant)," I shouted back, "I am not a *Zydek*, I am a *Zyd*, a full-blooded Jew, if that's what you want to know."

"Mankowski, cool down. My word of honour, I did not mean to offend you when I said *Zydek*. You know it's just a way of speaking. Forgive me." He stretched out his hand to me.

"*Dobrze* (good), Panie poruczniku."

"Now, Mankowski, what is interesting in all this is the fact that I would never have thought of you being a Jew."

"Why are you surprised? Am I, being a Jew, supposed to have horns?"

"You see, I mean to say that you never gave me any reasons to suspect you of being a Jew. Whenever we needed volunteers for a mission, you always came forward at once. You never stayed away from any effort. And all that is contrary to that what I heard about Jews. Therefore I was surprised."

"How many Jews have you met in your line of work, lieutenant?"

"The truth? None. But I read a lot about Jews."

"Well, I hope you'll have a different opinion of us now."

"Mankowski, you are a good man. I wish you the best."

"Thank you, lieutenant."

All the gathered units were told that according to the terms of surrender, the entire population of Warsaw had to leave the city within three days. All the participants in the uprising would be treated as prisoners of war according to the regulations established by the Geneva Convention. The civilians could take as many of their belongings as they could carry. The Germans promised not to make any reprisals against those leaving the city. People trying to stay behind in Warsaw would be shot. Everybody was advised to leave the city as quickly as possible.

The effect of these announcements was devastating. Not only had we suffered so many casualties in vain and lost the fight, but in addition to all that we would now become homeless too. Everybody had to leave that beloved city of Warsaw. I went back to Wilcza Street to prepare my wanderer's bundle, my meagre belongings.

"Panie Mankowski, what do you say to all that has befallen us now?" Mr. Lipowicz asked me that question when he saw me in the courtyard on Wilcza Street. Since the time when he had offered me gold coins in exchange for food, Mr. Lipowicz had taken a liking to me.

"What can one say? We all have to leave the city. That's all."

"Listen, Panie Mankowski, join me and my family leaving the city. It will be much easier in company."

I looked at Mr. Lipowicz. Just as once before, I was thinking that Mr. Lipowicz knew my secret and he was trying to be helpful and raise my spirits. "Thank you, Mr. Lipowicz. Let's leave together. When are you planning to go?"

"Early tomorrow morning."

"I'll be ready."

My dear Mrs. Lukaszewicz behaved very bravely. "Panie Jasiu, can you help me take down some things to the locker in the basement? I want to bury it there. When I return to Warsaw I'll dig it out. You can put your stuff there too."

"When are you leaving?"

"They told me that the elderly people will be taken out of the city by truck tomorrow morning. I have family living about fifty kilometres from Warsaw. I'll try to get to them."

I helped my landlady bury her things in the basement. I put in some stuff of mine and my wife's. I kept back the tears when I looked at Helena's blouses and skirts. Would I ever see her again?

For the rest of that day we lived as if we were in a bee-hive. Everybody was repeating all kinds of rumours. At noon the next day I joined the Lipowicz family: husband, wife and two daughters, twenty and twenty-three years old. Each family member carried a backpack and some bundles in their hands. I had a backpack too. In it were a few shirts, some underwear, bread and a jar of marmalade, courtesy of Mrs. Lukaszewicz. She cried bitterly when I left.

It was raining lightly. We were going in the direction of the train station. Thousands of people, everyone's back loaded, all walked in the same direction. When we reached the first German post, a German soldier motioned me out of the crowd. A moment of fear. Had I been recognized? I was sent to join a group of other people, more or less of the same age as I. Another soldier told us that before we left the city we had to work for a few hours cleaning the streets of barricades and other debris. We put aside our bundles and went to work. I was just sorry that I had to part from the Lipowicz family. Well, I had no choice.

I worked for about an hour when I noticed that the German soldiers were allowing some of the men to take their parcels and join the continuously flowing crowd. I decided to try my luck. The pavement was wet and slimy from the falling rain, I covered my shoes, trousers and hands with mud and went over to one of the supervising soldiers and said to him in German: "*Siehst du* (you see), I've been working here for three hours now, can I go?" I wiped the dirt from my hands as I spoke.

"Oh, *jawohl, du sollst doch schon gehen, Mensch* (Oh, yes, you should have gone already)."

It worked. Wearily now, faking tiredness, I took my backpack and joined the crowd. We were walking through a field when I noticed something red on the ground. I bent down; between the dried-out stems of summer vegetables I found a red tomato. It was bruised on one side. I wiped it clean and took a bite. How heavenly it tasted! Covering that unexpected precious gift from nature so that nobody could see what I had in my hands, I ate it all. I felt a pleasure that only people who had experienced the same kind of deprivation would understand.

We reached a field near the station. Crowds everywhere. Some were sitting on the wet ground, others walking around aimlessly.

"*Czesc, jak sie pan ma?* (hi, how are you?)," somebody tapped my shoulder and asked me.

Who was it, I knew him from somewhere.

"I can tell that you don't recognize me. Well, my wife used to work for your sister-in-law Gienia, when she lived on Panska Street. You stayed in my house in 1942 when you came from Parczew to Warsaw."

"Oh yes, I remember now." We embraced. This was the man who had received me so warmly when I first came to Warsaw looking for a hiding-place. "Panie Kazimierzu, it's unbelievable meeting you again. I remember your house on Twarda Street so well."

"I'm glad to see you alive. Where is your wife, the beautiful Helena, is she alive?"

"She was in Mokotow during the uprising. I haven't heard from her since."

"The Germans overpowered Mokotow right in the first week of the fight. There was almost no fighting there. Mokotow was evacuated then, so Helena must be alive. Don't worry, the *Schwabs* are on their last legs here. We will be free soon. *Trzymaj sie pan* (hold on, don't give up). *Czesc.* I have to join my gang now."

That was the first time in two months I had heard about Mokotow. My beautiful wife was probably outside Warsaw already. But where could she be? How did she feel in her pregnancy? Would we ever see each other again?

I sat down on a rock. The people around me told me that a trainload of evacuees had left the station about two hours before and that a new train of cattle cars would probably arrive soon and take us away. Where to, nobody seemed to know. I noticed one of Mr. Lipowicz's daughters. I ran over to her.

"Panno Lipowicz, where are your parents?"

"Oh, my God. Will my father ever be happy to see you! He can't stop talking about you. Come with me."

Mr. Lipowicz embraced me. "I prayed so much to see you again. Let me introduce you to a couple I met here. I told them what a nice man you are."

The young couple, looking to be my age, introduced themselves as Stach (Stanislaus) and Halina. He was handsome, she was exceptionally beautiful. The features of her face were full of grace and dignity. The Lipowiczes, Stach, Halina and I were now a family of seven.

The whistling and loud noises were signs of an arriving train, probably the one that was to take us away. A line of open cars, the kind used to transport coal or sand, stopped at the station. The scene of the train and the people boarding it looked familiar to me. I had seen that scenario when I was being taken to the death camp at Treblinka. However, there was a difference in the scenes between then and now: no Gestapo around, just ordinary Wehrmacht, the German army; no beating and pushing of the people, just directing them in an orderly manner. Even when we were waiting for the train, one could sit, stand or walk around, unlike the other time when we were ordered to sit crosslegged after first being robbed by the chosen breed of Nazi heroes.

My new family and I gathered our belongings and got into a boxcar. When the loading of about fifty or sixty people to a car was over, the train started to move. Unlike the other time, there were no guards at the front or the back of the cars.

Goodbye, Warsaw. So much happened while I lived within your limits, but in sum you were very good to me and my wife. I will never forget you — just as I'll never forget my home town Parczew. Indeed, you treated me better than Parczew. When I left my home town, it was in a cattle car — now I'm in a box car. Ironic? Perhaps, but the difference is like night and day.

Chapter Twenty

What a difference! The car didn't smell of excrement like the one that had carried me to Treblinka. And the people, my new fellow travellers? Everybody was serious, but not desperate. I suppose we were all thinking, "Well, it's hard, but eventually we'll rebuild our lives." As for myself, I remembered my thoughts on that previous ride: "Another twelve hours and....What do I do next?"

I whispered to Mr. Lipowicz: "I'm thinking of jumping the train at the first opportunity, I don't want to go to a labour camp. I have had enough of the *Schwabs*. Do you want to jump or stay on?"

"Let's talk it over with Stach and the girls."

It was a quick decision. Everybody wanted to run away. Stach said, "We'll do it once we get away from all the small stations around Warsaw. The *Schwabs* are all over around here."

Halina said, "We'll jump when it gets dark."

The train was rolling slowly. People were asking each other where we were being taken. Nobody could give a clear answer. Someone said that the Germans were going to stop the train in the middle of nowhere and make a selection. The young people would be sent away to labour camps in Germany, and the old folks and children they'd just dump anywhere and let them go. It was chilly and wet. Everyone tried to bundle up.

We noticed the train switching a few tracks. For safety reasons there were no lights on, and we couldn't see the sign on the station building we just passed. When the train stopped we asked the Polish servicemen on the ground where we were.

"Pruszkow," they replied. It was dark and drizzly. We saw people climbing out of the cars.

Stach said, "Let's go. Out, fast!"

We jumped out of the open box cars. Lipowicz whispered, "Hold hands, don't get lost."

About fifteen feet away from the car someone said, "*Bracia* (brothers), this way, quietly, this way, follow me." We followed the man. About one hundred feet now we heard the same voice as before. "*Bracia*, we are local Poles. Don't go to Germany, we'll hide you here. Don't talk. Follow me."

In no time we reached a building. One by one we were pushed through a small opening into a basement. Judging from the whispers, the place was already full of people. "*Ludzie* (people), you are among your own now. You are safe here. We'll take care of you tomorrow morning. Be quiet."

Everybody tried to find a spot on the bare earthen basement floor to lie down. I felt wet and cold all over. People used whatever they had to cover themselves and keep out the cold of the night. Mr. Lipowicz, the senior member of our group, was now directing how "the family" should place itself on the floor for most warmth. "Mankowski, I'm having a problem where to place you since you are all by yourself. Yes, I know. You will lie down between my two daughters."

"Joseph, what did you say?" Mrs. Lipowicz asked in surprise.

"Mankowski can't freeze. And I trust the three of them."

I felt that I was blushing in the dark. "Here's a place, lie down here," one of the obedient daughters said. It was certainly not an easy situation. The girls moved quite close to me and took their father's suggestion literally, that is, to keep me warm. The snoring of some people in the basement and the gender of my two neighbours kept me rolling from side to side. No, I was not cold.

For the sake of fun, Mr. Lipowicz asked me in the morning which of the girls was hotter, Irka or Stefa?

Laughing, Halina and Stach said: "Tell the father the truth."

"Panie Lipowicz, I can give you my opinion about Irka only. It was too short a night."

"Dad," said Irka, "Mankowski is a liar."

That was all the fun that morning. Before long, local people, mostly women, brought hot tea into the basement. Then a man told us that we had to leave, because the Germans knew a lot of people had jumped the train and they would certainly organize a search. The same thing had happened the previous day. It was the young people the Germans were especially after.

We talked about going away to a village, far away from towns that the Germans were milling around in all the time. Then Mr. Lipowicz took me aside and started to talk to me about a big problem of his. He thought of me as one of his own sons and talking to me always made him feel better.

"My daughter Stefa made a big mistake yesterday. She lost nearly all of my money. I had a lot of my money in Russian gold coins. You remember that I offered you some in exchange for food and you refused. I had a lot of these coins, and I was always hoping that when the war ended, I'd have something to start with. I'm not young any more, to start all over again with nothing. Nobody can undo what happened, but I feel like talking about it."

Slowly, Mr. Lipowicz told me his story. "When it became clear that everybody had to leave Warsaw, I baked a few loaves of bread. One loaf I loaded with the coins and then baked it. When we were leaving Warsaw I put the bread in Stefa's backpack, not telling her, for fear that she would panic about it. At the station in Warsaw, Stefa struck up a conversation with a woman who told her that she was a cosmetic saleslady and that she managed to save a few tubes of lipstick while leaving Warsaw. So Stefa exchanged one of her bread loaves for a tube of lipstick. When Stefa told me about the great deal I was horrified! I checked the bread. The traded loaf was the one with the gold inside. We looked for the woman but couldn't find her in the chaos at the station. And that's my story. What will I do at my age with no money left?"

I was certainly moved by what I heard from good Mr. Lipowicz. I tried to help by telling him that I, too, had lost a great deal in the past and that all we could do was retain our strength and hope that one day everything would be better again.

Mr. Lipowicz looked at me and said: "I don't know where to start. I have friends living about thirty kilometres from here. Maybe they'll have a place for us to stay until things blow over. I feel bad about leaving the three of you, but seven people might be too many guests to go to one house."

We joined the rest of our group and Mr. Lipowicz told them what he was planning to do. Stach, Halina and I decided to start our own odyssey together. We said goodbye, and wished one another luck. The Lipowicz family left us.

Stach, Halina and I were already on our way out from Pruszkow when we were stopped by two women.

"Are you from Warsaw?"

"Yes."

"Some of our family lived in Warsaw. We are trying to find someone who might have seen them." The two ladies gave the names of their relatives, but we had never met them. "We would be pleased if you would come to our house and tell us about the fights in Warsaw as you experienced them."

Another few questions and answers and we were invited to the ladies' house. Our getting acquainted proceeded quickly. We exchanged names. Kazia and Gusta were sisters.

"You'll stay with us for dinner," declared Kazia, the older sister.

Our resistance to that invitation was very low; we were too tired and hungry to argue. The house was not luxurious-looking, but tidy and neat: there were photographs of ancestors on the walls, a print of a landscape, handmade runners on the floors, a long sofa with hand-decorated pillows on it. There was a strong smell in that living room. When the two sisters departed for the kitchen to get busy with the dinner preparations, Halina put two of her fingers against her nose and said: "I smell *bimber* (moonshine)." Stach and I nodded. Gusta came back and asked whether we would like to wash up before having a light snack. We welcomed that suggestion and enjoyed the luxury of real soap.

The two sisters now began to show us what the proverbial Polish hospitality meant. They brought in two large trays with assorted canapés. Country bread with butter and cheese and ham (wow!) and tomatoes.

"Gusta, our guests would probably like a drink as well," Kazia said. I thought that Kazia had tea or milk in mind, but Gusta knew better what her sister meant. She took an unlabelled bottle out of a cupboard, then brought out drinking glasses. Kazia raised her glass and motioned us to do likewise: "Let's waste no time. *Na zdrowie, niech zyje Polska* (For good health, let Poland live)!"

Who wouldn't drink to that? The three guests sipped their drinks slowly, the two sisters beat us immediately, emptying their glasses in one go. "*Zakaski, prosze* (the small snacks, please)," one of the sisters said.

In an effort to neutralize the strong taste of the moonshine I took a canapé with cheese. Another sip, another bite, anything to please our great hostesses....

"Can you tell us now about the fights in Warsaw? We heard about so many brave fights. We are curious to hear more about it."

We talked on and on; the sisters listened attentively. When we described the German bombing, the two ladies got upset and interrupted, "*Psia krew, cholera na tych Schwabow* (a Polish way of cursing)." During the dramatic moments of the stories they couldn't resist taking big gulps of that homemade stuff, encouraging us to do the same. We had to be polite and comply....The "*na zdrowie*" toasts again and again made us (the guests only) very weary, half gone.

"Maybe you'd like to rest now, while we prepare dinner. It'll take us about an hour and a half."

I was grateful for that suggestion; so were Stach and Halina. We were shown to two rooms. After our rest time, Halina offered to help serve the dinner. "No, no, you are our guests and after the experiences you went through, you all deserve a rest."

When we were left alone in the living-dining room, Halina pointed a finger to her mouth and blew out some air. I understood well what she was trying to tell us, because I too felt the unpleasant aftertaste of the moonshine. None of us said a word about it.

Our two ladies put on a real show. They covered the dinner table with goodies I hadn't seen in a long, long time. We started with hors d'oeuvres and drinks of the same kind and consistency as before, but in small glasses now. Chat, chat, chat and a multitude of "*na zdrowies*" for our beloved land and the good health of everyone present at the table. Everything at a very leisurely pace. The soup was excellent. And the pork chops!

"Where do you get all this nowadays?" Halina wanted to know.

"Well," came the answer, "when you have the right currency, you know, the liquid kind, you can get anything you want."

It dawned on me then that the two chatty sisters were in the *bimber* manufacturing business. What a contrast to life in Warsaw and especially to my own secret life of the last few years. I told myself to forget the "before" and join the others in enjoying the "now" or else I might risk drawing attention to myself. At this point I proposed another *na zdrowie* for a quick end to the war. There could be no opposition to that kind of toast. There was a fantastically easy atmosphere at that table, as if all the bad yesterdays had never existed. It was great. Home-baked Polish *babka* and tea completed a great dinner. Afterwards, there was still plenty of talk.

Next morning we told our hostesses that the clean beds and calm of the night had made it seem to us as if we had slept somewhere on a strange continent. We were really rested and happy.

Kazia now said, "I don't know your plans. We would be very happy if you would like to stay with us for another day at least. We enjoy your presence here. I just want to ask you to go out somewhere, around ten o'clock, for one hour only. That's the time when our German clients come to buy *bimber* from us. They are very nosy and run around the whole house. They might suspect you of being from Warsaw and who knows what these *Schwabs* might do. I never trust a *Schwab*."

We talked it over and decided to leave Pruszkow. "Too many Germans here; they might round us up." The sisters served us breakfast. All that food! It seemed unreal! We kissed one another goodbye, and expressed wishes to meet again when the war was over and "our land is free."

We figured it would be wisest for us to settle somewhere in a village away from the main roads and away from German traffic, thirty to thirty-five kilometres from Pruszkow. It was a cloudy October day, not too cold. Taking all possible precautions not to be noticed by the Germans, we were out of Pruszkow after half an hour's walk. It must have been around four p.m. when it started to rain heavily. It was getting dark too. At the first house we reached we were told that they had no room for us and that we had better go straight to the town hall and talk to the *wojt*, the mayor.

We were soaking wet by the time we reached the town hall. What a pleasure it was to feel the warmth inside the building. I rang the bell on a little table, as the sign on the wall said to do. Out came a short, well-dressed man, with a narrow face, a moustache, two sharp-looking eyes. His looks instantly deflated my hope that he would help us.

"And what can I do for you?"

Halina stepped forward, turned her head to one side, brushed her hair back from her face and started to tell that we had come from Warsaw and....

"Don't tell me any more, there's no room for you here. Our area is already taking care of two thousand people from Warsaw," the *wojt* was shouting. "They are mostly old people. I can't send them away. You are three young people, you should go to Germany and work there. Nothing bad will happen to you there. I want you to leave Guzow immediately. Is that clear?"

Halina had promised a good performance but she gave up now and stepped back. The *wojt* turned to go. Realizing what we were facing now, I decided to act.

"Panie *wojcie*," I began in a raised voice, "Don't you go away."

"My decision is final. Go!"

"I didn't interrupt while you were shouting at us, so now don't interrupt me as I speak to you. And I mean it, don't interrupt." The *wojt* sat down in a chair and looked at me. I had the feeling that the man was impressed with the tone of my voice. I continued, "You have the nerve to tell us to go to Germany? You, a Pole, say that? You are sitting here comfortably. We are wet to our last thread. We are hungry; you are not. We have no place to go, but you will soon go to your house and eat your supper in comfort."

"But I can't do a thing. I'm...."

"Oh, yes you can. The first thing we want is a warm shelter for tonight, and something to eat. Tomorrow, if we really can't stay here, we'll go. I don't think this place is good for us anyway. Did you really mean it when you told us to go to Germany?"

"All right, I've had enough of this. I'll give you a note to a *soltys* (alderman) and he will place you, for tonight only."

Outside, I asked Halina why she had backed away from talking to that *wojt*. "When he was yelling, he sounded exactly like a Gestapo officer. He scared me. Even his accent was so German. Where did you find the guts to talk to him?"

"That *wojt* is an s.o.b. He'd never understand gentle talk. Besides, did we have a choice? I decided to speak forcefully to him. So far it's worked."

"I smell fresh bread," Halina said. "We are getting close to a bakery."

We really were. Inside, we asked the baker for a loaf of bread. The bread loaves of those times usually weighed two kilograms; they were called *zegars* (clocks) which was an allusion to the face of a big clock. When the baker noticed that we were having problems putting together the number of coins needed to pay for the bread, he said he'd take whatever we had. "You are probably from Warsaw. My God, what you have been through. The rotten *Schwabs* and their former friends, the Russians I mean. These Stalinist bastards didn't want to help out."

We asked the man whether we could get closer to the oven and dry our clothes out a bit. "Come, I'll put a bench right near the oven, and all three of you can sit down."

"Cut the bread, I'm hungry," Halina said. In no time, the three of us had finished with that *zegar*. The baker, impressed by our appetite, offered us another loaf free. Halina refused the offer.

"Take it, you'll eat it later or tomorrow," the man insisted.

We thanked him and left the bakery. Halina was now complaining of a stomach ache. "I ate that bread much too fast. It was so fresh and tasty."

Inside the alderman's house it was dark and the air was full of cigarette smoke. That smell and the smoke hurt my eyes. The people, mostly elderly, were staring at us curiously. The alderman's wife said, "The *soltys*, my husband, that is, is away on official duties and will be back around midnight."

"Can we wait for him here?"

"Of course. You look worn out. Can I offer you hot milk and bread?"

"Just milk will be fine, thank you," Halina replied.

While we regaled ourselves with the hot milk, the *soltys*'s wife said to us in a low voice: "It's so good to look at young people. We've got eight people staying here, all elderly. They never stop complaining, as if we were guilty of what happened to them in Warsaw. We do our best here to help. You'll stay here for the night. My husband will take care of you first thing tomorrow morning. Don't worry, we will help. Since there's no more room in the house, you can all sleep in the barn."

The woman gave us blankets and, a lamp in her hand, led us to the barn and showed us to a hayloft. After we spread out the blankets I noticed Stach and Halina kneeling. Oh, I thought, they are saying an evening prayer before going to sleep. I did the same.

Different thoughts came to my mind as I was falling asleep. What would it be like tomorrow? Where would I go? Village people were quick to recognize a Jew when they saw one — not like in Warsaw, where most of the people were preoccupied with their own problems and didn't care who the next person was. People in the country liked to analyse you when they looked at you. Would I be able to play my part the right way? Would it be up to me only?

I was thinking that in only one day we had experienced such warm hospitality from the two sisters in Pruszkow, the pleasant treatment by the baker, the kind attention of that *soltys*'s wife...and the *wojt*. He was only one out of four, and we had managed to persuade him to do something for us. How different was it when I jumped off the train that was taking me to the death camp? I was afraid then, afraid of everybody. It was different now. People were helping their brothers, and it was hard to imagine that Jews had always been strangers here.

And my dear wife. Where was Hindele? How did she feel with the baby inside her?

I fell asleep.

Chapter Twenty-One

The next morning, I talked to the alderman. "What did the *wojt* tell you yesterday?" he asked. I told him all the details of our conversation with the *wojt*. "He's crazy. He came here from the *Poznanskie* (a district right on the border between Germany and Poland). He thinks like a German, acts like one and even dresses like one of them."

"That's bad for us if he's the one to decide whether we can stay here or not."

"Don't worry. I'll take care of all that. We have to save our young people and we'll do it. See you at breakfast in half an hour."

At breakfast, his wife said, "Antoni, will you be able to do something for them? I wish they could stay here and not have to wander away into the unknown."

"I have a plan. At noon, the *wojt* has to go to Zyrardow to a conference. I'm taking over his duties for the rest of the day. It will be up to me to place the three of you wherever I please. Come with me to the town hall and I'll make the proper arrangements."

At the town hall, the alderman took out three pretyped forms, filled in all the necessary names and stamped the papers with the official seal. "This letter of recommendation obliges each of these farmers to provide shelter and food for one person from Warsaw. Good luck. Let me know how everything works out."

It was quite a nice afternoon. We arrived at the first farm, where the house and yard were clean and tidy. When the young farmer and his wife were told that Halina was Stach's wife and that she was assigned to another farmer, the farmer's wife said it wouldn't be fair to separate a young couple. "We have enough room for the two of you. We have no children yet and it won't be at all hard to manage."

I felt jealous. I asked Stach's and Halina's new hosts whether the farm family I was directed to was as nice as they. "Oh, the Zakutas are very good people. Once you're settled, come and visit us."

I had an uncomfortable feeling, saying goodbye to Stach and Halina. I knew that it couldn't be any other way, but as I walked through the soft field, I was just hoping that my farmer would be as nice as theirs.

When I reached the yard of the Zakutas' farm, a dog on a chain barked at me with all the power of his lungs. I went around him and knocked at the door of the house. No answer. The dog kept barking at me. I started to talk to him gently and moved a few steps towards him. He stopped barking and started to wag his tail. Encouraged now, I went over and patted his head gently. We became instant friends. I did the talking and the dog did the licking of my hands and face.

The farmer's wife, a woman of about forty-five years of age, arrived and I told her my story. "Come in the house, you'll have something to eat." While she treated me with bread and butter and cheese, she asked, "What did you do to the dog that he played with you? He's quite vicious and hard on strangers. Did you give him sweets?"

"No, *moja pani* (my lady). We had no sweets in Warsaw, believe me. I know how to talk to dogs because I've loved animals since I was a kid. That's all. A dog always likes a friendly person."

In the further conversation I found out that there were two children in the family, a son and a daughter, and they would soon be back from work. When Mr. Zakuta came home, he looked surprised to see a stranger in the house, but he didn't ask his wife or me anything. I felt strange in this situation. The wife took over and told her husband who I was and what I wanted.

"Sure, you can stay with us," the farmer said.

"Panie Zakuta, I'm a good worker. I'll make myself useful here."

"Oh, yes? What does a city man know about farming, eh? He knows that milk comes from a bottle and bread from the baker, that's about all the farmer stuff he knows."

I laughed out loud and Mr. Zakuta seemed happy with his witticism about city folk. When I had shaved my four-day beard, washed myself thoroughly and straightened out my good suit (the reincarnated former military German uniform), Mrs. Zakuta expressed her surprise at my new looks. "When I first saw you I took you for a man in his forties, you looked rumpled up and with a beard, yes, you looked old...I saw my mistake the minute you shaved and washed."

"And Pan Jan is good-looking too," daughter Marja added, smiling at me.

On the second day, I asked Mr. Zakuta whether he had anything urgent to be done on the farm. He looked at me, probably thinking, What does this city man know about real work? "I still have beets in the field. Sugar beets, you can help me get them out of the ground." Zakuta showed me his technique of beet picking. I improved it a bit my own way, but after four hours of work, the city boy's back started to remind him of its existence. Zakuta noticed that I kept straightening my body. "Half a day beet picking is enough, let's go for lunch," he said.

The following days I went to the field myself. Frost could set in any day now; everything still in the ground had to be removed. Every day I became more involved in the farmer's life. I was feeding the two cows and the horse, and spreading straw underneath them. When I started using the farm machinery, my farmer told me that I must have been lying to him and that most likely I was the son of a farmer.

Mr. Zakuta was most impressed with the way I used the plough. After everything was out of the ground, the field had to be ploughed before the arrival of winter. A horse-drawn plough was used for the purpose. The trick to that kind of work was to make the horse go in a straight line, and for the man to handle the drawn plough in such a way that the furrow was neither too deep nor too shallow. One improper move and the pointed front end of the plough either digs into or rides up out of the ground while the horse keeps going forward. When Mr. Zakuta handed me the reins and the plough, he had a grin on his face. He expected my performance to be a joke. I disappointed him. I put the reins over my head, on my shoulders; I adjusted their length for better control of the horse, took a firm grip on the handles and commanded a loud "*Wioh*" to the horse. The furrows I made looked very professional.

"I can't believe it. Who are you?"

"Panie Zakuta, my father was not a farmer, but my grandparents were. As a young boy I spent a lot of time on their farms. That's where I learned a few things."

When the family heard the father's report about my way of ploughing, Marja asked me whether I knew how to milk a cow so I could help her out sometimes.

"If you show Jan how to pull and squeeze he'll do it right. He's

young and he will learn fast," brother Feliks Jr. mixed in.
"Feliks, stop talking like that," their mother said.
"Don't worry, mom, Marja is afraid of her boyfriend. And you,
Jasiu, don't get ideas and don't start up with that guy of hers." Feliks
was laughing away.

I was becoming more and more a part of that family's life as each
day passed. I worked on my own. I knew what had to be done and when
to do it, and I did it without being told. I shared their meals, and one
dish in particular I will never forget; it was served almost daily. The
name of it was *zurek malopolski*, a sort of soup made with tiny bits of
pork fat and potatoes (lots of them).

That soup had a specific sourish taste from the added milk. But, considering the circumstances one had to be very grateful even for that
modest and simple food. When the war ended I couldn't stand potatoes
and I didn't eat any for ten or twelve years.

During that time, I made friends with a young Pole about my age
named Piotrus. He too was a refugee evacuated by the Germans from
Warsaw. He also, like me, belonged to the Polish underground fighters
in that ill-fated Uprising of August 1944. Piotrus was staying with Mr.
Bronkowski, a farmer right across from the Zakutas. Mr. Bronkowski
was a political activist in the left-oriented Polish Popular Front, and he
engaged Piotrus to work for the same party. There were many political groups in the villages then. The common goal of all of them was to
regain a free Poland. But where these groups, with ideologies ranging
from the extreme nationalistic right to the far left, did not agree, was
on how to organize the coming free state internally.

Differences of opinion were sometimes discussed among adver-
saries but more often they were fought out physically. Piotrus told me
many times about night-time gatherings in the woods, and about bitter
fights with other political groups. Since our past was in a way similar,
we liked to discuss things. Piotrus had access to underground radio.
He could tell me about the current news from the fronts; about the wor-
sening military situation of the German army. I told Piotrus what I was
reading in the German newspapers.

Many times Piotrus's way of thinking, his expressions and his secre-
tiveness about his past made me suspect him of being Jewish. To ask
him directly would have been dangerous for both of us. If I was mistaken and he was not Jewish, my question might have led him to suspect

me, and he might have started paying more attention to what I was saying, and the way I was thinking. Although he was a man of progressive ideology, he would not necessarily think in progressive terms when it came to Jews. I had seen that many times before. But Piotrus was good-natured and intelligent. Our discussions made my life in the village a lot less boring.

The farm was a small one, and towards the end of the season there was not too much to do. Feliks Jr. hired himself out to different jobs, while Marja worked in the nearby sugar refinery. Although nobody ever said anything to me, I felt that I was an imposition, especially in November when all the work in the field was finished.

I disliked sitting around and just waiting for the meals to arrive, and besides that, I was afraid that my hanging around and doing nothing might arouse suspicions about me. I decided to look for a job and get out of the house, at least for the winter months. The Germans were still masters of the situation and there were no signs of change. The Russian front seemed frozen. I thought the situation would probably last at least till spring. No, I couldn't stay on the farm and do nothing all winter long. It was unwise, and even dangerous too.

I decided to go to the *gmina* (town hall) and ask for a job. Remembering the way the *wojt* acted the day we arrived in Guzow, I had rather low expectations. But he didn't seem to remember me.

"Do you know German?"

"I've learned quite a bit in the last few years. I can make myself understood; I can write in German." (Out of fear of arousing suspicion as to my real identity, I never mentioned my formal education.)

"Good. I need somebody to help organize the social assistance to the refugees from Warsaw. The group in charge is part of the German Red Cross. It's called R.G.O." The *wojt* explained what my duties would be. I was to keep track of the incoming supplies — be it food, clothing and even money. I would oversee the proper distribution of the supplies among the refugees living in the surrounding villages. "There are over two thousand refugees in this district. You'll have lots of work and headaches too. You'll get help when you need it and you'll be responsible to me. I hope you are an honest man. You look like one."

"I'll certainly do my best."

The *wojt* asked the secretary to type out two *Bescheinigung* (certificates). One certified that Jan Mankowski was an employee of the

R.G.O., affiliated with the German Red Cross. The second one asked all the German authorities to give Jan Mankowski, employee of the R.G.O., all possible assistance in performing his duties. I loved the two new documents; I was now a regular person, officially that is. The two documents completed the status of my *Kennkarte*.

Every morning now I went to the *gmina* where the R.G.O. had its office. Checking the lists of the refugees in our region, I was always on the lookout for one person. I was looking for the name of Krystina Bartkowska, my wife. I did once come across the name Bartkowska, but neither the first name nor the age corresponded with those of my wife.

I had to face all kinds of situations and my reaction to them had to be swift. Taking time to answer a remark might have aroused suspicion regarding my secret.

One Sunday morning Halina came over unexpectedly. "Jasiu, come to church with me. Stach is busy and I don't want to go alone."

"Sure, Halina, I'll come with you."

"How come you're going to church?" Mr. Zakuta asked. "You told me that you are not too much of a believer, just like me."

"Panie Zakuta, when a beautiful young woman calls, one would be a fool not to go with her. First to church, then maybe to hell for a while."

All those present liked my answer and laughed. In church I discreetly copied the actions of the people around me. I tried to make all my movements during the service natural-looking.

Halina was a riddle to me. She looked like all good Jewish girls taken together — dark complexion, shiny hazel eyes, dark wavy hair, a nose that, although not typically Semitic, was still not of the Slavic variety. One could say the same thing about her lips: full-bodied, what one might describe as very sexy. I was even more intrigued by her way of praying. So much fervour and devotion! Was she trying to be holier than the Pope? That was how new "Aryans" usually acted, I thought. But her way of talking and expressing religious opinions was — one might say — "pure." Maybe she was a second- or third-generation convert, who realized she had Jewish looks, but covered for it by going to church and praying devoutly.

While in semi-hiding in Warsaw, I hadn't needed to be on constant alert in order not to betray my identity. Things were different in the country, whether I was on the farm or working at the R.G.O. I did everything I could to appear to be of the same fibre as everybody around me. One innocent remark by someone was enough to shake me up and give me the shivers.

In the evening, all the farmer's family sat around the kitchen table and talked. Pawel, Marja's boyfriend, usually joined us. Drinking *bimber* and smoking *mahorka* (cheap tobacco) were two activities never left out during these evening chats. A full, farmer-size drinking glass of alcohol was just "normal" consumption for one evening. I learned how to drink that homemade product; the quantity or quality of it no longer bothered me. Keeping up with the others was good for me, but I had to remember not to talk too much.

All the village gossip was traded during these evenings. Feliks Jr. once suggested that I should start going out with girls. "Why not have a good time? No use waiting for your sweetheart. She must have found somebody else by now." People at the table started to mention the names of girls in the village.

"Marja," the farmer's wife said, "invite the two Koziol sisters to our house. They are nice. Jan might like one of them, and old Koziol would for sure throw in fifteen acres as a dowry. What do you say, Jan?"

"The fifteen acres I can accept blindfolded. As for the girl I'd have to look her over...."

Everybody had fun now. "I don't think it will work," Pawel put in, "Jan is a city person and I always think of him as being different from us. Jan, am I right or not?"

(Different from us? *What did he mean?*)

"You're right. As a grownup, I never lived in a village. But if the girl is really nice, you never know what might happen. One should always look out for a good girl."

"Are you ready to forget your girlfriend?" Marja asked in surprise.

"It wouldn't hurt to get to know a girl now and decide about marriage later when I find out about my girlfriend."

"Marja, invite the Koziol sisters. If neither of them suits you, I'll get you another girl," Feliks Jr. sounded serious.

Later that night, it was Pawel's remark, and not the Koziol sisters, that I was thinking of.

Chapter Twenty-Two

One cold winter evening at the beginning of December, 1944 snow was coming down, not heavily, but it was driven by a strong whistling wind. We had just finished our modest supper when we heard a faint knock at the door. My farmer's lady opened the door and invited the visitor in.

"Thank you so much. I am almost frozen stiff from the cold."

She was an older woman. The way her lower and upper jaws looked when her mouth was closed indicated that our guest was toothless. Her eyes were small and moved very fast. The farmer's wife offered her some food, but she asked instead for some hot milk. She had her own food, she said. When the hostess served her a big jug of hot milk, the guest reached into one of her mysterious-looking bags, and brought out a chunk of dried-up black bread.

"This is the kind of bread I like best for my evening meal." She broke the bread into small pieces and dipped each morsel in the hot milk. When they were soft enough for her toothless mouth, she spooned them out of the mug and ate them. When she'd finished, we asked her who she was.

"I go from place to place. I often come across people who need help in the house. I am very good with babies, because I love them. People are nice to me and pay me for my honest work. My problem is that I never like to stay in any one place longer than one or two weeks at the most. Something drives me from place to place."

She bent down and from somewhere among the numerous folds of her long skirts, she produced a well-used deck of playing cards. "I am also a fortune-teller. Let me tell you what the future holds for you. I don't want any money from you. My cards always tell the truth."

Everyone urged Marja to go first. The fortune-teller laid down her cards, looked closely at Marja and told her that she would make someone a good wife — but she should wait a while. The farmer's wife turned to me now. "Jasiu, ask the lady to tell your fortune. Maybe she can tell you about your girlfriend. You've waited for her so long."

I didn't want to get involved in all that. My fears grew in intensity as the lady looked at me with her penetrating eyes. Was she looking at me that way because it was part of her game, or was she really seeing something in my face that I wouldn't want anybody to know? I had to reply without hesitating, and in a natural-sounding way. "I would rather not have my fortune told," I said. "I wouldn't want to hear that anything bad has happened to my girl in Warsaw."

"Jasiu," the farmer's wife said, "you are not married. And if your girl has lost her life, well, there are many more girls around. It's not good to be alone."

"Well, Madame? Tell me what you see in your cards for me."

The lady shuffled her cards, cut them and looked at me. I looked at her, trying to keep the I-couldn't-care-less smile on my face. The butterflies kept growing inside me. But hadn't I successfully concealed my inner fears many times? I decided to laugh at everything she said. I would make everything sound like a joke.

The lady told me to pull two cards out of the deck and lay them side by side, face down, on the table. She flipped them. They were a king and a queen. The lady looked at the cards, then glanced up at me. Everybody was very quiet and attentive as she began to give her reading of the cards. "It happens very seldom that a king and a queen are drawn at the same time. They are even of the same suit. That alone means that she is alive. She thinks of you and worries about whether you are alive. That means also that you and your girl love each other with the true kind of love. Is she blond?"

"Yes," I answered in a firm voice, giggling at the same time. That was part of my game now.

The lady took six more cards out of the deck and placed them, face up, around the queen. Moving the index finger of her right hand from card to card, she continued. "Your sweetheart is well liked by everyone around her. As a refugee from Warsaw, she has no real hardships. She manages well. But this card suggests that she is suffering some kind of discomfort. Is she a sick person?"

"When I saw her the last time...that was in July, she was having a summer cold," I said, laughing. My dear wife was seven months pregnant, and the fortune-teller was talking about my "girlfriend" suffering "a discomfort." I was getting panicky for fear of what that card reader might still come up with! But I was laughing. It was the kind of laughter I had trained myself to use in ambiguous situations.

The lady shuffled the cards again, laid them out in four rows, rearranged them in a pattern that was mysterious to us, and told me, "She is worth waiting for. She loves you, and you will be very happy together."

While I was scrabbling in my pockets for change to pay the lady, the door to the house opened and in came Piotrus, my political friend, who worked for farmer Bronkowski. He was immediately introduced to the fortune-teller. Everyone insisted that he too ask the lady what she could see of his future in the cards.

The lady shuffled her cards, and while doing so, she looked intensely at Piotrus. "What is your first name, young man?"

"Piotr," he answered. "They call me Piotrus."

"Piotrus, your eyes tell me that you are an open person. You seem to be very straightforward, not complicated. My cards will have no problem revealing your future."

She cut the cards three times, divided the deck into three parts, studied the figures, then turned sideways to look at Piotrus. Her face expressed bewilderment. Not saying anything, she put the cards together, shuffled them again, and made three parts again. When she looked at the turned cards now, her face became serious. She gave Piotrus a short look, then sighed slightly, put her cards together, and again spread them out in three rows, face down. She asked Piotrus to turn over one card from each row. When Piotrus did that, she turned one card on each side of those uncovered by Piotrus. She looked at the cards in silence. We all felt a certain tension.

And then she spoke, "Piotrus, you are nice, you are helpful to people. But you have many enemies. You seem to be mixing with people who will disappoint you. I see danger surrounding you." She collected the cards and laid them out again in a different pattern. "Piotrus, you are with people too much. You go out too much at night. I am frightened for you. Someone is after you. Maybe it's the Germans and maybe it's someone else. But you are definitely in danger." She was going over each card with her eyes. She continued, "If I were you I would change location. I would disappear for a while, so your enemies can forget about you. I don't think I can tell you much more. Good luck, Piotrus."

Pawel, Marja's boyfriend, was the first to comment. "I say don't listen to that yackety-yak. One time they make you feel good, another time, they scare the pants off you. I've seen it in Warsaw. Only stupid people go for that stuff. They'll never get me!"

A sip of moonshine lightened the serious feelings the lady's predictions had left in the air. Everyone was now jokingly telling Piotrus not to see so many girls every evening, because one of them might be jealous, and attack him in a place where it really hurts. The joking, the talking, and the moonshine came to an end. And to save naphtha in the lamp, everyone went to bed. It took me a while to fall asleep that night. I was thinking about Hindele, who was in discomfort. I was praying for her comfort. I was praying to see and be with her again.

The fortune-telling lady left next morning, and the daily chores made everyone forget her stories, until one morning about two weeks later, three days before Christmas. We were awakened by a knock on the door. It was four o'clock in the morning. Farmer Bronkowski walked in.

"Good morning. Bad news, Mr. Zakuta."

"What happened?"

"Piotrus was killed."

"What? How did it happen? Who killed him?"

Everybody dressed in a hurry and Mr. Bronkowski told the story of the killing. "A group of people came to the house and asked for Piotrus. Piotrus didn't open the door of his room — he asked them who they were and what they wanted. So then they just fired a machine gun through the door and killed him."

The warnings given to Piotrus by that fortune-teller two weeks before flashed through my mind like lightning. Mr. Bronkowski told us that the preceding evening Piotrus had gone to a meeting of his political group, in the woods. Apparently, the different factions were in conflict. Piotrus went home about midnight, and probably it was those political opponents who killed him.

Poor Piotrus, only thirty years old! He hadn't listened to the advice of the fortune-teller, and had gone on attending meetings and getting into arguments with his foes. He paid a high price for not being careful, in those emotion-loaded times. I was shocked. I dressed fast and went across the road to take a look at my dead comrade from Warsaw with whom I had discussed so many things.

A thought came to my mind. If Piotrus was Jewish, it would come out now, and a new twist to my problems would appear. A twist that might lead to me. I realized that my mind was not in balance now, and that my way of reasoning might be illogical. I no longer knew what made sense, and what did not. I went into the room where Piotrus was lying and closed the door behind me. I pulled back the heavy linen sheet. Piotrus's eyes were open, but his face was stiff and unchanged. I folded back more of the sheet. And there, right in the chest, was the deadly wound, with dried blood still around it.

My fear of being discovered was overwhelming, but I had to know if Piotrus was Jewish — if he was circumcised. I moved the sheet further down and looked. Then I stretched the sheet back over Piotrus. No, he was not Jewish. No, there would be no extra talk or suspicion.

Later that morning Mr. Bronkowski and two of his friends called me away from my work. "We have to arrange a decent burial for Piotrus. But he was killed by the ultranationalists, so we can't do it openly, in case the Germans find out about the whole business and arrest us. We want you to take care of all the funeral arrangements. It will look more natural for you to take care of giving the last respects to a friend who fought with you in the Uprising."

The three men looked at me expectantly. I could see that not accepting their suggestion would be most disappointing to them, and unreasonable on my part. With no way out, I said, "Sure, I'll do it."

One of the men said, "We will come back to you within an hour, and bring money to cover the expenses."

The three men left. I became very panicky. I busied myself in the barn. I wanted to be alone to think. My prewar self, the old Ben, was protesting: how in the world could I take part in a Catholic ceremony? I knew nothing at all about the rituals involved. One inappropriate step, and everyone would look at me with wide eyes. And it would take only one person to come up with a suspicion — and that would be the end of me.

It was ironic. The end of the German tyranny seemed so near, but I had no other choice; I had to play the game. I had learned enough in the last few years to be prepared to face another test. I had to remember, whatever I did, to act naturally and forget the fear.

The three men came back shortly. They gave me 200 zlotys to buy a coffin and an outfit consisting of a suit, shirt, socks, tie, and shoes. They gave me addresses where I could find all these things. They were the addresses of people who could be trusted not to talk too much. A man with a horse and a wagon would come and take me over to make the purchases. Then I was to go to the local parish priest and ask for his permission to take the deceased's body out of his parish and over to the parish of Zyrardow, to be interred there. The reason for the transfer was that, when the war ended, Piotrus's family might be looking for him. If we buried him in a small village cemetery, they might never find him. Zyrardow is a big city, and burials there were properly registered.

"Take care of everything today, because the funeral will take place first thing tomorrow morning. This afternoon we will arrange the death certificate and the permit for a five-wagon convoy."

At the coffin-maker's place, I found two customers ahead of me. I was all ears and eyes to learn what they were asking for and the language being used. It was a fast introduction to coffin-buying, the Catholic way. When my turn came, I asked to be shown something simple, but decent-looking, and not too expensive.

"It's for a friend of mine who was blown here by the winds of war. There isn't much money around, you know."

"Was he religious?"

"I know he was a believer, and that's all I know."

"How about this one with the cross on the cover?"

"How much is it? Forgive my asking, but I am limited in money."

"Seventy-five zlotys."

"I'll take it." I paid, and they put the coffin on my wagon. I went to the address given to me for the clothes. "How tall was the deceased?" they asked.

"About eight to ten centimetres taller than I am. And bigger in the chest."

The store owner took a jacket off the rack, and asked me to try it on, just for an idea of the size. Something moved in my throat, but "Now, no silly reactions," I heard a voice inside me say. I paid for the suit and other garments, and returned to Mr. Bronkowski. I still had to go to the priest for permission to transfer the body. Mr. Bronkowski insisted that I eat a meal with him before I left. I didn't know what I was eating.

I had to walk to the priest's place. It was only two kilometres away. All the way, I was thinking how I would approach the priest, how to present myself as one of the flock. I tried to recall similar situations I had read about. The housekeeper let me into the priest's chamber. He was young. He was sitting at a desk, a big cross on the wall behind him.

I knelt, crossed myself, and said, "Let Him be praised." I stood up, and told the priest what I came for.

Apparently he knew about it already, because he had everything ready. When he handed the permit to me, he said, in a very gentle voice, "The Almighty will bless you for your good work."

I thanked him, crossed myself, and backed out of the priest's chamber. I thought I had done very well.

Early in the morning of the next day, five wagons, each with two horses, were ready in front of Mr. Bronkowski's place. I took a look at Piotrus before closing the casket. He looked very elegant, all dressed up. His eyes were closed now, and his face arranged in a nice expression. The casket was placed on the first wagon. The other wagons carried three or four mourners each.

I was given all the documents, and off we went on the road to Zyrardow, about fifteen kilometres away. When we were about one-third of the way there a German military vehicle stopped us. Three Gestapo officers jumped out of their car, and one of them called out, "*Was ist los hier?* (What is going on here?)"

"It's a funeral," I answered, pointing to the coffin.

"*Haben Sie Waffen?* (Do you have any weapons?)"

"No, it's a funeral." One of the Germans went over to the coffin and uncovered it. They always suspected a coffin of serving as a disguise for weapon-smuggling.

"*Es ist doch ein junger Kerl, was war los mit ihm?* (It's a young chap, what happened to him?)"

One of the mourners shot back, "They suspected typhoid."

Like magic, the three Germans jumped into their car. One of them called out: "*Machen Sie es ja schnell—vorwärts.* (Move on quickly.)"

When the Germans disappeared, we had a good laugh at the typhoid joke. We took the coffin off the wagon at the gate of the cemetery. I thought that we would take it straight over to the grave, and that that would be it. I was wrong. The six pallbearers — I one of them — were told to take the coffin into the chapel, where a priest would say mass.

I followed the other pallbearers to the back seats. Everyone had a prayer book in his hand. I took one too. When I heard the verbal responses to the prayers, I looked in my prayer book and moved my lips. I couldn't have been on the right page number, but I tried to be close just in case anyone was looking at me. When I saw the other pallbearers forming a line and walking to the coffin, I quickly followed. The service was over. The priest said a few sentences of eulogy, praising the patriotism of the deceased. Then we carried the coffin out to the cemetery. When it was lowered into the grave, I, the close friend of Piotrus from Warsaw, was given the honour of putting down the first shovel of earth.

I had to go back to the office of the chapel, and together with another local person, I signed my name as witness to the fact of interment of Piotrus. I put down the name of Jan Mankowski in the registry of the cemetery of Zyrardow, December 22, Anno Domini 1944.

On my way back to the farm, I could hear my other self saying, "Jasiu, remember, you are not smart, you are just lucky. Keep praying for your luck to continue."

Chapter Twenty-Three

Anew year had started. 1945. What would that new year be like? How much longer would the war last? Would I ever be myself again? Would I find my wife? For no special reason I was growing more and more restless, but nothing gave any indication of forthcoming change. The German apparatus worked flawlessly, at least in the area where I was staying.

At night I talked to myself, trying to keep my mind under control and go on playing my game. After all, I reasoned, the front was only about forty miles away; by March or April something was bound to happen on that front. The Germans were on the defensive on all sides now. So, Jan Mankowski, I thought, watch yourself a little while longer, arm yourself with patience and soon, soon, they will pay the price for what they did to you and yours — and you will see it with your own eyes. Oh, how I wanted that moment to arrive!

I was always sensitive to what was being said about Jews. I was always on my guard not to say anything that might have resembled a Jewish way of thinking. Past experience taught me that there was always someone eager to denounce a Jew to the Germans. It was very difficult to be careful all the time.

One cold January morning, my task for the day was to go over to one of the villages and distribute clothing to the refugees from Warsaw. For these distributing days in remote villages, a farmer with his wagon and two horses were assigned to me by the R.G.O. With the wagon loaded, and bundled up against the bitter cold, we set out. We were driving along not saying much to each other.

After a while, the farmer commented, "It's cold. Look at the air coming out of the horses' nostrils."

"Yes," I answered, "it looks like a decoration." Without thinking I added, "In weather like this one should take a glass of vodka and a chunk of baked goose."

"Baked goose, eh? You sure talk like a Jew."

I forgot about the cold weather, I felt a wave of heat in my blood. "Ha, ha, ha. It was the Jews who once treated me to vodka and baked goose in the winter and I liked it a lot. I wouldn't mind having the same thing now. I would warm up real fast."

"No more Jews, no more baked goose," said the farmer.

"Were there any Jews living around here?"

"Not many. The Germans took them away."

"I'm cold in my feet."

"Get off and run after the wagon and you'll warm up."

I was glad to get off the wagon and not prolong that dangerous conversation about vodka and goose, the Jewish remedy for the cold of winter. While running after the wagon, I scolded myself for not being careful enough.

A few days later, I arrived in a village with a wagonload of assorted provisions for distribution among the refugees. I went to the gymnasium of the local school, where people had lined up for whatever I had brought them. I had two bags of sugar, each weighing one hundred kilograms, to dispense. I weighed one kilogram of the precious commodity for each person waiting in line. When I got the knack of the job, each scoop came up weighing exactly one kilogram, or very close to that weight.

The work was moving swiftly when I heard someone saying, "He weighs out that sugar just as skilfully as the Jew Yosel did when he had his store here."

"That's right," another man agreed.

I felt my hand losing its steadiness. Still, I managed not show any reaction to what I had heard. Gradually, I lost my "skilful" touch and the sugar scooped out of the bags was of assorted weights. I was glad to see the weighing coming to its end.

Finally...it happened.

When I arrived in the Community Centre of Guzow early one morning, six farmers with their wagons were waiting for me. We were to go to a place called Milanowek in order to pick up a load of supplies for the refugees. The farmers told me about unusual goings-on inside the administration building. Despite the very early hour of the morning all the lights in the offices were on. There were rumours that the *wojt* and the chief of police were packing their belongings and preparing to leave the place. But soon everything looked normal again. We decided there was no reason to hesitate about taking our trip to Milanowek, and we started out.

We had travelled for about an hour, in full daylight now, when motorized German vehicles loaded with soldiers started crowding the road. After half an hour the highway was empty again: no more military in sight.

It must have been just a routine military exercise, I thought.

But no, something looked different this time. German tanks were crossing the fields, all going in one direction: west. There was a noise in the skies. Two airplanes, Russian airplanes, flew over low enough for us to see their markings clearly. Then it was quiet again. The Russians from the other side of the Wisla River must have been looking for a soft spot in the German lines, I was thinking.

"I think the *Schwabs* are shitting in their pants," the farmer, on whose wagon I was sitting, said to me.

"That would be good, you think?"

"I don't expect anything good from the Russkies either."

We passed through a village packed with German vehicles and soldiers. One of the soldiers, carrying a box, came running to our wagon. *"Wollen sie Schnapps kaufen, zwei zlotys eine Flasche?* (Do you want to buy whisky, two zlotys a bottle?)"

My farmer bought one bottle. For lack of money I didn't buy any. The soldier lowered the price and the farmer bought the rest of the case, nine bottles, for fifteen zlotys. The German ran to his truck and returned with another case of alcohol to offer to another farmer in our convoy.

"He probably needs the money to buy himself a civilian suit. Then he'll throw away his uniform and defect from the army," my farmer said.

About one kilometre away from the village, we saw some German soldiers lying dead. Right beside the road, there was a body dressed in a uniform, but not a German one. He was a *"Wlasowiec,"* a member of an army unit, organized by the Ukrainian general Wlasow, that had the reputation of working zealously for the Germans and being extremely cruel to the civilian population. I felt no pity for the dead man lying beside the road, only a pleasure in revenge. Such a huge body that man had; who could say how many civilians he had killed while serving the Germans? His death was very right then; he paid for his cruelty. But I couldn't help the sudden thought: What if the man was innocent? An innocent victim of the war?

A few abandoned artillery pieces in the field indicated that the Russians were machine-gunning the retreating Germans.

"Panie," I said to my farmer, "it seems that the Russians have started their offensive."

"It sure looks like it. Let's hope we can get home in one piece."

When we arrived in Milanowek, everything seemed normal: no signs of disorder of any kind. German police were patrolling the streets in the usual way. I was disappointed. Another false alarm?

We drove over to the warehouse for our pick-up. Everything there was absolutely normal. We loaded our wagons and I signed the receipts for the goods. I found out from the clerks in the warehouse that the adjoining building housed the main offices of the R.G.O. I went over and asked for the registry of the people from Warsaw living in the area. I looked through the lists from all the villages around. I didn't find there the name of Krystina Bartkowska.

When we were ready to leave Milanowek the sirens began wailing. An air raid. People were running in all directions. It was winter, and there were no leaves on the trees to provide any camouflage. We stayed near our wagons. The sirens stopped wailing, but now German trucks were crossing the town in droves. We couldn't move. There was panic, complete chaos, then...everything was over. German police were patrolling the streets again. It was unbelievable.

It was dark when we took to the road again. No military movements could be seen, but artillery fire could be heard from far away. The Germans abandoned their burning trucks on the sides of the roads.

Yes, the Russians had started their offensive. But would they continue it, or retreat for some reason? It was still winter. Wouldn't they wait until spring to make their big move? I was afraid to build up my hopes too high. It was cold and dark. Artillery fire was splitting the dark sky. *Boom! Boom!* Frightening, scary.

Suddenly I heard a shout: "*Stoi!*" It was the voice of a Russian soldier, ordering us to stop our wagons. He wanted to know who we were, what we were doing on the road, what was in our wagons. I answered everything in Polish. Since we were not Germans, he became friendly and told us that we were right in the middle of the front-line and should not be travelling now.

"*Smotri*," he said, pointing to the red sky over the burning city of Zyrardow. If we insisted on proceeding he warned us to take side roads.

I heard more Russian voices nearby. I could see silhouettes of tanks and a group of soldiers near them. One man, probably an officer, was lecturing the group.

It had happened. The Germans were gone and I was alive. I had made it, I had survived Hitler, and lived to see with my own eyes the downfall of that tyranny, just as I had prayed!

My farmers decided to take side roads and go home. Not saying a word, I remained with them. We were moving ahead. Heavy artillery fire sounded from all sides. We were passing some farmhouses when we heard "*Halt*."

A group of twenty-five or thirty German soldiers encircled our convoy and ordered us out of the wagons. They lined us up against a wall of a barn, ordered us to face the wall and put our arms over our heads. While some of them threw everything out of our wagons, the others lifted their rifles and held them aimed at us. At that moment, I thought I hadn't made it after all. I was about to lose my life, in the last stage of that terrible struggle. I waited for the last salvo. I could have survived the war, I thought, if only I had chosen to go to the Russians a short while ago. Now, it was the end of me.

Suddenly, out of nowhere came a German officer riding a bicycle. He asked what was going on. The soldiers told him that we were suspected of carrying weapons and other supplies for the Russians. The officer ordered his men to check the wagons and if nothing suspicious was found to let us go unharmed.

"*Schnell, kein Zeit verlieren* (Swiftly, no time to lose)." A minute later the Germans took off. We were free. That German officer was this time the proverbial angel who saved lives.

It was past midnight when we reached the *gmina* building in Guzow. The farmers leaving the wagons loaded unhitched their horses and ran home. I rushed to my house. My farmer lit the kerosene lamp. Both he and his wife embraced me; she was crying. "Listening to the shooting all day long we were very afraid that you might get killed on the road."

"Jasiu," said the farmer, "you know I'm not a believer, but this time I was praying for your safe return. Now that you are back in one piece, I might even be inclined to change." He gave me a big grin. Next morning we learned that four people from the village had lost their lives in the erratic shooting. The Germans were gone, this time for good.

My farmer wanted to know what happened to the merchandise we brought back from Milanowek. I told him that we had left everything on the wagons near the *gmina*. "I'll take my horse and wagon and we'll go and see. The war is over. You are poor, why not take that stuff for yourself? It belongs to you. You almost lost your life getting it. Come on, let's go."

We found empty wagons. People had taken everything before we got there. Only one thing was left: a double-size barrel of salted herring. It must have been too heavy to carry away in a hurry. We took the barrel on our wagon, brought it home and put it in the shed adjoining the house.

"Listen, Jasiu," my well-wishing farmer told me, "the Russian soldiers are herring crazy, you can barter with them the herring in exchange for things you need for yourself."

My farmer was right. The Russian soldiers came to every house asking for milk or boiled water and other small things. I offered them *solotki* (herring). In no time I acquired a few shirts, socks, towels and soap, everything of poor quality but still, it was more than I possessed. For six herring I even bought a bicycle. On the advice of my farmer I hid it in the barn. "There are no rules with the Russians. One soldier will sell something to you and then he will send his companion to take it back."

Mr. Zakuta was right. A group of Russian soldiers came to the house, and asked: "*Solotki u was da*? (do you have herring?)"

"*Da.*"

They offered handkerchiefs and gloves for sale. When I went to the shed to get my "money" (herring), the soldiers followed me, pushed me aside, rolled out the barrel with the herring and put it on one of their trucks. When I pleaded for my treasure, they just laughed at me: "*Uhodyi* (get lost)."

I was bitter and angry and so was my farmer.

There was a change beginning in my way of thinking. I couldn't figure
it out. Just two days before I had wished to see the Germans wiped off
the map of the world completely. My deep desire for revenge for all
that the Germans had done to us Jews, their murder and robbery, had
always made me pray for an opportunity to take part in wiping out the
German gangrene, the gangrene of the human race. But a feeling of
pity was awakening in me now. Was I getting crazy, abnormal? Or was
I getting to be human again? A struggle between two forces was taking
place inside me.

It was a rainy, wet day. A few Russian soldiers came to our house,
unpacked their food and asked for water. While they were eating, they
saw through the window a German soldier with his hands above his
head walking towards our house. One of the Russian soldiers, a tall,
broad-shouldered man with delicate facial features, got up from the
table and went outside. I followed him. The German outside, still in
his uniform, but with no cap on his head, looked to be about twenty
years old; he was slight and blond. His face was full of fear and his
eyes were asking for mercy. The Russian took out his revolver
and...*click...click*...the revolver did not fire. The German fell to the
Russian's feet begging for his life. The Russian kicked him and moved
away from him. He aimed again...*click...click*...no shots.

Other Russian soldiers came out of the house. "Take him prisoner,"
I said in Polish to the Russian who had tried to shoot the German.

"*Uhodyi*," he yelled at me in anger and asked another Russian for
his gun.

The other gun worked. The German fell to the ground and rolled
over. The Russian fired again. I turned away my face. I heard one of
the Russians saying that the German was still alive. The Russian who
did the shooting told the other soldiers in an angry voice not to give
the victim a mercy shot.

We returned to the house. I was shaken. When I composed myself,
I couldn't help asking that mild-faced Russian why he hadn't taken the
German as prisoner. "He was not armed. He looked like an ordinary
young soldier, probably a completely innocent person."

The Russian looked at me in silence as if to say, "What do *you*
know?" But then he began to speak, to justify his seemingly un-

reasonable act of cruelty. Slowly, so that I could understand him, he explained.

"I am a very average person. All my life I worked as a mechanic in an industrial complex. When I was drafted in the army and went to war, I left behind my wife and two children, a boy of seven and a girl of six. Never in my life had I hurt anybody. I always used my free time for doing things around the house, to play with my children and read books. I was a happy man. After we pushed back the invading Germans, I went home to my village in Byelorussia hoping to find my wife and children. I did not find them. What I found out was that Tanya and my two children had been rounded up together with others and just machine-gunned, in cold blood."

The Russian stopped talking. His eyes were shining with tears. He continued, "As I stood by my burnt-out house, I swore to take revenge. I swore to kill any German I met. I didn't want to think who he might be. I knew that my wife and children were innocent. I decided to kill out of the desire to make German mothers, fathers and children cry over the loss of their families. I'll keep that promise, yes, I will — as long as I live and am able to."

As if to cool down and regain balance after that emotional talk, the Russian went outside. He did not go to look at the German. I did. He was still in convulsions. I felt something breaking down in me. What was happening to me? Why did I feel pity? I had no answer to my own question.

Chapter Twenty-Four

We were sitting in the farmhouse one afternoon when we heard the noise of a small plane. It seemed to be flying just above the roof of the house. When we looked out, the plane had landed about five hundred feet away from the house. It had landed with the wheels up. We rushed over and found the pilot crawling out of the plane. Unharmed and completely unperturbed, he lifted his flying machine and, singlehanded, put it back in the right position, landing wheels down. It was a small, single-engine biplane. The pilot, dressed in the uniform of a Russian officer, took a wooden suitcase from his plane and came over to us.

"*Zdrastvity tovarisce* (Good day, comrades)." Without saying anything else he went straight to our house. It looked as if he was leading us. In the house, he looked around the first big room (that was kitchen and sitting-room together) and the look of it did not seem to please him. He opened the door to the only other room in the house, the farmer's bedroom. He went in and closed the door behind him. We heard from him about half an hour later when he called for hot water in a basin, to wash up. Then, clean and groomed, he entered our room and in a matter-of-fact tone announced that he would be staying for a few nights. To my farmer's remark that he and his wife slept in that room, the Russian calmly replied, "You can sleep in the barn. As for the *shenstsina* woman, she can stay in the room with me, I don't mind. You do understand it's war and everybody has to contribute something." He spoke very casually and he seemed to expect the farmer to take it that way.

The officer went back to "his" room and returned holding in his hand a bottle of whisky and a little package wrapped in a newspaper. He then asked for some *stakany* (glasses), filled them generously and invited everyone present to drink with him. After the first gulp, he unwrapped the package. It contained shrivelled-up pastry. *"Davay, bieryi* (Go ahead, take some)," the officer said. He became talkative and told us that he was operating behind the first front line as a communication man. His job was to deliver and collect messages to different army units, messages that could not, for security reasons, be relayed over the radio. He never stayed in a place longer than two or three days. He had not been flying a lot in the last few months, but he expected to do so now that the *Krasnaia Armia* (Red Army) was closing in on Berlin.

I was completely flabbergasted when the officer, in answer to my asking where he was stationed for the last few months, said, "In a small *gorod* (town) called Parczew."

"Parczew? Is that somewhere near Lublin? I once visited a friend of mine living there. It was a pretty town. Is it still a nice place?"

"*Da*. First our partisans, and then our army, saved that place from destruction by the Germans."

"You had Russian partisans there?"

"We sent our trained agents in there and together with the Jewish partisans who had run away from the Germans to the forests, we gave the fascists lots of trouble."

"Jewish partisans?" my farmer was wondering.

"*Da*, the *yevrecy* were very good fighters, and they saved their lives that way."

I was anxious to ask the officer for more details about these *yevrecy*, but I considered it to be unwise and unsafe for me to show too much interest in that subject. I didn't ask any more questions. I was happy to hear that some Jews from Parczew had survived and my thoughts were now directed to a new objective: to get home to Parczew as fast as possible.

It was only a few days before the Russian front moved west, away from us. Warsaw was free. Halina, Stach and I concluded that it made no sense to stay in Guzow any longer. While I told them I planned to go to a place near Lublin, they told me that their plan was to follow the Russian army. As soon as the coast on the Baltic Sea was freed, they would return to their family farm there.

We loaded our possessions on the bicycle I had bought from the Russians, thanked our farmers for all their hospitality and the help they had given us for almost four months, and left Guzow.

We decided to go to Warsaw. I was thinking of going to Wilcza Street in the hope of finding my belongings buried in the basement of the house where I had last lived. Stach and Halina wanted to get to the place they lived in, because they buried a real treasure in their basement: a large amount of leather, all ready to be used.

"Jasiu," Stach said, "if I recover that leather, I'll give you some of it. We'll all be rich. You'll remember our friendship."

We started our march from Guzow quite early in the morning; the weather was cold but bright and sunny. We hoped to reach Warsaw, about 70 kilometres away, within two days. Stach and I alternately walked the bike with our belongings. At one point, when Halina and I were ahead of Stach, Halina told me that she wanted to ask me something and, since the war was over, I should be frank with my answer. I knew instantly what Halina wanted to know. I just looked at her. She moved away the woollen shawl covering her face from the winter cold, looked at me with her dark hazel eyes and asked shortly, "Yes or no?"

"Yes," I answered her. "And you, Halina?"

"Half, yes. Jasiu, I knew it the minute I met you."

"I only suspected you. I was not sure, Halina. Does Stach know?"

"He knows everything about me. We love each other. He is a prince of a person."

We reached the outskirts of Warsaw late the following day and spent that night in an empty basement. The streets were mostly empty, some buildings were completely undamaged, others in ruins or half-ruined. Pieces of tin roof dangled and swung back and forth. I watched the bundled-up people in the street, concentrating on their way of walking in the hope that I might recognize someone I knew. Maybe one of my many benefactors. I didn't expect to see Krystina in Warsaw now, figuring that, if she was alive, she wouldn't move around in the last weeks of her pregnancy.

Early next morning we went straight to the place where Stach and Halina used to live. It looked as if the place had been dug up before we got there. It was hard just to give up hope, and we started to dig in the spot where Stach thought he had hidden the leather.

Suddenly, four armed men stood before us, and one of them declared solemnly: "In the name of the citizens' committee of the City of Warsaw you are all under arrest. Get moving upstairs." In the courtyard we were informed that unless we could prove that we had lived in the building, we would be brought before a court and accused of being marauders intending to steal someone else's property. Halina and Stach had documents to prove that they had lived there and they even met two old neighbours. "And who is he?" the committee people wanted to know, pointing at me. I was cleared too.

We went back to the basement but our digging was in vain. Somebody else had found Stach's hidden treasure. "Well, that's war," Halina said philosophically, "we are young and we'll make it up." Stach couldn't stop swearing. The three of us went on to Wilcza Street, to my place. The part of the building where I had buried my "treasure" was completely demolished. All our illusions about a quick recovery of our fortunes were gone. We decided to continue on the road to our individual destinations. Halina and Stach gave me the address of the farm they were planning to live on. I told my friends that since I didn't know where I would end up, I couldn't give them an address. Halina looked at me. She knew well what I was saying.

Riding the bicycle now, I pedalled to Praga, the suburb of Warsaw. At the Eastern Station I got on the train to Parczew, loading my bike on with me. I was taking the same route as I had more than two years before, but in the opposite direction. Then I was running away from Parczew, now I was returning there. Sitting in the train, I had lots of time to compare the "then" and "now." When I was hiding in Warsaw, I had prayed that, if my fate was to die at a young age, my end would come after the Germans had been humiliated and put to shame for what they did to us weak and powerless Jews. Now, since I had witnessed their destruction, I was superstitiously thinking that I would die soon. I had told God that I wouldn't mind dying after their defeat. My prayer had been answered, so why should I not die?

No, I was not sorry for myself. I had had my satisfaction. But what about my wife? Maybe she was alive and would still give birth to my baby? If I died, the baby would probably never know his or her father. Or perhaps Hindele and the baby, too, would pay for my having witnessed the destruction of the Germans.

I was travelling in a cattle car again, but there were no Germans around this time. The train was full of people returning home after selling their wares, mostly farm produce, in liberated Warsaw. This new breed of traders was mostly women, carrying on the tradition of the German occupation when, as women, they were better treated than men. Watching them — they were mostly between the ages of twenty-five and fifty — one couldn't help being surprised at how easily they drank alcohol. Teaglass after teaglass of that homemade moonshine disappeared in their mouths.

We arrived in Siedlce in the early hours of next day. We were halfway between Warsaw and Parczew. This was the station where I had jumped the train taking me to the death camp of Treblinka about two and a half years before. What memories!

The train was continuing now in a different, eastward direction, away from Parczew. Instead of waiting for a train connection, I decided to bicycle there. I ate the leftover bread and I climbed on my bike. There was no snow on the road that January day; I was lucky. I passed the city of Lukow, the first thirty-kilometre stretch done. I used to know quite a few people in Lukow. I wondered if any of them had survived. I rode on. Another thirty kilometres to the town of Radzyn. The last time I had been in that town was September 2, 1939, on my way from Warsaw to Parczew. There was no point in stopping there now. All my friends and acquaintances were gone. The Lichtsteins, the Nusbaums, the Bermans, Kleinbaums, Zytos, Turkieltaubs — all but a few, who had left for Palestine before the war, were gone.

I stopped in the village of Suchowola, about seventeen kilometres from Parczew. I went into a house closest to the road and asked for a drink. The place happened to be a carpenter's shop and the owner was working when I walked in.

"Let Him be praised."

"For all the time to come."

"I'm on my way to Parczew. May I ask you for a drink of water? I'm very thirsty."

"Sure, sit down and have a rest."

I was treated to tea. The man wanted to know where I was coming from and where I lived. I told him all about myself except that I was Jewish. Just to be on the safe side. Years ago this place, Suchowola, had a reputation for being very anti-Semitic. Jews travelling through that village were the object of attacks. Remembering all that now was a good reason not to tell the man everything about myself.

I asked the carpenter if he knew how Parczew looked. Had the town changed a lot under the Germans? "I haven't been there since 1939," I told him.

"I would say that nothing much has changed, except that there are no Jews there now. The Germans slaughtered them all. No more Jews, thank the Lord. I'm told that about one hundred and fifty Jews returned from the forests but I'm sure they won't stay there too long."

"Does Count Tchetwertinski still live here in Suchowola?"

"Are you crazy? The Count here? Under the Russian rules? He had to flee."

I was getting ready to leave when the carpenter suggested that I stay with him for a few days: "Suchowola is a nice place. Our priest here would be glad to welcome you and listen to your first-hand stories about the Uprising against the Germans in Warsaw. He talks about Warsaw in church every Sunday."

I explained to the man that I was very anxious to see my old friends, and that most probably I'd be back in Suchowola soon to enjoy his hospitality for a couple of days. I thanked him for the drink and left.

It seemed that some Poles hadn't learned a thing from the war or changed in their thinking about Jews. That church-going Christian thanked the Lord for what the Germans had done to the Jews. His priest must have been feeding that devoted soul with special teachings.

Where was I going? What would I do in Parczew? What could I expect there, even with the Germans gone? But I had to start somewhere.

After another hour and a half on my bicycle, I came to the outskirts of Parczew and passed the Jewish cemetery, with the fence torn down and the monuments broken and scattered. I didn't want to awaken all those memories; I rode by the place quickly.

Who would be the first person I'd recognize and who would recognize me?

And yes, there was a man I did recognize. A Pole, a former alderman whom I had once, at my father's request, invited to our house for a discussion about cobblestones for one of the streets in the Jewish district. I got off the bike and asked him where I might find a restaurant in town? He looked at me and gave the wanted information. No, he didn't recognize me.

I went right to the centre of town and looked around. I did see a Jew I knew. During the war years, David had come to our house often, always sharing a special admiration for my father. When he looked at me, I turned away. Even though I wanted to talk to him, I wanted to make absolutely sure that I could pass unrecognized if I had to.

David didn't give up. He came over to me. "I think I know you," he said in Polish.

"I don't think so. I've never seen you before."

"I'm sorry, I made a mistake."

Each of us walked away in opposite directions. I turned around slightly and saw that he had turned too, and was standing and looking after me. I couldn't control myself any longer and called, "David!"

"Benjamin," he called back.

I dropped my bike to the ground. We embraced and cried silently. "Come with me to my house. You'll have to wait downstairs for a moment. I have to break the news to Feigele gently, I'm afraid she might get a shock from the excitement. Oh, my God, Benjamin, you are alive!"

The news that Benjamin Mandelkern was back alive spread quickly. All the Jews came to greet me. The "*l'haims*" went on and on. Feigele (that good Jewish mother) and David explained over and over to the well-wishing visitors that I was tired from the long trip and they should come and talk to me next day. Some listened to the appeal, others not at all. And my dear hostess followed me around, offering all kinds of products of her culinary craftsmanship.

While I was taking a rest, my hosts invited about twenty selected guests for the rest of that evening. What an evening it was! Talking? Lots of it. Drinking of vodka? Well, lots of that, too. My training in the art of drinking alcohol, acquired on the farm, came in very handy now. I could keep up with some and surpass others. (I was told later that my way of talking that evening resembled a lot that of a drunken person, which I, of course, denied.) My problem that evening was that I couldn't communicate freely with people because I had forgotten my Yiddish. I kept talking away in Polish and German.

There was no end to the number of questions I was asked. The women wanted to know about my wife. Where's Hindele? they wanted to know. They became suspicious when I told them that I didn't know her whereabouts. And when I mentioned that when I and Hindele parted, she had been about three months pregnant — the women looked at each other. All that seemed to confirm their belief that Hindele found another man in those turbulent last months of the war. In my state of haziness from the vodka, I could still make sense of the stories these women were telling about cases of Jewish wives leaving their husbands during the war for more convenient Gentile partners. "And, you know, Hindele is a beautiful woman, she would certainly have had no problems finding a good man." I felt hurt listening to these whispers about Hindele.

I went to see Lola next morning. She was still carrying on the business in the store we had once owned together with the Goldreich family. When I walked in, Lola was busy with customers. Then she saw me and yelled, "Jesus Maria!" I ran up to the counter and we embraced, while the customers looked on in surprise.

"Have you heard from Ludwik?" I asked.

"He's home."

"Lola, I'll be back."

I ran to Ludwik's place and pounded on the door. Ludwik opened it and we embraced without saying a word. We sat down at the table and looked at each other, not knowing where to start. He had come home only a few days before me.

We talked for hours about our experiences since we were forced out of Warsaw at the beginning of October 1944. We talked and we drank vodka, again lots of it. When Ludwik suggested that he would take me to Feiggle's place because I was too drunk to go by myself, I protested, but to no avail. The truth was that both of us were very drunk. Grownups and children stared at us as we walked in zig-zags from one side of the street to the other.

When I sobered up a bit, I was informed that according to regulations I was supposed to get a permit from the local Russian authorities allowing me to stay in Parczew. Not getting that permit could result in my deportation. I had to go to see a *politruk* (political commissar) for the document. I was advised to go to there in the company of Leibl Bocian who, being a purveyor of vodka, was influential with that official. Good-natured Leibl Bocian was happy to be of service to Benjamin Mandelkern, son of Leib, for whom he had worked years ago. "I'm honoured to help you, Benjamin," Bocian said.

I did not realize what that help meant until I found myself before the representative of Stalin's regime. "*Tovarich* commissar, my name is...I've just arrived in Parczew, and I was told by my friends that I must get your permission to remain in town," I said all that in Polish. Leibl translated.

"*Pravlno* (that's right). Where were you during the war years?" I told the man all the details. "*Slushyi tovarich* (listen, comrade), you go back where you stayed before coming here. I don't know you and I don't want you here. *Eto vsio* (that's all)."

Apparently, the alcohol I had been drinking that day had not evaporated from me completely. I got angry. Raising my voice, I said, "You are telling me to leave Parczew? I was born and raised here, went to school here, lost all my family here and now you, a complete stranger in this place, are telling me to go?"

Leibl Bocian pulled my arm, "Keep quiet, you are drunk. *Tovarich* commissar, he is drunk but he is a good man."

The Russian looked at me and laughed out loud. Leibl wasted no time. Pulling a bottle of vodka from under his coat, he uncorked it by hitting the flat end of it against the palm of his other hand and filled the empty glass on the Russian's desk. The whole operation took seconds only. "*Tovarich*, you can tell that my good friend Benjamin is drunk. I assure you he is one of us." (Oy, what a family.)

Leibl took an empty glass out of one of his pockets and filled it with vodka too. "*Na zdrovie.*" Both men had a drink. After emptying a second glass, the commissar signed the permit allowing me to stay in my hometown.

When we left the office, Leibl explained to me the new realities here. I'd better keep my mouth shut or else I'd be in trouble in no time. In other circumstances I might have been more outraged by how the commissar had treated me. But I had no shoes, I was full of lice, the lining of my German soldier's suit was crawling with insects. I had to stay in Parczew for now anyway and make new plans. All I wanted was to find Hindele and the baby, and, if I was lucky, recover my parents' possessions. And then I thought I would probably leave this place because for me it wouldn't be much of a life under Russian domination and in the prevailing anti-Semitic surroundings.

My third day in Parczew, Lola saw me on the street and called me into her store. "I received a letter you might be interested to read," she said, as if she had just thought of it. It was in my wife's handwriting! She was asking Lola whether she had heard anything about Benjamin. She, Hindele, was living in Milanowek and the baby was due to be born. "Lola dear, help me if you can," she wrote.

There was no time to waste. I had to get to her fast. She was in Milanowek, the same place where I had been the day I was liberated and where I had looked for her name in the refugees' registry. The problem now was how to get to her quickly. There were no fast trains, and no bus system. Through friends, I found someone who was driving a truckload of flour out west. I talked to him and he, a former partisan, agreed immediately to take me to Hindele. He remembered her from the time when he used to take mathematics lessons from her father.

We arrived in Milanowek in the early evening hours of next day. I ran up the stairs of the house and knocked. The landlady opened the door.

"Good evening. I came to see Krystina Bart...." I hadn't finished pronouncing her name when I saw my wife at the far end of the room. She was looking towards the door but she didn't recognize me, since I was still standing in the poorly lit entrance. In seconds we were embracing each other, though it was not at all easy because of her sizeable tummy.

I kept looking at my beautiful wife as if I were trying to make sure that the miracle had really happened. We were together again, and free now. The scene of that moment will remain with me for the rest of my life. She was wearing a white blouse and a wine-red skirt that was too narrow to close at the top. We talked and talked all evening long.

The same night, about four a.m., my wife woke me, saying that she felt pains. "The baby must be coming."

The landlady went to get the midwife. I was preparing hot water. The midwife arrived.

At five-thirty in the morning my wife gave birth to our oldest daughter. The midwife showed me the baby, then handed her to Hindele. "She looks so much like you," Hindele said, and the midwife agreed.

The landlady commented to me, "The excitement of your arrival brought on the birth of the baby."

A new life was born, the beginning of a new generation.